2285

D0545377

DESMOND MORRIS is the bestselling a
The Human Zoo, Intimate Behaviour and *I*
became the Project Director for the Gestu.. ...._...
backed by the Harry Frank Guggenheim Foundation of New York.

PETER COLLETT is a research officer and member of staff at the
department of experimental psychology at Oxford. He is the editor
of *Social Rules and Social Behaviour*.

PETER MARSH is a social psychologist lecturing at Oxford. He is
the co-author of *The Rules of Disorder* and *Football Hooliganism*,
and the author of *Aggro : The Illusion of Violence*.

MARIE O'SHAUGHNESSY is a language graduate of Cambridge
University who, after taking a course in Social and Administrative
Studies at Oxford, spent three years as a social worker before joining
the Gesture Maps research team as project organizer and principal
interpreter.

Gestures
their origins and distribution

Desmond Morris
Research Fellow, Wolfson College, Oxford

Peter Collett
Department of Experimental Psychology, Oxford

Peter Marsh
Department of Experimental Psychology, Oxford

Marie O'Shaughnessy

TRIAD
GRANADA

Published by Triad/Granada in 1981
Reprinted 1982

ISBN 0 586 05361 1

Triad Paperbacks Ltd is an imprint of
Chatto, Bodley Head & Jonathan Cape Ltd and
Granada Publishing Ltd

First published in Great Britain by
Jonathan Cape Ltd 1979
Copyright © Desmond Morris, Peter Collett, Peter Marsh,
and Marie O'Shaughnessy 1979

Printed and bound in Great Britain by William Clowes (Beccles)
Limited, Beccles and London

Contents

Illustrations

Diagrams

Maps

Histograms

Histograms for each gesture individually are to be found on the
following pages: 9, 22, 41, 59, 64–5, 77, 91, 97, 114–15, 131,
144–5, 159, 166, 175, 182, 195, 204, 210–11, 221, 239, 243.

Picture Credits

The authors thank the following for permission to reproduce illustrations: the Pitt Rivers Museum, Oxford (pp. 27, 139, 140); the
British Museum (pp. 6, 29, 32); Muggiani Editore, Milan (p. 49);
Nicholas Treadwell Gallery (p. 84); Mansell Collection (pp. 115,
243); La Soprintendenza Archeologica per l'Etruria Meridionale
(p. 128); Politikens Presse (p. 141); Percy M. Young and the pub-
lishers of his book *A History of British Football*, Stanley Paul
(p. 228); Associated Press (p. 229); *Punch* magazine (p. 230); Barker
and Dobson (p. 234 *top*); Syndication International (p. 234 *bottom*).
The endpapers are reproduced by permission of Geographia Ltd.

Preface

The importance of human gestures has been greatly underestimated. Students of linguistics are everywhere, and the analysis of human languages is a widely accepted scientific subject, but the gesture specialist is a rare bird indeed — not so much a vanishing species, as one that has hardly yet begun to evolve.

There are two reasons for this. In the first place, gestures have quite wrongly been considered a trivial, second-class form of human communication. Because verbal exchanges are man's crowning glory, all other forms of contact are viewed as somehow inferior and primitive. Yet social intercourse depends heavily on the actions, postures, movements and expressions of the talking bodies. Where communication of changing moods and emotional states is concerned, we would go so far as to claim that gestural information is even more important than verbal. Words are good for facts and for ideas, but without gestures, human social life would become a cold and mechanical process.

If this is so, then why has the science of gestures lagged so far behind the science of linguistics? The second factor working against such studies is a curious one and is difficult to express. It is as if, by their very nature, gestures do not like being written about. They resist verbal analysis. On reflection, this is not so surprising. Their very existence depends upon the fact that they provide a non-verbal channel of communication, and attempts to verbalize it are bound to meet with a special set of problems. These are problems that every art critic will understand. To describe in words the visual qualities that make a painting by Rembrandt a great work of art is a daunting task, and to convey the precise significance of a fleeting gesture is equally challenging. But there is a way. We can greatly deepen our understanding of great works of art by investigating the geography and history of art movements. And with gestures, too, we can learn much from a detailed examination of the geographical and historical background of the so-called 'trivial actions' we all take so much for granted.

We each of us use hundreds of expressive movements every day as we pass through the social events that engulf us from waking to sleeping. Each of these actions has a particular history — sometimes

personal, sometimes cultural, and sometimes more deeply biologi-
cal. By tracing the geographical range and the antiquity of these
actions we can begin to see them more clearly as an understandable
pattern of human behaviour. To do this systematically is to open up
a whole new area of comprehension, and one that is as exciting as
any other area of the sciences of mankind.

This is what we have attempted to do in the present book. Because
it is a new type of study, it has an essentially preliminary quality. We
are fully aware of its limitations, but it is at least a start, and presents
a fresh approach to the whole topic of human gestures. It will be easy
to criticize it for what it does not do, but we hope that instead it will
be accepted for the new ground that it does cover, and for the new
possibilities for future research that it opens up.

Desmond Morris, Peter Collett,
Peter Marsh, Marie O'Shaughnessy

Oxford, 1979

Acknowledgments

During the three years it has taken us to complete the field work for this project, many people have helped us. In particular, we wish to acknowledge the assistance of eight colleagues, each of whom accompanied us to more than one of the foreign locations. They were:

Robert Attenborough
Rosemary Canter
Karen Chessell
Alberta Contarello

Daniel Jessel
Annick Jorand
Peter Macphail
Ramona Morris

In addition, there were a number of interviewers and local interpreters who each assisted us at one particular location. We would also like to register our gratitude to them: Gary Boyles, Anne Marie Sloth Carlsen, Solvie Erikkson, Ahmet Giritli, Tony Kalçic, Jane Kelly, Raffi Kunter, Anna Lambidi, John McLeod, Domenic Magri, Hella Naura, Ingeborg Ramm, Bryan Richards, Alda Tavares, Beate Tischler, Lucy Vouvou, Randi Winsnes and Mohammed Zeribi.

Others who supported the project or provided help in a variety of ways include: Michael Argyle, Robert Barakat, Ian Craig, Jean-Pierre de Waele, Peter Hancock, Roger Lamb, Michael Maguire, Tom Maschler, Pär Nygren, Giovanni Pelleciari, Georg Rapp, Chris Riley, William Stokoe, H. A. Swan, Stella Triantafyllides, Jan Van Hooff, George Vassiliou and Vasso Vassiliou. We would like to record our thanks to them all — and to the 1,200 people across Europe and the Mediterranean who patiently answered our many questions and gave us such valuable information about their local gestures.

For permission to quote from *The Works of Mr Francis Rabelais*, we thank the Navarre Society, London.

Finally, and most importantly, this research investigation would not have been possible without financial support. For this, we are greatly indebted to the Harry Frank Guggenheim Foundation of New York, especially in the person of Robin Fox, whose encouragement from first to last was greatly appreciated.

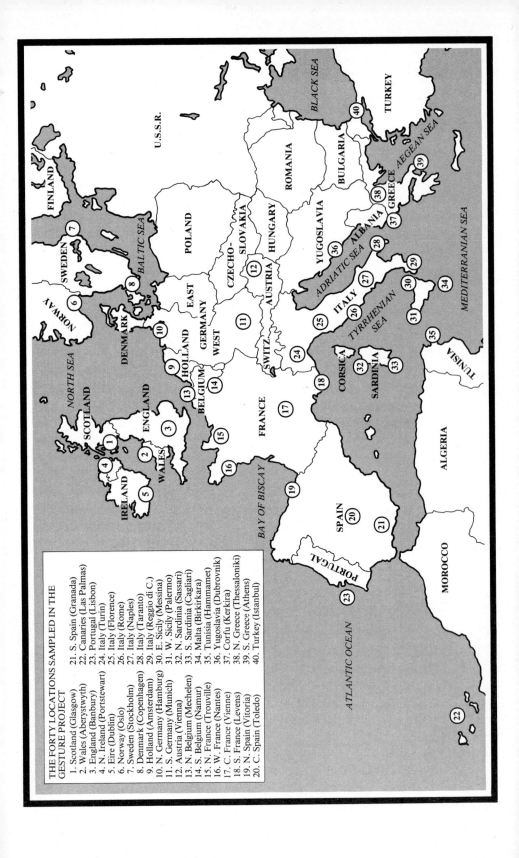

THE FORTY LOCATIONS SAMPLED IN THE
GESTURE PROJECT

1. Scotland (Glasgow)
2. Wales (Aberystwyth)
3. England (Banbury)
4. N. Ireland (Portstewart)
5. Eire (Dublin)
6. Norway (Oslo)
7. Sweden (Stockholm)
8. Denmark (Copenhagen)
9. Holland (Amsterdam)
10. N. Germany (Hamburg)
11. S. Germany (Munich)
12. Austria (Vienna)
13. N. Belgium (Mechelen)
14. S. Belgium (Namur)
15. N. France (Trouville)
16. W. France (Nantes)
17. C. France (Vienne)
18. S. France (Levens)
19. N. Spain (Vitoria)
20. C. Spain (Toledo)
21. S. Spain (Granada)
22. Canaries (Las Palmas)
23. Portugal (Lisbon)
24. Italy (Turin)
25. Italy (Florence)
26. Italy (Rome)
27. Italy (Naples)
28. Italy (Taranto)
29. Italy (Reggio di C.)
30. E. Sicily (Messina)
31. W. Sicily (Palermo)
32. N. Sardinia (Sassari)
33. S. Sardinia (Cagliari)
34. Malta (Birkirkara)
35. Tunisia (Hammamet)
36. Yugoslavia (Dubrovnik)
37. Corfu (Kerkira)
38. N. Greece (Thessaloniki)
39. S. Greece (Athens)
40. Turkey (Istanbul)

Introduction

This is the first study to make a serious attempt to map the geographical distribution of human gestures. It is common knowledge that gestures do vary from culture to culture, but the precise nature of this regional variation has never previously been analysed by means of an objective field study.

Earlier attempts to localize a particular gesture have been limited to labelling it as 'French', or 'Italian', without endeavouring to find out how common or rare it may be, whether it is restricted to one area of the country, or whether it extends across several national boundaries. The result is that we have a number of local gesture guides, but no precisely expressed gestural ranges.

Clearly a worldwide study of all human gestures would be a monumental task, but a start can be made by selecting one major region, covering a number of adjoining, but distinct linguistic areas, and by selecting a number of key gestures known to be important there. The region we have chosen is western and southern Europe and the Mediterranean. Twenty key gestures were selected, on the basis of a preliminary study of the area, and research teams then went into the field to question a large number of subjects on the local use and meaning of these gestures in as many localities as possible.

The field research began early in 1975 and continued until late in 1977. During these three years we visited 40 localities in 25 countries, involving 15 different languages, and we were assisted by a total of 29 research workers and interpreters. As far as we know, no other field study of human gestures has ever been conducted on this scale before, involving, as it did, detailed interviews with 1,200 informants and covering almost a whole continent.

In addition to the standard interviews carried out at every site, we also made direct field observations of gestures 'in action', and made both still and cine film records wherever possible. But the main source of information, nevertheless, came from the standardized and systematically repeated interviews. It is the answers obtained from these that provide the basis for the quantitative information presented in this book. The interviews were conducted as follows:

At each of the 40 locations, 30 adult male subjects were selected at random in public places, such as streets, squares, parks, bars, quaysides, or restaurants, and were shown a sheet of standard drawings depicting the 20 key gestures. If they were in any doubt about a particular drawing, the investigator would then enact the gesture to provide additional information.

The first question asked for each gesture was: Is it used locally? This was important because some subjects (as emerged from a pilot test in England) knew gestures that were not employed locally, either because they had travelled abroad, or had seen them at the cinema or on television. If the answer to this first question was *yes*, they were then asked what the gesture meant to them, and their answer was recorded in their own words. Investigators worked in pairs, one member of each pair being an interpreter, who conducted the interview, while the other recorded the translated replies on a standard, printed sheet.

Additional notes were made concerning local variants of gestures and their rarity. At the end of each interview, the subject's approximate age and, where possible, his occupation were recorded. He was finally asked two additional questions concerning his methods of beckoning and waving: 'Please show us how you beckon someone to come to you', and 'Please imagine someone is leaving, and signal goodbye to them'. When they demonstrated these two actions, their precise form was recorded on the questionnaire sheet.

Each interview took approximately 40 minutes. Occasionally, where an informant was particularly helpful, we extended the discussion to ask about other local gestures and to obtain further background information.

We restricted ourselves to male informants because it was known that in some areas women would be reluctant to co-operate, especially where 'taboo' insult gestures were concerned. In general, very old and very young informants were also avoided. A typical informant could be characterized as a middle-aged male in the middle- or lower-income bracket, who was relaxing in some public place, with a little time to spare. In general, our informants were immensely helpful and patient, and responded seriously and thoughtfully to our queries. If we ignored the more sophisticated and better educated of the males who were available it was simply because we feared that they might be too well travelled and know too much about gestures foreign to their particular locality. There was always a danger that, in such cases, they would wish to show off their knowledge, and in so doing would slightly distort the true, local picture.

The only source of error that seriously concerned us was the over-helpfulness of certain informants. Particular males felt it incumbent on them to provide as many answers as possible. We stressed that nobody was expected to know all the gestures, that we were not conducting an intelligence test, and that many of the gestures were restricted to only small sections of Europe, and most men accepted this readily. As a result, if they did not know a particular gesture, they were happy to say so. But, even so, some individuals were reluctant to appear ignorant of gestures and preferred to invent some meaning for them. It was nearly always obvious when this was happening, usually because of the hesitancy of the reply, but once a reply had been given we were forced to accept and record it, to avoid any subjectively biased selection on our part. Fortunately, in the end, this did not lead to the distortion of the results we initially feared, because the 'wild guesses' of the over-helpful informants were always so varied that they never combined to form a significant group to be set against the major, genuine replies. Out of every 1,200 replies for a particular gesture, there were never more than about 20 – 30 of these wild guesses, and since they were nearly all different from one another, they hardly registered in our final scores and caused no serious interference with our results.

In choosing our 40 locations (details of which are given on page xxiv) we had to balance the need for wide coverage against our wish to examine variations within national boundaries. We spread our net from Norway and Sweden in the north, to Tunisia and the Canary Islands in the south, and from Ireland and Portugal in the west, to Greece and Turkey in the east. But we also managed to include several sites in many of the major linguistic zones — 5 in the English-speaking region, 5 in the French-speaking region, 4 in the Spanish region, 3 each in the German-speaking and Greek regions, and as many as 10 in the Italian region. Italy was particularly favoured because it included the two separate land masses of Sicily and Sardinia, and because we already knew that significant differences in the gestural repertoire existed between the northern mainland of Italy and the southern zone. Geographically speaking, the odd-man-out in our survey was the sample from the Canary Islands. This was included because, although the islands are in the Atlantic, off the west coast of Africa, they are culturally European and the inhabitants consider themselves to be very much a part of Spain, in spirit as well as in law. In fact, Spain is not referred to as 'Spain' by the Canarians, but simply as 'the mainland', or 'the peninsula', despite the fact that it is about 500 kilometres away, while the stretch of water between the Canaries and the west coast of Africa is little more than 80 kilometres wide. It therefore became interesting to examine an island population that was culturally close, but geographically remote from its national centre.

Had it been possible to extend the study further, it would have been valuable to include the other North African countries, the Middle East, and the whole of Eastern Europe. We are convinced that such a study would be rewarding and hope that, at some point in the future, it will be undertaken. To take the project still further to other continental land masses would not, however, be sensible without changing the selected group of 20 key gestures. These were chosen as significant for the European scene and, if comparable projects were to be undertaken on other continents, it would be necessary to revise our list of 20 gestures to suit the local gesture repertoires. Ultimately, of course, the goal must be to map all gestures in all countries, and to produce an encyclopedia of human gestures, but such a task would necessitate the establishment of a specialized research institute of a kind which does not exist anywhere at the present time. Until such a development occurs, we have to accept the fact that, although linguists have massive, authoritative dictionaries to serve them, the gesture-student is without any major reference work for his subject.

This brings us to the question of how we selected the 20 gestures on which we based our enquiry. The choice was not an easy one. Clearly, there were hundreds to choose from and the process of elimination was a painful one. To explain how we did it, we have to distinguish between two basic types of gesture, sometimes referred to as 'illustrators' and 'emblems'. Illustrators are those actions which accompany verbal statements and serve to illustrate them. Emblems are actions which replace speech and can act as substitutes for verbal statements. To give two examples: a man is talking excitedly and, as he does so, his arms gesticulate vigorously, beating time to his words and emphasizing the points he is making. These illustrators are not performed consciously or deliberately, are largely unidentified and unnamed, and are difficult to recall. Ask a man who has just been gesticulating wildly, what movements his hands were making, and he will be unable to tell you. He will remember that they *were* moving, but their postures and the shape of their movements will be beyond his powers of description. A second example, this time of an emblematic gesture, differs markedly: a woman crosses a road watched by two young men. One man turns to the other and winks at him; the latter replies by shaking his fingers as if they have been burned by something hot. No word is spoken between them. Here the gestures have replaced speech and, if the young men were asked later what precise gestures they had used, they would be able to recall them and, in the case of the wink, actually name one of them.

These emblems are essentially *symbolic gestures*. There are other kinds, such as *mimic gestures*, which imitate manually certain specific objects or actions, but this is not the place to present a complete classification of gesture types, since in our present project we have concentrated on the symbolic. We did this because they have the most interesting histories and the most clear-cut regional restrictions. Anyone can mimic the act of drinking, if he is thirsty, and he will be understood almost anywhere in the world. But a symbolic gesture involves a process of abstraction requiring the acceptance of a local convention, and it is this that makes such gestures particularly useful for the preparation of distribution maps. An example will help to clarify this and, in order not to preempt later discussions, we will select one that we did not employ in our present project — the 'temple tap'.

If a man taps his temple with the tip of his forefinger, it can mean one of two things, either 'crazy' or 'intelligent' — two opposing meanings, but both relevant to this particular gesture. There is no mimicry involved. A simple hand action stands for — symbolizes — an abstract quality — craziness or intelligence. In a culture where this particular symbolic convention is totally absent, the gesture might well be meaningless. It requires the acceptance of this particular symbolic equation, an acceptance born of local, cultural exposure and learning. If it is particularly useful, it will soon spread throughout the population where it first arises and may then go on to invade new territories, crossing linguistic boundaries and eventually becoming familiar at a broadly international level. If it is less useful, it may travel badly and remain restricted to one small part of the culture that spawns it, perhaps, in rare cases, to only one city. Its spread will depend on a number of factors, and it is these factors that our present investigation seeks to discover and describe. But to return to our temple-tapping example, it is possible to present a gesture diagram which summarizes its inherent qualities, as follows:

Basic morphology	*The tip of the forefinger of one hand is tapped lightly against the temple.*	
Distinctive feature	*The hand-to-brain 'contact'.*	
Selected symbolism	Bad brain	Good brain
Generic meaning	Craziness	Intelligence

Specific messages	*1 He's stupid.*
	2 Idiot!
	3 What a fool!
	   etc.
		1 He's clever.
		2 Brilliant!
		3 Very bright!
		   etc.

GESTURE DIAGRAM — THE TEMPLE TAP

When we demonstrate a symbolic gesture to one of our informants in the field, what he gives us as a reply is one of the Specific Messages. From our eventual collection of hundreds of these, it soon becomes clear that they can easily be split up into a small number of major categories. These are the Generic Meanings of the gesture and it is these meanings that we can then map and plot as histograms.

There was seldom any difficulty in assigning specific messages to generic meaning categories. In the example we have given here, for instance, there is only one type of danger, namely the sarcastic use of a word like 'Brilliant!', which would put the response into the other category. We were always careful to check for sarcastic usages of this kind and to prevent errors of this type arising. Another type of error might occur, for instance, with a different gesture, where the message was, say, 'Take care!'. This could be a friendly warning or a hostile one, and we quickly learned to avoid such ambiguities by insisting on elaboration of such a reply. Usually this was best done by requesting the informant to give us an illustration of the way he would use the gesture in question.

Frequently it was necessary to make the Generic Meaning categories rather broad, because many gestures are, by their nature, able to cover a wide range of related messages. A particular gesture, for example, might give us a range of messages from 'tasty' to 'beautiful'. One informant, thinking of good food, would find words of praise that would be applicable to eating; another, thinking of an attractive girl, would select words of praise that suited the female form. As more and more such messages were collected — delicious, great, fine, magnificent — it would soon become clear that they all shared the one common factor of *praise*, and this would be the final title we would then select as the Generic Meaning for that particular gesture. But we would still have to make one final check. If all the 'tasty-delicious' words came from one region, and all the 'beautiful-glamorous' words came from another, then we would be able to sub-divide the main meaning into two sub-meanings and map them separately, to show the small, but distinct shift in the usage of the gesture. This is why, on the pages that follow, some of the Generic Meanings we have employed are broader than others. The impor-tant feature of the categorization into basic meanings is that it should expose as clearly as possible the regional differences, and this has been our guiding principle throughout.

Having decided to base our main study on 20 key symbolic gestures, it remained to choose those out of all the many possible alternatives. Following a number of preliminary interviews at Ox-ford, with people from different regions of Europe and the Mediter-ranean, we were able to select a group of gestures that had two essential properties:

1 Each gesture had to be difficult to interpret, merely from its form. By picking such a gesture, we could be sure that, unless it was genuinely employed locally, the informant would not be able to identify it.

2 Each gesture had to be well known somewhere in our study-area and comparatively unknown elsewhere in the area.

In addition to these two considerations, we also tried to make sure that a wide variety of types of meaning were covered — including several insulting gestures and several complimentary gestures; some that were threatening, and others that were protective or friendly. We also made certain that at least some of the gestures were popular in each of the major zones of the study-area, to avoid making foreign trips that resulted in largely negative responses.

As it turned out, our original choices were fruitful ones, and it is doubtful whether, even being wise after the event, we would have selected differently. Our only regret is that we could not have tested a greater number, but had we imposed a longer interview on our informants we might well have taxed them beyond the limits of their patience.

In presenting the results for our 20 key gestures, we have followed a set formula. In each case, we provide first a picture of the type shown to our informants, along with a verbal description of the gesture, and a brief table summarizing the main meanings we discovered for it. Alongside each of these main meanings we give the number of our informants, out of the total of 1,200, who interpreted the gesture in that particular way. There follows a discussion of the origins of the gesture and its history as far as it is known. Finally there is a report summarizing our findings concerning the present distribution of the gesture in the study-area. This is accompanied by gesture maps of the main meanings and, for more detailed information, histograms showing the level of response at each of the 40 locations. At the end of the book (p. 271) we also provide a complete tabulation of all our figures, for anyone wishing to analyse them further.

We conclude the book with a summary of the Gestural Concepts that have emerged from our field study. Without wishing to anticipate that summary, we feel that there are certain points of interest that emerge from the investigation, that should be borne in mind while reading the pages that follow. They are:

1   Many of the gestures had several major meanings. We had expected this in certain cases, but were surprised by how commonly this occurred. The phenomenon of the *multi-message gesture* stems from the frequent, local selection of different symbolic pathways. Just as, in the example we gave earlier, the gestural feature 'brain' could lead, via 'bad brain' or 'good brain' symbolism, to two distinct meanings of 'craziness' or 'intelligence', so many of the gestural features of our 20 key gestures led to a number of varied and often conflicting meanings in different zones. Ignorance of such differences could easily lead a traveller or visitor into embarrassing misunderstandings.

2   Many of the gestures extended their ranges across national and linguistic boundaries. Remarkably few of the gestures we studied could be labelled as exclusively British, French, Italian, or as belonging to some other specific country. This discovery contradicts a great deal of what has been written in the past about so-called 'national gestures'. There are, however, a number of gesture *meanings* which are truly national in their territorial restriction.

3   Certain of the gestures showed ranges that stopped, sometimes abruptly, *within* a particular linguistic area. This phenomenon, the Gesture Boundary, is of particular historical significance, as it reflects a cultural division within a nation that requires a special

explanation relating to past events. One such case was of such interest that we made it the subject of a more detailed field study. This is reported on p. 247.

4 Some gestures showed a colonial pattern, giving high scores in an old imperial power and also in one of its ex-colonies, despite being absent or rare in the geographically intervening regions.

5 In some cases, there was *gesture-meaning overlap*, with a particular gesture having more than one meaning in one particular region. This, too, was unexpectedly common, and in one or two cases was difficult to explain.

6 A large number of distinct, but highly characteristic *gesture ranges* emerged as we completed our maps. Cases of randomly scattered peak-points, with a meaningless, disjointed distribution, were extremely rare. It was almost as if we were ornithologists mapping the geographical ranges of a number of bird species across Europe. This regional patterning provided us with ample justification for our initial decision to map gestures, rather than to study them in some other way.

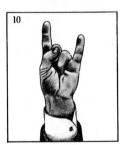

The Twenty Key Gestures

Reproduced on the page opposite is the sheet of 20 key gestures, as shown to our 1,200 informants in the field. Some were clear from the posture of the hand, but others involved a characteristic movement which was difficult to illustrate. If the subject was in any doubt, the interpreter would supplement these drawings with a brief demonstration of the movements involved. The 20 gestures were as follows:

1 The Fingertips Kiss
2 The Fingers Cross
3 The Nose Thumb
4 The Hand Purse
5 The Cheek Screw
6 The Eyelid Pull
7 The Forearm Jerk
8 The Flat-hand Flick
9 The Ring
10 The Vertical Horn-sign
11 The Horizontal Horn-sign
12 The Fig
13 The Head Toss
14 The Chin Flick
15 The Cheek Stroke
16 The Thumb Up
17 The Teeth Flick
18 The Ear Touch
19 The Nose Tap
20 The Palm-back V-Sign

The Forty Locations Sampled

1 Scotland (Glasgow)
2 Wales (Aberystwyth)
3 England (Banbury)
4 N. Ireland (Portstewart)
5 Eire (Dublin)
6 Norway (Oslo)
7 Sweden (Stockholm)
8 Denmark (Copenhagen)
9 Holland (Amsterdam)
10 N. Germany (Hamburg)
11 S. Germany (Munich)
12 Austria (Vienna)
13 N. Belgium (Mechelen)
14 S. Belgium (Namur)
15 N. France (Trouville)
16 W. France (Nantes)
17 C. France (Vienne)
18 S. France (Levens)
19 N. Spain (Vitoria)
20 C. Spain (Toledo)
21 S. Spain (Granada)
22 Canaries (Las Palmas)
23 Portugal (Lisbon)
24 Italy (Turin)
25 Italy (Florence)
26 Italy (Rome)
27 Italy (Naples)
28 Italy (Taranto)
29 Italy (Reggio di C.)
30 E. Sicily (Messina)
31 W. Sicily (Palermo)
32 N. Sardinia (Sassari)
33 S. Sardinia (Cagliari)
34 Malta (Birkirkara)
35 Tunisia (Hammamet)
36 Yugoslavia (Dubrovnik)
37 Corfu (Kerkira)
38 N. Greece (Thessaloniki)
39 S. Greece (Athens)
40 Turkey (Istanbul)

The fingertips kiss as a salutation by a modern Neapolitan.

1 The Fingertips Kiss

**THE FINGERTIPS
KISS MEANINGS:**

1	Praise	601
2	Salutation	375
3	others	49
4	not used	175

(Based on 1,200 informants
at 40 locations)

DESCRIPTION

The tips of the fingers and thumb of the right hand are pressed together and pointed towards the gesturer's own lips. At the same time the hand is raised towards the lips and the fingertips are lightly kissed. As soon as the kissing movement of the mouth has been made, the hand is tossed lightly forward into the air, the fingers opening out away from one another as this second movement is executed.

The true fingertips kiss is usually a rather gentle performance, the movement having little vigour, but when it is imitated by foreigners who do not normally employ it, it is nearly always heavily over-emphasized. When used frequently, it often lacks the actual hand-to-lips contact, the fingertips stopping just short of the mouth. Some individuals reduce it even further, bringing together only the thumb and forefinger and brushing them gently against the lips.

ORIGINS

Kissing the fingertips is a symbolic version of the basic mouth kiss. The mouth kiss itself, contrary to popular opinion, is global in distribution. Careful modern field studies of the behaviour of widely separated tribal cultures have revealed that mouth kissing, in some form, occurs even in societies that have traditionally been labelled as 'non-kissers'. Where there are strong taboos on social or public kissing, the mouth kiss still survives during private moments of lovemaking or between parents and infants as part of tender caressing.

If the mouth kiss exists as a fundamental pattern of human behaviour in a loving or affectionate context, it is worth asking how it has arisen. The German ethologist, Irenaus Eibl-Eibesfeldt, in his book *Love and Hate*, puts forward a convincing case that 'kissing with lips and tongue by human beings is certainly a modification of feeding movements. Mouth-to-mouth feeding between mother and infant is practised in widely differing cultures.' It seems that the primitive version of weaning the young from the breast to solid food was via an intermediate stage in which pre-masticated food was passed from the mother's mouth directly into that of the infant, and the oral contact involved is seen as the precursor of the loving kiss, the primary food reward of the mouth-to-mouth action endowing it with a lasting quality of intimate caring and affection.

Starting from this basic human kiss many formalized variants of the action have developed: kissing the cheek, kissing the hand, kissing the knee, kissing the hem of a garment, kissing the foot, and even kissing the dirt. The lower the status of the kisser, the lower the site of the kiss he offers to a dominant individual.

In ancient religions, the worshipper who wished to demonstrate his love for the deity by offering a kiss to an idol, or some other religious symbol, was forced to formalize the kiss even further. Unable to approach close to the sacred object, either because it was raised up and physically inaccessible, or because he was forbidden to come near to it, he was driven to make a 'long-distance kiss'. Simply to mouth a kiss with the lips, in the direction of the symbol, was visually inadequate. Some form of mime that displayed the transmission of the kiss was needed, and the obvious answer was to use the hand, kissing that and then moving it in the direction of the revered object. In this way, the fingertips kiss was born.

The precise antiquity of this gesture is not known, but it is certainly more than 2,000 years old and was common in ancient Greece and Rome, and in biblical times in the Near East. It is recorded that the Greeks and Romans, when entering and leaving a temple, threw a kiss towards the image of the deity, and kisses were also thrown towards sacred objects, such as altars, graves, statues and sacred stones. In the same way, early Christians gave the finger-tips kiss towards the crucifix.

In its original form, this action was therefore one of adoration, restricted to a specifically religious context, but as time passed it slowly extended its range, sinking in intensity from adoration to praise. The fingertips kiss was now offered, not only to symbols of the deity, but also to priests, holy-men, god-kings, emperors, and eventually to any lordly or dominant individual, as an act of rev-erence, adulation or flattery. Eventually it passed into general use as a form of humble salutation, though not without criticism. Tacitus, for instance, records his disapproval of the use of this gesture by the Roman emperor Otho who, on the occasion of his ascension to the throne in A.D. 69, threw kisses to the cheering crowd. His action was attacked as unsuitably 'slavish'.

Over the centuries the European courts continued to use the fingertips kiss as a formal obeisance, a flowery and falsely exag-gerated way of saying to an overlord: 'You are god-like, and I am your humble slave.' Such obsequious displays were criticized again in the sixteenth century by the Italian archbishop Giovanni della Casa, in his *Galateo*, an instruction book on good manners. He accepts the gesture as properly belonging to 'Those solemnities that church men do use at their Altars, and in their divine service both to God and to his holy things', but scorns the use of the fingertips kiss towards other men, because it treats them 'as if they were holy things'. He adds that this fashion is not of Italian origin, but is 'barbarous and strange and not long since, from whence I know not, transported into Italy'. He points towards the Spanish court as a probable source of what he calls 'superstitious ceremonies', and it is certainly true that, at the time, Spain was the country with the most elaborate system of court etiquette in the whole of Europe. It has been suggested that the fingertips kiss may have flourished there because of the long Arab influence in that region, the Arabs having retained (even to the present day) the fingertips kiss as part of their formal greeting ceremony, in which the fingers are touched to the chest, mouth and forehead when bowing.

Caroso, in his *Della Nobiltà di Dame*, published in Venice in 1600, gives us the most detailed description of how the gesture was per-formed in courtly circles. It was always executed with the right hand, which should not touch the mouth, being kept 'somewhat distant, and bending it a little, not keeping it straight'. The action was accompanied by a bow or a curtsy. The arm, as it approached the

The fingertips kiss performed as an act of adoration. From John Bulwer's *Chirologia* of 1644.

mouth, with the wrist and the hand curving inwards, brought the index finger nearest to the lips, this being the 'showy' finger of the period, often adorned with a large ring.

In Elizabethan England, both Shakespeare and Ben Jonson, in several of their plays, had satirical comments to make on the use of this gesture in the fawning manners of court circles, and it was clearly not employed by the general population. By the seventeenth century it had become more popular, although in a rather abbreviated form. As a Restoration greeting, it was no more than the flourish of the hand in the direction of the mouth and then forwards, as part of the elaborate bowing ceremony: 'You must always pull off your glove, and kiss your hand when you take from or present

The fingertips kiss as part of a seventeenth-century bow by a French nobleman. Before the act of salutation, the glove is removed and held in the other hand. From a drawing by Jacques Callot.

anything to, a person of quality, or when you return anything to them.' But it was important not to keep them waiting, so the correct form was to hand over the object first and then afterwards 'not to forget to kiss your hand'.

In her study of the history of courteous behaviour, *The Polite World*, Joan Wildeblood traces the history of this gesture through to the eighteenth century, where she notes that the action is even more curtailed, becoming 'a mere circular motion of the hand and arm as it is extended forward'. English etiquette books of that century no longer refer to the kissing element, and as we pass into the nineteenth century and beyond, the formal gesture fades completely out of sight. In a late edition of della Casa's *Galateo*, published in England in 1774, the criticism of the use of the fingertips kiss has been intensified by the translator. It has now become a 'ridiculous custom' ... 'a practice, wretched in itself, and still further prostituted by a promiscuous use of it on all occasions ... and has its whole existence in superfluous titles and empty words.' This stronger interpretation of the original reflects the changing attitude towards exaggerated displays of subordination, a shift which influenced, not only the use of the fingertips kiss, but also the whole range of bowings and scrapings that had once been part and parcel of social etiquette.

Given this shift, and its acceleration in the twentieth century, it is surprising, at first glance, that the fingertips kiss should have survived at all in modern Europe. The secret of its survival, however, lies in its removal from the formal sphere to the informal. Just as it moved originally, from the strictly religious, adorational role, to the more generally subordinate, respectful role, so it sank again to a third level — the cheerfully, almost playfully informal.

Today no one employs the fingertips kiss in a solemn act of greeting or praise towards a powerful dominant figure on an important occasion. Instead it is used in a light-hearted way towards a loved one, or in an exuberant moment of praise for something tasty or beautiful. In becoming informal in this way, it has split into two. It is either a salutation or an act of praise. In its earlier existence, it was transmitting both messages simultaneously, since it was only ever used as a salutation to a praised individual (or religious symbol). To kiss the fingertips to someone was both to salute *and* to praise them. Since then, the double message has divided and the gesture now transmits one or other signal. Which signal dominates in which region has now emerged from the present field study.

DISTRIBUTION

Of the 1,200 informants questioned in our field study, 1,025 of them reported that the fingertips kiss was used locally. In none of the 40 locations was it totally absent, although it was rare in the Celtic regions. In many places it was known by all the subjects interviewed. The majority (601) identified it as a complimentary gesture, nearly always with reference to attractive girls or tasty food. In such cases, the gesture was not performed *to* someone or something, but *about* them, for the benefit of a third party.

In contrast to the kiss-as-praise, the kiss-as-salutation was always performed directly *towards* the saluted person. This was reported to be the primary meaning of the gesture by 375 of our informants.

The specific messages, as reported to us in the field, were as follows: *Kiss-as-praise*: beautiful, cute, delicious, divine, excellent, exquisite, fantastic, fine, good, great, lovely, magnificent, marvellous, nice, O.K., perfect, pleasant, pretty, sexy, splendid, stupendous, super, superb, supreme, tasty, wonderful. *Kiss-as-salutation*: affectionate salute, blow a kiss, blowing greeting, goodbye, greeting kiss, hullo, parting kiss, sending a kiss, throw a kiss, welcome.

When these specific messages are combined into the two major categories and plotted as histograms (p. 9) or as a gesture map, it soon becomes obvious that there are some significant trends as one moves across Europe. Instead of a random scatter of high-praise and high-salutation sites, they appear in major groupings. The first cluster, the high-praise group, extends from Spain in the west, through France, Belgium, Holland, Denmark, Germany, Austria and Yugoslavia, to mainland Greece and Turkey. In all these cases, more than half the informants gave *praise* as the primary meaning of the fingertips kiss. The second cluster comes in mainland Italy where, at all six sites visited, the responses were more mixed, with roughly equal totals for *praise* and *salutation*. This Italian trend away from high-praise continues in the islands surrounding the Italian mainland. In Sardinia, Sicily, Malta and Corfu, there is always a dominance of the *salutation* meaning. A fourth cluster is found in the north of Europe, in the British-Norwegian zone, where no particular dominance appears because there is a generally low level of response.

There are four exceptional, isolated cases that do not fit in with these major groupings. Tunisia and the Canary Islands are both high-praise sites, while Portugal and Sweden are both high-

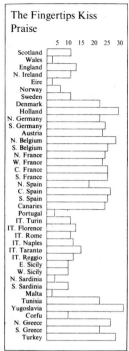

The Fingertips Kiss
Praise

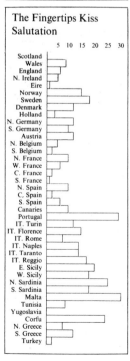

The Fingertips Kiss
Salutation

salutation sites. Tunisia appears to be following its late colonial rulers — the French — and the Canaries are reacting as part of Spain (which, of course, they still are). But it is difficult to understand the Portuguese and Swedish figures. Portugal contrasts vividly with neighbouring Spain, and Sweden with nearby Denmark. It is almost as if, in these two cases, the gesture difference reflects a tradition-polarization — part of a general social trend to keep identities distinct between close neighbours. But such a contrast does not occur between many other neighbours, where this gesture is concerned, so the explanation is a weak one.

It is possible to sum up the general situation by expressing the praise/salutation balance across Europe, arranged in its four major clusters:

Group 1 Continental Europe excluding Italy (and Portugal): *4-to-1 in favour of praise.*

Group 2 Mainland Italy: *1-to-1 balance praise/salutation.*

Group 3 Islands around Italy: *3-to-1 in favour of salutation.*

Group 4 British–Norwegian Zone: *1-to-1 balance (low levels).*

It is tempting, when looking at these groupings, to explain the differences on the basis of variations in local temperament, with the dour northerners and the unsophisticated islanders being too reserved to perform effusively complimentary displays. But such interpretations, although popular, do not stand up to close examination. There are too many contradictions. The Portuguese and Canarians do not fit the pattern; and why should the supposedly volatile Italians differ so markedly from the rest of Continental Europe? At this stage we can give no simple answers, merely record, for the first time, the facts. But one myth that the facts do explode is the idea that the fingertips kiss is an essentially 'French Gesture'. G. J. Brault, for instance, writing in 1963, calls it 'perhaps the best-known Gallic gesture' and points out that it has become so strongly identified with the French that it is often used by a foreigner wishing to imitate a Frenchman's actions. This is certainly the case, and yet our figures show that the gesture is no more French than it is Spanish, Yugoslav, Dutch, Greek or Turkish. And the suspicion must be that the 'foreigner' imitating the gesturing Frenchman is probably English-speaking, rather than one of the other inhabitants of mainland Europe, who is unlikely to see anything odd about the Gallic addiction to blowing kisses of appreciation into the air. Indeed, it is safe to say that remarkably few gestures are specific to one nation, and most of the comments that have been made in the past, concerning 'French Gestures' or 'Italian Gestures' must be re-examined. Just because a gesture is used in France or Italy, or any other country, does not make it exclusive to that place. We would think it absurd to refer to the 'French Smile', simply because Frenchmen smile, or the 'Italian Frown', because Italians often frown, and the same is true today for the vast majority of symbolic gestures. Once, at some distant point in their history, they must presumably have originated in some restricted locality. But since then they have nearly all spread, by gradual cultural diffusion, until many of them are now commonplace right across Europe and, via colonial expansions, far beyond.

The interesting feature of the expanding, cross-cultural spread of early symbolic gestures is that it seldom leads to a úniform coverage over the entire range. The degree of penetration into neighbouring cultures varies considerably. The fingertips kiss may now be seen in most European and Mediterranean countries, but not, as we have observed, to the same extent in each region. This leads on to the question of what forms of local resistance exist. If *some* people in a particular culture know and use the gesture, and it is a useful social signal, what is it that stops it from becoming so generally popular that it is known to *all* members of that culture?

One form of gesture-resistance has already been mentioned: the desire to be different from near neighbours. This could be called the 'cultural-prejudice factor' — the dislike of behaving like foreigners — the need to be different from 'them'.

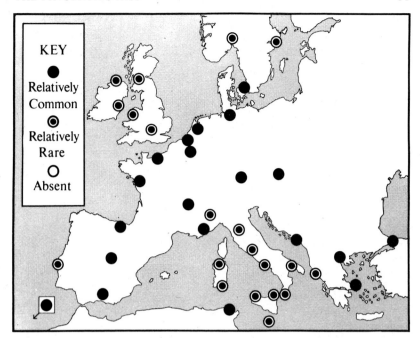

THE FINGERTIPS KISS Meaning: praise

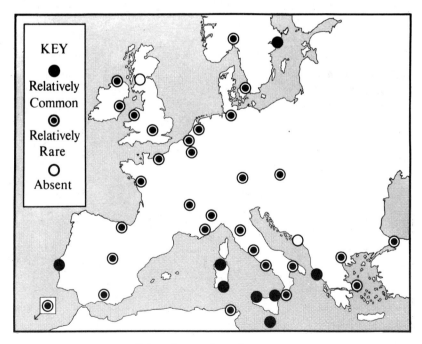

THE FINGERTIPS KISS Meaning: salutation

Another form of resistance can arise because of the existence of an already indigenous gesture that performs the same task — what we can call the 'gestural-niche factor'. If, for example, the British already employ a thumbs-up gesture, or some other signal when making a sign of approval, then the spread of the fingertips kiss gesture into the British cultural region may be impeded. Its gestural niche is already occupied.

This may partially account for the lack of dominance of the kiss-as-praise gesture in both the British and the Italian regions. In the latter, there is a rich repertoire of complimentary signs, one of which, the cheek screw, is dealt with later in this book, and which is a dominant praise gesture for many Italians.

Another factor reducing the popularity of a particular symbolic gesture is the phenomenon of 'gesture-replacement'. A new gesture arises locally and becomes fashionable, partially or largely replacing the old gesture, which begins to look quaint and 'old-fashioned'. The new gesture has the double value of transmitting its basic signal and, at the same time, displaying that the gesturer is 'in the know' and up to date.

Local taboos may also impose restrictions of a special kind. If, for instance, a culture prohibits public kissing, then this may work against the use of a symbolic version of the basic action, such as fingertips kissing. Despite its remoteness from the original mouth action, it may nevertheless be tainted by its association with the idea of sending a kiss, even at a distance.

Finally, there is the factor of 'gesture-obscurity'. Some gestures are based on a symbolism that has only a restricted, localized meaning. A Swedish 'reindeer gesture', to take an imaginary example, would be obscure to any southerner. Such gestures will often travel badly, because they become essentially 'abstract' in foreign regions. This resistance cannot, of course, apply to the case of the fingertips kiss which, as already pointed out, is based on the globally distributed action of mouth kissing.

It is too early yet for us to state with any conviction which of these various resistance factors are operating across the gesture map of the fingertips kiss. Probably the first three are all playing a part, but precisely how, where and in what proportions remain to be investigated.

MINOR MEANINGS

With every gesture investigated in the field there have inevitably been a few unusual or idiosyncratic interpretations by a small number of our informants. These fall into several categories: the misunderstood, the over-helpful, the inventive, and the rare but significant.

Misunderstandings arise where the informants do not know the main meanings of the gesture in question, and mistake it for a similar gesture which they do know. In the case of the fingertips kiss, a total of 28 informants at no fewer than 12 different locations, interpreted it as 'eating'. This is because of the existence of a common mimic action of putting imaginary food into the mouth. Not knowing the 'kiss' version of the gesture, they 'saw', as it were, only the hand-to-mouth element of the movement, and explained that as an eating signal. In a similar way, 11 informants, at 7 different localities, described it as a 'whistle' gesture, based again only on the hand-to-mouth element, and ignoring the 'throwing' element of the kiss. They interpreted it as a mime of the action of placing fingers into the mouth to produce a piercing whistle. Three others, at three sites, based their answers on the idea that the hand-to-mouth action had something to do with speaking, or being unable to speak — a silent pointing of the fingertips towards the mouth being the indication of someone 'dumb' in certain regions.

The over-helpful category, unable to understand the gesture, searches desperately for some explanation, no matter how unlikely, in order to 'be of assistance' to the investigator. One informant, for example, obviously searching for an answer, finally stated that the fingertips kiss gesture meant 'I couldn't give a damn'. The links in such cases are so tenuous that it is often impossible to see what they might be. Perhaps in this case, he felt that the flicking out of the hand was in some way dismissive (relating it, possibly, to the chin flick gesture discussed later on).

The inventive category includes those informants who, not wishing to appear ignorant, invent some strange answer in order to 'score a point'. In this case, one reported that the gesture meant 'nonchalant', another that it meant 'he's a poof'. In both cases they were seeing the hand movement as a flourish, and then applying an inventive interpretation which might vaguely fit.

Fortunately these idiosyncratic or mistaken responses are comparatively uncommon — in this case, no more than a handful out of the 1,200, and they do no damage to the results for the major interpretations. And occasionally, there is a rare but none the less interesting reply amongst this group of minor categories. In the present case it occurred in Tunisia, where one Arab informant gave the answer that the fingertips kiss means 'Thanks to God'. This relates to the Tunisian greeting ritual of touching first the chest, then the mouth, then the forehead, and then finally moving the hand up towards the sky. The four actions are brief, swift movements of the hand, following one into another, but sometimes the action is abbreviated from the four elements to three, two, or only one. When one element occurs alone, it is usually the hand-to-mouth gesture, and this is the form which was being identified as the fingertips kiss. Although only one of the 30 Tunisian subjects reacted in this way, his response is nevertheless historically significant. In fact, he is almost certainly the only one of the 1,200 informants who was still linking the modern fingertips kiss gesture with its original, ancient role as a sign of religious adoration.

The fingers cross as a Stars and Stripes good luck patch for attachment to denim clothing.

2 The Fingers Cross

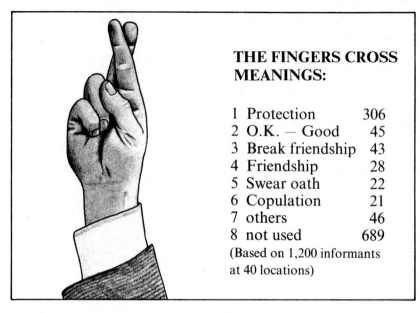

**THE FINGERS CROSS
MEANINGS:**

1	Protection	306
2	O.K. — Good	45
3	Break friendship	43
4	Friendship	28
5	Swear oath	22
6	Copulation	21
7	others	46
8	not used	689

(Based on 1,200 informants
at 40 locations)

DESCRIPTION

The middle finger is twisted over and around the forefinger, while the other fingers are bent back fully and held under the thumb. The hand may be raised slightly as the fingers are crossed, so that the 'locked' forefinger and middle finger point upwards, or the hand may be held forwards, with the crossed fingers in a horizontal position. The posture is usually held for only a few seconds. A common variant occurs with the hand held behind the back or in some other hidden position, so that, although visible to a companion, it is concealed from a third party.

ORIGINS — As the Sign of the Cross

The most popular explanation of the dominant use of this gesture is that it is a religious sign that has broken loose from its devout origins to become a 'common superstition'. Viewed in this way, the act of crossing the fingers was originally a cryptic version of making the sign of the Christian Cross. Instead of crossing himself openly in the usual way, a Christian could protect himself from the powers of evil by making a 'cross' with his fingers, an action small enough to be easily concealed from unwelcome eyes. Assuming this interpretation to be correct, the belief of the gesturer would be that the presence of the powerful Holy Cross would ward off evil or hostile influences. Such protection would be called upon if the gesturer was facing some kind of risk, and felt the need of God's aid, or if he was behaving badly in some way — telling a lie, for instance — and wanted to protect himself from retribution.

Today, many people who use the gesture as a 'good luck' sign are unaware of these Christian origins and think of it merely as a joke — a token of mild alarm. The common phrase accompanying it, in English, is usually 'I am keeping my fingers crossed for you', indicating the existence of a shared fear of risk and a common desire to avoid it.

In its original form, when the action was presumably being used secretively, it was not, in our sense, a true gesture, since it communicated nothing to a human observer. In a religious sense, however, it *was* acting as a gesture because the devout believer was intending it to communicate with his God.

Since crossing the fingers was such a highly stylized way of making the sign of the cross, and did not look overtly cruciform, it is easy to see how it could drift away from its sacred role and become a simple piece of folklore, more repeated than understood. Eventually, its origins obscured, it could then come out into the open as a light-hearted social gesture, performed by Christians and non-Christians alike.

Although there is very little early evidence to go on, this is the explanation we tend to accept. However, three other suggestions deserve mention. The first sees it as a special form of the *Mano Pantea*, the ancient hand posture used as a Christian blessing. In this the hand is held up with the thumb, the forefinger and the middle finger erect, and the other two fingers bent. The three erect digits represent the Holy Trinity, with the thumb standing for God, the forefinger for the Holy Ghost, and the middle finger for Christ. By placing the middle finger over the top of the forefinger, a gesture is formed which is said to indicate 'Christ Victorious'. According to Macdonald Critchley, in his book *Silent Language*, this 'is to be seen in El Greco's Christ in Toledo Cathedral and in the sixteenth century mosaic of Christ Pantocrator in St Mark's, Venice, and in still earlier mosaics at Ravenna'. But the fact that the modern gesture is called *crossing* the fingers, seems to favour the idea that the sign of the cross, rather than this somewhat esoteric explanation, is the underlying source. Even if this is not the case, and Critchley's explanation is correct, the protective significance is barely altered. In both instances, the gesturer is, in effect, calling upon Christ to help him.

A second alternative ignores Christian influences. In his book *The Story of the Human Hand*, Walter Sorell states that 'To cross one's fingers ... when wishing someone luck goes far back to a belief in magic that can tie things together.' Here, presumably, the two fingers are seen, not so much struggling to form a convincing cross, as straining to tie themselves into a knot. Again, the title of the gesture is against this alternative suggestion. If it were true, one might expect the action to be called 'tying one's fingers', rather than crossing them.

An entry in the *Standard Dictionary of Folklore Mythology and Legend* interprets crossed fingers more in the spirit of a childlike act of 'crossing something out', a familiar enough act in the world of clumsy childhood writing: 'To keep the fingers crossed while lying is a child's trick. The idea is that to do so "crosses out" the wickedness of lying or protects the soul against the Devil's seizing it at the moment of sin.' It is certainly true that children commonly use the gesture in this way, and Iona and Peter Opie, in their study of *The Lore and Language of Schoolchildren* include the children's rhyme: 'Cross my fingers, cross my toes, hope I don't go in one of those', used when an ambulance goes by. But there is something unconvincing about this explanation. It explains the word 'cross' in the title of the gesture, but it ignores the form of the action. To twist one finger over another bears no motoric relationship to the back-and-forth movement of crossing something out.

Bearing these comments in mind, it seems safest, at present, to accept the initial interpretation that to cross the fingers protectively is to make a stylized form of the Christian sign of the cross.

ORIGINS — As a Sign of a Couple

There is a second major meaning for the crossed fingers gesture that bears no relationship to the protective meaning, and here the symbolism employed is quite distinct. Because there are two fingers involved and because they are tightly applied to one another, they can readily be seen as representing two people with some kind of close connection between them. The connection takes two basic forms: simple friendship and sexual contact. When describing two close friends, the gesturer holds out his crossed fingers and says: 'They are just like that.' In such a case, the juxtaposition of the

The fingers cross gesture used as a protective device in a school
playground in England.

fingers indicates nothing more than togetherness, rapport, or unity,
but when used in a sexual context, the one finger on top of the other
represents one lover on top of the other in an act of copulation. This
is sometimes made more explicit by rhythmically tapping the upper
finger on the lower finger. A rare but amusing variant of this sexual
symbolism involves an inverted finger-crossing, with the forefinger
above the middle-finger. This means 'the woman on top of the man',
and is used as a joke about a supposedly domineering female.
Related to this is another rare interpretation, in which the relationship of the two people symbolized by the two fingers is based
on their status rather than their sexual activity. Here, the gesturer
assumes the role of the uppermost finger, and the meaning is 'I'm the
boss', or 'I'm on top'.

Going to the other extreme from friendship, but still employing
the two fingers as symbolic of two people, is the use of the gesture as
a signal of breaking off a relationship. In this case, the crossed
fingers are held out towards a friend with whom there has been a
violent argument or disagreement, as a sign that the friendship is
about to be ended. If the friend agrees to the break, he may thrust
one of his fingers between the crossed digits and forcibly tear them
apart with a sudden snatch of his hand. This function of the crossed
fingers gesture is essentially parasitic on the basic friendship gesture
and only exists because of it. Here, holding out the fingers, crossed
tightly, acts as an intention movement of what is to come, because if

the friend does not actively tear the fingers apart, the gesturer himself will go on to flick them vigorously away from one another, shifting them from the crossed position to a widely splayed out posture, signifying the separation that is about to take place.

To someone who does not use the gesture in this way there seems to be an inherent confusion between the friendship gesture and the break-friendship gesture. Both look the same, and yet the latter can clearly transmit its message *without* the separation of the fingers occurring. Lack of ambiguity in this instance is achieved entirely by the context in which the gesture appears. It is unlikely to occur in silent isolation. Usually, there is an angry verbal exchange to accompany it.

DISTRIBUTION

As a result of its two major derivations, and their several subdivisions, the distribution of the crossed fingers gesture was complex and difficult to analyse. Several of the meanings, although widespread, were at a rather low level, in terms of frequency, and this makes quantitative statements difficult. But in its role as a protective signal it was common enough, and we can look at this dominant meaning first, before considering the rarer forms.

Of the 1,200 informants questioned in our field study, a total of 511 reported that the crossed fingers gesture was used locally, for some meaning or other. Of these, the majority – 306 – identified it as a protective sign. If we examine the specific protective messages given to us, it is clear that they fall into three categories. These can be summed up as (1) Good luck (2) Defence against bad luck, and (3) Cancelling a lie.

The good-luck messages included: for luck, good fortune, hope for the best, hopeful, hoping for good, hoping for luck, optimism – here's hoping, to wish good luck.

The defence-against-bad-luck messages included: against bad luck, against the evil eye, child's pax, defence against evil omen, protection against evil, protection when passing a cemetery, self-protection, superstitious protection, used for exorcisms.

The lie-cancelling messages included: annul a bet, cancel a lie, cancel ill-effects of having done something wrong, cancel praise (presumably false praise), cancel white lie, lying cross, to nullify something, witch's cross, word-of-honour cancelled.

Although this covers a fairly wide range, it is clear that, in all cases, the gesturer is seeking protection (1) against the failure of something good happening in the future (2) against the likelihood of something bad happening in the future, and (3) against the consequences of something bad that is being done now.

Combining together these three closely related groups of messages, under the general heading of protective finger-crossing, produces an interesting gesture map and histogram (p. 21). It becomes immediately clear that, as a popular gesture, it is restricted to N.W. Europe, with the British Isles as its stronghold. However, although it is uncommon in continental Europe, it nevertheless occurs everywhere except in the far S.E. region. Amongst our 40 sites, it is totally absent only from Turkey, S. Greece and Tunisia. Its absence from our two non-Christian locations, Turkey and Tunisia, supports our feeling that this is indeed a Christian gesture in origin. Furthermore, it seems likely that its primary source is British and that it has spread outwards from the British Isles, reaching a wide, but low-level scatter across the continent. It is tempting to read into the map a 'Catholic factor'. In other words, a suggestion that, in predominantly Catholic countries, there has been a greater resistance to the spread of the gesture than elsewhere. But there is only a faint suspicion of this, and it would require much more detailed surveys to test the significance of this. The reason for supposing that there might be such a factor at work is the survival in strongly Catholic communities of the full 'crossing oneself' gesture, not only as a church-going sign, but also as an informal protective gesture, whenever danger threatens. (The full gesture, as is well known, involves the making of the sign of the cross by moving the hand from forehead to chest, then from left breast to right breast.) Because they still use this larger gesture in a wide variety of circumstances, devout Catholics hardly have need of the 'meaner' gesture of crossing the fingers, and, as a result, the progress of the British sign across Southern Europe would be expected to be sluggish and its success poor. This is certainly what seems to be happening, although there are a few sites, such as East Sicily and the Canary Islands, that do not fit the pattern particularly well.

Related to the general, protective category are two additional meanings that require passing mention. The first is a category that can be roughly labelled as 'O.K.—Good' signs. Here, the informants make no mention of being protected, or of needing protection, when making the crossed fingers gesture, but the implication is that, instead of needing it *now* (as when lying), or in the *future* (as when

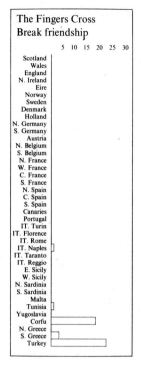

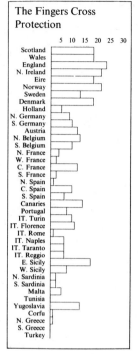

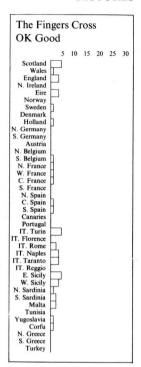

faced with some risk), they are celebrating having had this protection in the immediate *past*. The messages reported included: all is
well, all right, everything all right, everything is O.K., fine, I'm all
right, O.K., well done, we're fixed — it's O.K. To the Englishman,
these are messages to which he would automatically attach a thumbs
up sign in most cases, but to a small number of people (45) scattered
right across Europe, they are messages for which the crossed fingers
gesture seems most appropriate. They can best be summed up under
the generalized message: 'I have *had* good luck.'

Also related to the sign-of-the-cross derivation of the crossed
fingers gesture, is its use, according to 22 informants, during the act
of swearing an oath. This was recorded in 13 sites and was most
common in the Sicily–Sardinia–Malta area, but was rare everywhere. It is probably a survival of what was once a much more
frequently employed sign, clinging on today mostly in isolated island communities. Specific messages included: assurance of truth,
for swearing, guarantee of truth, oath-taking, oath that I am telling
the truth, swear I am sincere, swearing the truth, used when promis-
ing something. Interestingly, some informants said that the correct

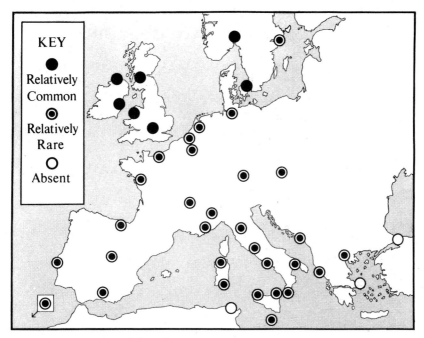

THE FINGERS CROSS Meaning: protection

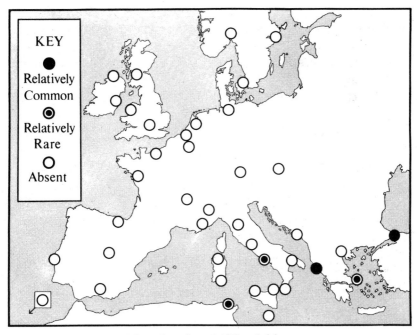

THE FINGERS CROSS Meaning: break friendship

way to swear an oath was to cross, not the forefinger and the middle finger but, instead, the forefinger and the thumb. One even said that the ordinary crossed fingers gesture contrasted with this thumb-cross, and meant '*bad* fortune to you'. This tied in with three informants at the same sites who simply gave a blunt 'gives you bad luck' interpretation to the crossed fingers gesture. It seems as if, on these Mediterranean islands, there is the remnant of an ancient digit-crossing system that has somehow come to clash with the now dominant method of finger-crossing that has spread all over Europe. On these same islands were individuals who agreed with the general, modern European trend, so there must obviously be some local confusion. Confirmation of this came in one incident, where Sardinians began to argue amongst themselves about the correct way to make these crossing gestures, the younger people disagreeing with their elders.

Moving on to the second major derivational category — the gesture as a sign of a couple — it is clear that the break-friendship category is grouped in the S.E. of our general range, with Corfu and Turkey as the main centres. The curious feature of this distribution (see gesture map on p. 23) is that mainland Greece, between Corfu and Turkey, hardly knows the gesture in this role. The history of Corfu gives no clue as to why it should share with Turkey this special meaning for the crossed fingers. We would have predicted a long Turkish occupation at some point, to explain the link, but there is no support for this from the historical records for the island, and the similarity between the two sites remains a mystery.

The use of the gesture to signal simple friendship or copulation is so rare and so widely scattered that little can be said about these two distributions at present, except perhaps that the copulation signal is more common in the S.E. than in the rest of the range.

Other minor meanings were even smaller in number and of little interest. Most were apparently wild guesses by over-helpful informants. Only one seemed to have any validity. That concerns five people at widely scattered sites, who interpreted the raised arm with crossed fingers as a request by children to go to the toilet, someone making a query, or a man calling a waiter. Whether they were simply seeing the action as a raised arm demanding attention, or whether in some places there is a special significance about holding the fingers crossed when seeking attention, it is hard to say, but our informants seemed quite certain of this, in which case we must add yet another message to the already long list for this particular symbolic gesture.

The tandem version of the nose thumb, seen in an Italian village just north of Naples.

3 The Nose Thumb

THE NOSE THUMB
MEANINGS:

1	Mockery	1,058
2	others	14
3	not used	128

(Based on 1,200 informants at 40 locations)

DESCRIPTION

One hand is raised so that the thumb touches the tip of the nose, with the fingers spread out in a fan and pointing upwards. The face may be expressionless, or may be grimacing, often with the tongue protruding. A more elaborate version of the gesture is the double-handed or tandem nose-thumb in which the thumb of the second hand is joined on to the little finger of the first. In either the one-handed or the two-handed version, the fingers may be held stiffly erect, or may be waggled back and forth.

ORIGINS

There are three unusual features of this gesture. First, it is known to more Europeans, and over a greater range, than any other symbolic gesture we studied. Second, it has been subjected to a more lengthy and exhaustive historical investigation than any of the other gestures. Folklorist Archer Taylor has published a paper running to over seventy pages, devoted to this single action. Third, it has acquired more names (fourteen in English alone) than any of the other gestures.

Despite these three facts, the origins of thumbing a nose remain puzzling. Why the act of holding the hand up to the nose in this particular posture should be so universally insulting is not at all clear. The clues are vague and often conflicting. Even the antiquity of the gesture is uncertain. Some authors have claimed to recognize it amongst the graffiti of ancient Rome, but others have rejected this as a case of mistaken identity, and no really convincing case has been established. The problem arises from the foreshortening effect of two-dimensional representations of the gesturing human figure. Hands raised in adoration, prayer, surprise, or some other simple gesticulation can easily appear to be in contact with the gesturer's nose, when in reality they are nowhere near it. As a result of this, the earliest convincing records are verbal rather than visual.

The oldest reference we can find comes from Godefroy's dictionary of the French language covering the period from the eleventh to the fifteenth century, where the gesture is given the title of '*Un nez de cire*' — a wax nose. The phrase 'to make a wax nose at someone' suggests a link with the ancient practice of making ugly, derisive wax effigies in which people were represented with unflatteringly long noses. A much later title of 'making a long nose', which is one of the most widespread of all the various names for this gesture, and which appears not only in English, but also in French, Italian, Dutch and German, could well be a descendant of this earlier 'wax nose' title. In other words, the distinctive feature of the gesture could be its elongation of the nose, reminiscent of the mocking effigies. But there is no hard evidence from ancient writings to support this.

The earliest detailed description of the gesture dates from 1532

The tandem version of the nose thumb insult, shown by a red devil figurine collected in Europe in the nineteenth century by Frederick Elworthy. Pitt Rivers Museum, Oxford.

The nose thumb gesture as a sign of mockery. From De Jorio, 1832.

and occurs in the writings of François Rabelais, who devotes a whole chapter to a duel of gestures between Panurge and an English scholar. As the chapter proceeds, the gestures become more and more rude and bizarre, with the Englishman becoming increasingly 'pale and trembling' under their accumulated impact. In this gesture-communication parody, Rabelais exaggerates wildly, but the description of the nose-thumbing phase of the duel is clear enough:

> Panurge suddenly lifted up in the aire his right hand, and put the thumb thereof into the nostril of the same side, holding his foure fingers streight out, and closed orderly in a parallel line to the point of his nose, shutting the left eye wholly, and making the other wink with a profound depression of the eye-brows and eye-lids. Then lifted up he his left hand, with hard wringing and stretching forth his foure fingers, and elevating his thumb, which he held in a line directly correspondent to the situation of his right hand, with a distance of a cubit and a halfe between them. This done, in the same forme he abased towards the ground both the one and the other hand. Lastly, he held them in the midst, as aiming right at the English mans nose.

The Englishman then retaliates against this gestural onslaught in the following way:

> Then the English man made this signe, his left hand all open he lifted up into the aire, then instantly shut his fist the foure fingers thereof, and his thumb extended at length he placed

upon the gristle of his nose; presently after, he lifted up his right
hand all open, and all open abased and bent it downwards,
putting the thumb thereof in the very place where the little
finger of the left hand did close in the fist, and the foure right
hand fingers he softly moved in the aire; then contrarily he did
with the right hand what he had done with the left, and with the
left what he had done with the right.

Neither Panurge's elaborate gesture, nor the Englishman's response
to it, is precisely what we know today as the thumbing-a-nose
gesture, but both are close enough for us to be sure that we are
dealing with basically the same action. Furthermore, both occur in a
suitably insulting, teasing context that matches well with the modern
usage of the nose thumb gesture.

After Rabelais, the next appearance of the action is in the work of
Pieter Brueghel. In a 1560 print of his entitled *La Fête des fous*, a
fool is shown making the two-handed version of the gesture in the
centre foreground of the picture. Again, there is a slight difference in
the form of the action, when compared with modern times, the
thumb touching the gesturer's head, not on the nose-tip, but just
beneath the nose. A sketch by another sixteenth-century artist,

Detail of a Pieter Brueghel drawing showing one of the earliest
representations of the nose thumb gesture. Sixteenth century.

Bernardo Passeri, also shows the gesture being performed by a fool, or jester. The context is clearly one of mockery and, in this instance, the thumb is placed, in the modern manner, against the tip of the nose.

It has been suggested to us by an informant in Germany that the gesture may have originated specifically as a jester's signal. It seems that a medieval jester named Till Eulenspiegel, who was born in Belgium, travelled through Germany taunting and mocking the locals as part of his act, and he is said to have employed the nose-thumb gesture as one of his main insults, making it popular over a wide area. Whether or not this is true, it would appear that by the sixteenth century the gesture had become associated with fools and jesters in a context of light-hearted teasing.

From this period onwards, the gesture is referred to by many authors, and Archer Taylor has traced its history right through to the present day. So many names have become attached to it over its long history that it is worth listing them here as a brief glossary:

1   To thumb the nose
There is no mystery over this title — it is simply descriptive of the action of putting the thumb up to the nose. It is the most popular name in English today for the gesture, and has taken over from most of the earlier, more obscure titles. It dates back at least to 1916.

2   To make a nose
This is a slightly earlier, simpler version of the previous name, dating back to 1903.

3   To cock a snook
This is the only one of the more obscure English titles to have survived from earlier times. It is well known today, although few people understand its wording. Even some dictionaries refer to it as 'of obscure origin', but it is not too difficult to trace its source. The word 'cock' is used in the same sense as in 'cock an eyebrow', a dog 'cocking its ears', or the 'cocking of a gun'. In other words, cocking means simply 'moving upwards'. The word 'snook' is a modification of 'snout', and was used, in particular, to refer to a long, projecting nose. A 'snooker' was one who 'smells an object like a dog' — that is, who pushes his nose forward to scent or smell out something. From all this it is clear that 'to cock a snook' was to 'thrust up a long nose'. Seen this way, the gesture has two elements: sticking the nose in the

air, and projecting it forwards in the direction of the insulted victims as though insolently sniffing them out. It dates back at least to 1904.

4   To pull a snook

A variant of 'cock a snook', with the emphasis on pulling the nose out into a long shape, as in a 1928 reference to someone 'pulling a long snook at the gallows'.

5   To cut a snooks

An even earlier variant, dating from 1879, with the word 'cut' presumably referring to the extending forward of the nose in such a way that it 'cuts through the air'.

6   To make a long nose

This title, which can be dated to 1868 and probably much earlier, is sometimes applied only to the two-handed version of the gesture. It has equivalents in a number of other languages, where it is often the most popular expression today when speaking of the gesture. In France it becomes *le nez long*, in Germany *die lange Nase*, and in Italy *il naso lungo*. Whether it stresses the thrusting of the nose into someone else's business, or the crude miming of a long, ugly nose, is not certain.

7   Taking a sight

This appears to have been one of the most popular titles used in the nineteenth century. Charles Dickens refers to it in 1840 in *The Old Curiosity Shop*, and it lasts through almost to the end of the century, but then fades out. It relates the form of the gesture to the naval action of taking a sight with a sextant, the arms of the sextant being in a similar position, in front of the nose.

8   Taking a double sight

Dating from the same period, this was the name given to the two-handed version of the gesture. The one-handed form was sometimes referred to as 'taking a single sight'. The earliest recorded date for the double sight is 1836.

9   The Shanghai gesture

Like the title 'taking a sight', this name seems to relate to the way the gesture resembles the use of an instrument. Shanghai is the name given to a catapult in Australia, and the action of holding the forked

Early nineteenth-century cartoon of the nose-thumb gesture.

catapult up to the face when firing it, is seen as reminiscent of the gesture. *The Shanghai Gesture* was the name of a play by author John Colton in 1926, but it has been used rarely since that time.

10 *Queen Anne's fan*

Because the fingers are fanned out when thumbing the nose, the gesture has a mild resemblance to holding a folding fan close to the face. Fans became immensely popular in Europe during the late seventeenth century, when Queen Anne was on the throne, and their popularity survived right through the eighteenth century and into Victorian times. A whole language of fan movements and positions grew up, so that a lady could silently indicate her mood and her feelings to her companions, merely by the way she directed, flicked, folded or unfolded her fan. For instance, hiding the eyes behind an opened fan meant 'I love you'; covering the left ear with a closed fan meant 'do not betray our secret'; touching the tip of the nose with the closed fan meant 'you are not to be trusted'; and slowly lowering the open fan until it pointed down towards the ground meant 'I despise you'. With these and many other such signs a lady of fashion could encourage or discourage male attentions without uttering a word. We know that the nose-thumb gesture was in use during this period and it is not surprising that it came to be looked upon as a crude pastiche of a fan gesture. The name 'Queen Anne's fan' does not appear to refer to any specific, queenly use of the fan, but simply to the fact that she ruled at the time of the fan's first wide popularity. The term was not current, apparently, until late Victorian times, and the people who used it were no doubt searching for a title that somehow epitomized fanmanship.

11   The Japanese fan
A similar explanation applies to this name. Folding fans originated in Japan, spreading from there to the western world, via China. Another way of giving the nose-thumb gesture a title that epitomized fan-using, was to name it after the original source of the fans.

12   The Spanish fan
The same explanation applies here, the ladies of Spain having retained the folding fan longer than their more northerly counterparts. This title for the nose-thumbing gesture was used in the present century, when Spanish ladies would be almost the only 'model' left, from whom a fanning name could be borrowed. As a popular title for the gesture, it appears to have faded in more recent years.

13   To pull bacon
This was a popular description of the nose thumb in the 1880s, but became rare later and the phrase 'to pull bacon' only makes sense in terms of early slang. Bacon was the name given to a stupid rustic, and the term 'bacon-faced' meant clownish and dull. So, to pull bacon was to pull a stupid, clownish face. A police report dating from 1887 uses the phrase in the following way: 'The officers spoke to him, when he put his fingers to his nose and pulled bacon at them.'

14   Coffee-milling
In the middle of the last century the action of turning the handle of a coffee-mill was taken as the title for a gesture very similar to the nose

thumb — so similar, in fact, that no distinction has been made between them in the past. In reality, the details of the actions were significantly different, because although the first hand performs the ordinary one-handed nose thumb, the second hand, brought up to touch it, does not repeat the posture of fanned fingers, but instead revolves, like a hand rotating a coffee-mill. The following quotation from Farmer and Henley's *Slang Dictionary* gives a clear description: 'Coffee-milling: To cock snooks or "take a sight" by putting the thumb of one hand to the nose and grinding the little finger with the other, as if you worked an imaginary coffee mill.' It is clear from this that the gesture *is* being equated with the ordinary nose-thumbing gesture, despite the fact that there is a vital difference in the movement of the second hand. A quote from a ballad of 1854 gives a clue to the way the phrase was used: 'When I went the pace so wildly, caring little what might come, coffee-milling care and sorrow, with a nose-adapted thumb.'

15   *To take a grinder*

Equated with the phrase 'take a sight' by early writers on slang, this title relates closely to the last one. Barrere and Leland, in their *Dictionary of Slang, Jargon and Cant* published in 1889, describe the action in the following words: 'to take a grinder is to make an insulting gesture by applying the left thumb to the nose, and turning the right hand round it as if in the act of grinding an organ.' In 1836, Dickens had used it in *The Pickwick Papers*: 'Here Mr Jackson smiled once more upon the company; and, applying his left thumb to the tip of his nose, worked a visionary coffee-mill with his right hand, thereby performing a very graceful piece of pantomime (then much in vogue, but now, unhappily, almost obsolete) which was familiarly denominated taking a grinder.' According to Eric Partridge, this name for the gesture did not finally become fully obsolete until the year 1919. As with coffee-milling, the gesture involves minor differences from the nose-thumbing action. Again, however, these are not sufficient for it to have been considered as a distinct and separate gesture.

16   *The five-finger salute*

A modern name for the gesture, used by school-children who pretend to make a respectful salute and then let their hand slip down from temple to nose. According to Iona and Peter Opie in their recent study of *The Lore and Language of Schoolchildren*, there was a rhyme at the time of the First World War that went: 'Salute the King, Salute the Queen, Salute the German Submarine.' On the word 'king', a smart military salute was given; on the word 'queen', a smart naval salute, and then, on the word 'submarine', the saluting hand was dropped to the nose to make a derisive nose-thumb gesture. During the Second World War, the routine changed slightly: 'Salute the captain of the ship [smart naval salute]. Sorry, sir, my finger slipped [dropping the hand to the nose].'

In addition to these sixteen English names for the nose-thumb gesture, there are many foreign titles. We cannot list them all, but a few of the more important ones in use today include:

FRANCE: *Pied de nez*. This means literally 'a foot of nose', but a slang meaning for the word 'pied' is 'fool', and the origin of the phrase is more likely to be 'fool's nose', which fits well with the early role of the nose thumb as a jester's taunt.

Un pan de nez. The word 'pan' has several meanings, but in this instance it probably means 'a flap of the nose'.

Le nez long. The long nose.

ITALY: *Marameo*. This is by far the most common name for the gesture in Italy today, and derives from the sound of a mewing cat. In some regions it is pronounced *Maramau*.

Palmo di naso. The second most popular title, meaning simply to palm a nose.

Tanto di naso. 'A nose so long', or 'so much nose'. Similar to it is *Naso lungo*, the long nose, another common name.

GERMANY: *Die lange Nase*. The long nose is the most popular term in Germany for the gesture, but a common phrase given by children is '*Atsch! Atsch!*', uttered as they make the two-handed version.

DENMARK: *Raekke naese*. Meaning an extended nose.

YUGOSLAVIA: *Sviri ti svode*. This means 'to play a flute', a name based on the accidental resemblance of the gesture to the action of fingering a flute.

PORTUGAL: *Tocar tromfete*. Another musical analogy, this time the meaning is 'to play the trumpet'.

MALTA: *Neena-neena*. Meaning unknown.

These, then, are the many names acquired by the nose-thumb gesture during its long history, but there still remains the question of its true origin. The various titles give us certain clues — often conflicting — but they do not provide a final answer. Some names are merely descriptive, while others do no more than offer a visual analogy. The question of why the hand, or hands, held up to the nose, with the fingers fanned vertically upwards, should be so widely accepted as a mocking insult, still demands an explanation. The vital information from earlier centuries is missing, and the best we can do is to consider a number of possibilities. They include the following:

1   The gesture as a deformed salute
Archer Taylor, at the end of his history of this gesture, concludes: 'I am inclined to regard the gesture as a parody of the military salute.' He points out that, during the period when the nose thumb became popular and widespread, there was a great deal of development in military procedures, and the method of giving a military salute became standardized in its modern form. As a sign of respect, the raising of the hand to the temple would then be available for deliberate distortion, the deformed salute carrying the opposite meaning, namely disrespect. This suggestion ties in with the war-time use of the gesture, as the five-finger salute, by modern school-children.

Our attitude to this explanation is that it is more likely to be a secondary factor. It seems more probable that the rude gesture came first and was then available to a saluting man as a means of parody-ing his signal of respect.

2   The gesture as modified version of thumb-sucking
When a child sucks its thumb, it often does so with its fingers held upward, so that its hand is in a posture similar to that of the nose thumb. To make such a gesture is tantamount to saying 'you're just a baby', a suitably mocking insult. But if this were the true origin, it remains to be explained why the thumb is moved up from contact with the lips, to contact with the nose-tip.

3   The gesture as a threat of snot-flicking
The childish insult of flicking snot or spittle has given rise to certain other rude gestures, and could be a relevant factor here, too. In the earliest record of all — the quotation from Rabelais — the gesturer inserts his thumb in his nostril, and in the earliest picture — the Brueghel print — he places his thumb just below the nose. Both these examples support the idea that the person thumbing his nose is performing the intention movement of flicking forward, at the in-sulted person, dirt from his nose. However, if this is the explanation,

it is surprising that no further reference is ever made to it in any of the names or phrases associated with the action.

4   The gesture as a grotesque nose

The many references to the 'long nose' that appear in various countries may be more than purely descriptive. As already mentioned, in one case, the action is called 'making a wax nose', and it could be that the ancient practice of making ugly, long-nosed effigies in wax, as a way of mocking people, is the true origin of the gesture. In other words, the gesture says 'you have an ugly nose like this', the precise posture of the fingers being of little importance, and the hands merely acting as an extension of the nose. It is interesting to read in Grimm's dictionary of the German language that, to be given this gesture is to be reprimanded, because 'those who were reprimanded used to have to wear a colourful paper nose'. This relates to a mid-nineteenth-century German reference, and it is just possible that the custom of long-nosing someone is the basis of the gesture, but hard evidence is not available.

5   The gesture as a phallic nose

Some psychoanalysts, such as Otto Fenichel, have, inevitably, seen the gesture as creating an 'erect' nose, with the nose playing its well-known role as a penis symbol. In such a case, the nose-thumb gesture would be similar in origin to the many other familiar phallic insults, where a stiff finger, or a forearm, take the role of 'threatening penis'. Against this interpretation is the fact that the gesture has hardly ever been criticized as obscene, a fate which always befalls other phallic gestures.

6   The gesture as a threatening cock's comb

This is the only explanation that takes into account the posture of the fingers as the nose thumb is performed. In their vertically fanned position, they resemble the comb of a fighting-cock. When such a bird is in a fighting posture, it leans forward, and this is also a common characteristic of the nose-thumbing gesturer, as if he is mimicking the fighting bird, about to strike. In support of this idea is the fact that cock-fighting was widespread and popular at the time when the gesture was gaining ground. Furthermore, a keen supporter of cock-fighting was sometimes called a 'cocker', which suggests the phrase 'cock a snook' should perhaps have been written 'cocker snoot'. Remembering that the word snoot derives from snout, or nose, the phrase then becomes 'a cocker's nose', that is, the kind of nose made by a cock-fight supporter when imitating one of the birds. Again, there is no hard evidence to reinforce this.

7 The gesture as an implication that someone stinks

The act of thumbing a nose is generally more popular as a child's insult, and a common schoolboy's insult is to accuse someone of making a bad smell. Holding the nose when an enemy enters the room is the obvious way of converting this insult into a simple gesture, but it is just possible that thumbing a nose has a similar origin. It has the effect of thrusting the gesturer's nose forward, as if to sniff the victim, implying that there is something unpleasant to smell. The face of the gesturer often makes an expression of disgust at the same time, with the features wrinkled up in distaste, and sometimes with the tongue protruding, as if its owner feels sick. On this basis, it is possible to consider the meaning of the gesture as 'you stink — if I push my nose in your direction like this, it makes me feel ill.'

It would be pleasant to conclude this survey of the origins of the nose-thumb gesture by arriving at a firm conclusion, favouring one particular source, but this is not possible. Each of the seven possible derivations has something to support it, but none is totally convincing. If we say that they may *all* be correct, this may sound nonsensical, but it is worth considering for a moment. The point is that each gesture has an *initial, primary source* — the origin from which it first sprang. This may often begin with one man in one place on one particular day — the first man to invent the particular act of symbolism. We know this to be the case with some modern gestures. But in addition it may also have a number of *reinforcing, secondary sources*. These are explanations given to the gesture some time after it has spread and become popular. The true, original source, now forgotten, may have lost its validity and its social relevance, so some new explanation has to be concocted. Once this has been done, and becomes talked about, it will actually start to influence the further spread of the gesture.

As an example of this process, let us suppose that the nose-thumb gesture originated in the cock-pits of London, where one particular, rather flamboyant cock-fighting personality started to imitate the threatening posture of his victorious bird, as a way of taunting and annoying his rivals. From his creative act of introducing, probably

on the spur of the moment, a new gesture into the narrow social
sphere of the cock-pit, there will have been a gradual spread, first to
other people at his own haunts, then to other cock-pits. Eventually,
the gesture will have been taken out on to the streets and used by
children when teasing one another. From there, it will start to spread
further and further, even into areas where no cock-fighting can be
seen. As time passes, the original source of the gesture becomes
forgotten. It is performed and its message understood, but every so
often someone will wonder about its derivation, and will ask a
question. His companions will think about it and then offer their
explanations. One will say that there used to be long noses on ugly
statues, another that he remembers someone using it as a funny
salute in the army, behind the officer's back, and another will
remember the old saying that a man with a big nose also has a big
penis, so the gesture must be a way of making an obscene phallic sign
without being too obvious about it. If any of these explanations is
accepted by the people who hear them, they will automatically start
to act as *pseudo-sources* for the gesture. They may not be the true,
original source, but the fact that they provide a reasonable background to the gesture will be enough to carry the gesture on, with
more conviction, from generation to generation.

Bearing this in mind it becomes difficult to say that any particular
explanation of a gesture has no significance. The very fact that
someone has proposed it or suggested it at some point begins to
make it a supportive factor in the survival of the symbolic action.
Nevertheless, a true beginning to a symbolic gesture must have
taken place, and it is worth continuing the search for it. Sadly, most
of these beginnings, especially with the very old gestures, are now
lost to us. They were not matters that attracted the attention of the
writers of the past. Sometimes, the present-day distribution of a
particular gesture can give us a clue as to its possible place of origin,
and from this we can make a better guess at its source, but in the case
of the nose thumb, even this does not help us, since the gesture, as we
shall see in a moment, has spread with such enormous success over
such a large expanse of territory.

DISTRIBUTION

Apart from being the best-known gesture we studied, and the most
widespread, the nose thumb was also the least ambiguous. Of the
1,200 people interviewed, 1,058 — 88 per cent — gave mockery as its

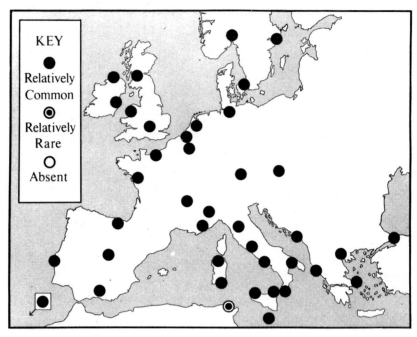

THE NOSE THUMB   Meaning: mockery

basic meaning. Only 128 said it was not known, and a mere 14 gave
other meanings for it. Of these 14, all were meaningless, wild guesses.

The range of words used, as specific answers, in the general
category of mockery, was large, but nevertheless close in meaning.
They included: abusive defiance, annoyance, buzz off, cheeky, contempt, derision, disparaging, get knotted, get lost, go to hell, humil-
iating, idiot, impolite, jeering, leg-pulling, making a fool of someone, making fun of someone, mickey-taking, mocking, piss off,
playful teasing, provocation, pulling someone's leg, ridiculing, rude,
sarcastic, scoffing, stupid, taunting, teasing, to belittle, to hell with
you, unfriendly, you're a fool, and you're crazy.

In 39 of our 40 locations, more than 20 out of 30 informants gave
this basic meaning of mockery. The reaction was so high in all these
39 cases, that it was impossible to detect any 'centre' for the gesture
in Europe. The statement that has been made in the past by certain
authors that this is a British gesture is unsupportable. On the evidence we have collected, the gesture could easily have begun
anywhere in Europe and then spread, without resistance, to all other
regions.

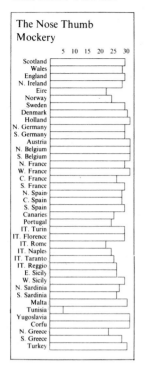

The Nose Thumb
Mockery

	5	10	15	20	25	30
Scotland						
Wales						
England						
N. Ireland						
Eire						
Norway						
Sweden						
Denmark						
Holland						
N. Germany						
S. Germany						
Austria						
N. Belgium						
S. Belgium						
N. France						
W. France						
C. France						
S. France						
N. Spain						
C. Spain						
S. Spain						
Canaries						
Portugal						
IT. Turin						
IT. Florence						
IT. Rome						
IT. Naples						
IT. Taranto						
IT. Reggio						
E. Sicily						
W. Sicily						
N. Sardinia						
S. Sardinia						
Malta						
Tunisia						
Yugoslavia						
Corfu						
N. Greece						
S. Greece						
Turkey						

The one location that stood out as an exception to this general rule was Tunisia, our only Arab site. There, no more than 5 of our 30 informants knew the gesture as an act of mockery. The Arab resistance to the spread of this gesture may be due to the gestural niche for mockery already being fully occupied. Arab cultures, we know from the work of Robert Barakat, are extremely rich in gestural insults, probably more so than anywhere else. Amongst the 247 Arab gestures he collected were many different kinds of mocking insults, but in none of the countries he visited did he find the nose thumb as a common gesture. In Tunisia the local population must certainly have seen the gesture, because of the strong French colonial influence. This influence has left behind a number of other French gestures which are still used today, long after the departure of the French. In France today, 92 per cent of our informants knew the gesture as mockery, so that it is highly unlikely that Tunisians did not become exposed to it during colonial days. But this exposure did not lead to imitation. Where mockery was concerned, the Tunisians remained traditionally Tunisian.

One final and rather curious observation is worthy of mention. Despite its enormous popularity and its huge range, the nose-thumb gesture appears to be on the wane. All our informants were adult and many of them commented that they remembered the gesture from their school-days. They also said, in many instances, that the gesture is 'only used by children' — meaning themselves and their friends when they were children. Amongst today's British school-children, according to Iona and Peter Opie, there is a rapid falling off in the use of this gesture when teasing or insulting. In its place, new and more daringly obscene gestures are being used. So perhaps, in another generation, the nose thumb will begin to go into a decline, to be replaced by the phallic and masturbatory gestures that are gaining ground at the moment. This trend, if it really is general, is no doubt due to the more relaxed attitude towards taboo words and taboo subjects that is spreading in western culture. In its wake, this trend may see the demise of some of the more subtle and obscure gestures from yesterday's repertoire. It is worth quoting the Opies at some length on this point:

> Having shown that minor customs and practices tend, under children's propulsion, to spin on quietly from generation to generation, it is almost a greater curiosity when a practice, recently commonplace, and with a long tradition behind it, suddenly ceases. That peculiar form of recognition ... 'nose thumbing' ... used, thirty years ago, to be demonstrated by every child in the country, both in private and national schools. Today the gesture is no longer in fashion; indeed it is more often seen performed by obstreperous grown-ups than by children; and at most schools it has altogether fallen out of use.

The Opies later give a list of the new favourites amongst children's insults. At the top of the chart comes the obscene V-sign (No. 20 on our list), the most virulent of all adult signs in Britain today. Alongside this, the homely nose thumb must seem tame indeed.

4 The Hand Purse

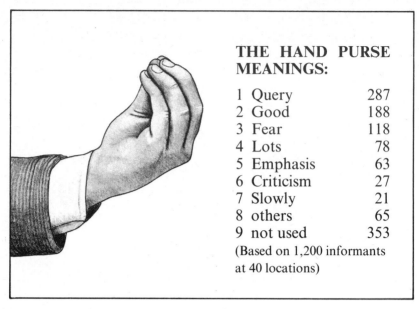

THE HAND PURSE MEANINGS:

1	Query	287
2	Good	188
3	Fear	118
4	Lots	78
5	Emphasis	63
6	Criticism	27
7	Slowly	21
8	others	65
9	not used	353

(Based on 1,200 informants at 40 locations)

DESCRIPTION

The fingers and thumb of one hand are straightened and brought together in a point facing upwards. Held in this posture the hand may be kept still, or moved slightly. A low intensity version of this action involves a bringing together only of the thumb and forefinger, but with the hand held in the same, palm-up position.

ORIGINS

The hand purse is a multi-message gesture. Many gestures have more than one meaning, as you travel from place to place, but it is unusual to find one with such a variety of meanings, even over a wide range of territory. The explanation lies in the primary source of the hand purse, as a 'baton signal'.

Baton actions occur when the hands 'beat time' to the spoken words. When a speaker emphasizes his words in this way, he uses a variety of hand postures, depending on the mood of his statements. If in a forceful or hostile mood, he tends to employ a clenched fist, his fingers unconsciously adopting a 'power grip' posture. If, by contrast, he is making a fine point, or requesting greater precision or clarity, he is more likely to display the typical 'precision grip' so characteristic of the human species, namely the bringing together of the tips of the digits as if holding some very small object. The digits involved vary, but there are two basic arrangements, the thumb-and-forefinger-tips touch, and the five-fingertips touch.

Speakers perform these precision grips without, of course, actually gripping anything. The small object is imagined, not held, and the hands make the gripping action *in vacuo*. Because this is done unconsciously, as part of the general flow of gesticulation during animated conversations, the movements, like most baton signals, are not identified or named as specific gestures. In the case of the five-fingertips touch, we have therefore had to invent a name — the hand purse. We have used this term because the action is similar to 'pursing the lips', that is, bringing them tightly together, as if pulled close by the draw-string of a purse.

Pursing the hand, as a basic form of baton signal, is common and widespread. Indeed, such is the repeated need for precision during verbal interactions, that it is probably worldwide, like the clenched fist, the begging hand, the repelling hand, and many of the other fundamental baton postures. But in the case of the hand purse, special developments have occurred. In certain regions it has gone beyond the simple act of beating time for emphasis, and has grown into a specific symbolic gesture. In this role it is no longer dependent on verbal exchanges, but can also be performed *instead* of speech.

It is this growth, from a simple baton signal into a fully fledged, symbolic gesture, that has enabled the hand purse to have different meanings in different parts of the world today. The original precision message is capable of a variety of special extensions, evolving separately as distinct local traditions. In one region, the primary signal of 'precise emphasis' has changed into 'please be more precise', or 'what are you trying to say?', or 'you idiot, what *are* you trying to say?'. In this way, it can become a gestural equivalent of a question mark. It can either accompany a spoken query, or act as a substitute for it. When performed silently, the gesturer simply purses his hand at his companion, who infers from the context why he is being questioned and answers accordingly.

The use of the hand purse as a symbolic query was commented on as long ago as 1832 by the Neapolitan Andrea de Jorio, who wrote: 'bringing the fingers together in a point means bringing your ideas together: "make one word out of all the other words and tell me what you mean; what are you talking about?"' In other words, make one, small, precise statement that will clarify the situation. This implies a certain degree of impatience on the part of the gesturer

The hand purse gesture employed as an insistent query by a modern Neapolitan.

and, although irritation is not always implicit, it is frequently present when the gesture is used in this way.

A totally different meaning has arisen elsewhere. From the basic statement of precise emphasis, the message has become transformed into 'this thing has precision'. From there it has changed to 'this has class', to 'high quality', to 'excellent', to 'good'. So, although the hand purse may be a query, often an irritable one, in one region, it can also be a satisfied or excited signal of excellence in another.

To confuse matters further, in a third region the gesture has an additional meaning, namely strong criticism or sarcasm. To transmit this signal, the pursed hand is pulled downwards through the air, while the face makes a glum grimace. The verbal equivalent would be 'that's marvellous', spoken with heavy sarcasm and meaning the exact opposite. At a sporting event, the gesture would be saying '*what* a good team you have', meaning 'what a *bad* team you have'. In this special case, as a sarcasm gesture, it appears to be a corrupted version of the hand purse meaning 'excellent' or 'good', because in areas where the gesture is used as a straightforward signal of excellence there is also a frequent tendency to use the down-pull movement of the hand. It seems likely that, in the 'sarcasm region', the gesture has simply 'gone sour' in its usage. The same fate can befall a word. For example, to say that someone is 'precious' today would be taken by most people to be an insult, rather than that he was 'of great value', even though that is the original meaning of the word. Once such a process has begun, it is difficult to put into reverse, and it can quickly spread throughout a whole culture, the original complimentary meaning of the word or gesture becoming too risky to use because it can so easily be misread.

In yet another region, the hand purse message 'be precise' has become 'be careful'. From there it has changed to 'take it slowly' and to the simple message 'slowly'.

So, from the simple baton gesture there have evolved four apparently completely separate symbolic messages in different parts of the world: *query, good, sarcastic criticism*, and *slowly*. But in addition to these modified baton signals, there are also several other distinct hand purse symbolisms. In certain areas, the gesture means 'lots'. It might be 'lots of people', or 'a crowd', or it might simply mean 'many', 'plenty', or 'much'. The symbolic root here is the bringing together of all the fingers in a clump or cluster — the combining of individual units into a tight group.

Another, more complex piece of symbolism concerns the use of the gesture as a signal of fear. Here the symbolic starting-point appears to be the squeezing together of the fingertips 'like a tight sphincter' of a frightened person. Some gesturers take this symbolism further by slightly opening and closing the pursed hand, as if the panic has become so great that the anal sphincter is no longer able to control itself. In some regions there is even a special word associated with the use of the gesture, which, roughly translated means 'to dirty yourself'. Others who use this same fear gesture ascribe it to a different symbolism, with the opening and closing of the fingers representing either the fast heartbeat of panic, or the trembling of terror, but these are probably no more than polite, modern alternatives. The image of the pursed hand as an orifice is certainly an old one, as this passage from the sixteenth-century writings of Rabelais will testify: '... the Englishman lift up on high into the aire his two hands severally, clunching in all the tops of his fingers together, after the manner, which, *à la Chinonnese*, they call the hen's arse ...' Strangely, this particular image seems to have survived in a few places, because to some people today the hand purse means 'you've laid an egg', and is employed as a gross insult, true to the original Rabelaisian usage.

All together this totals six major symbolic meanings which can be transmitted by this simple hand gesture in different regions today. This multi-message potential of the hand purse can obviously create a problem for the traveller or tourist, who can easily make mistakes when using the gesture, or when interpreting its use by others. In almost every area of Europe it has a special local meaning, and as the visitor passes from one to the other, his own way of understanding the gesture must be repeatedly revised if he is to avoid embarrassing misunderstandings. The results of our field research can help to clarify the present position.

DISTRIBUTION

1   The hand purse as a query
If any symbolic gesture can be said to be truly national, it is this. The hand-purse-query is not only widely understood throughout the Italian-speaking world, it is also largely confined to that world. Cross the border from northern Italy into southern France, for instance, and the local understanding of the gesture drops dramatically from 90 per cent of the population to 3 per cent. Go north to Austria, east to Yugoslavia, or south to Tunisia, and the figure drops to 0 per cent. Even the island of Malta, which is only 58 miles south of Sicily shows the same striking contrast — from 100 per cent on Sicily to a mere 3 per cent on Malta. In fact, nowhere outside the Italian region did we find the hand-purse-query understood by more than 6 per cent of the local population. Inside the Italian region we studied ten locations — six on mainland Italy, two on Sicily, and two on Sardinia — and nowhere there did we find it understood by less than 73 per cent of the local people, with the national average being even higher, at 92 per cent.

It is easy to see how a whole nation can come to use the same gesture meaning, but it is surprising to find it so neatly confined to the national borders. As we pointed out earlier, when talking of the fingertips kiss, it is often a mistake to call a particular gesture French, English, or German. There are numerous cases where, on closer examination, it emerges that the gesture is equally well known in other, neighbouring countries. But here, with the hand-purse-query, we can ignore this caution and talk safely of an Italian Gesture. Bruno Munari, when writing his gestural *Supplement to the Italian Dictionary*, was therefore entirely justified in using an illustration of the hand purse on its front cover.

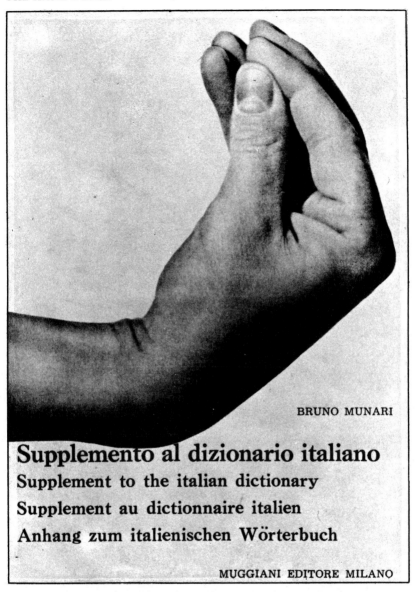

BRUNO MUNARI

Supplemento al dizionario italiano
Supplement to the italian dictionary
Supplement au dictionnaire italien
Anhang zum italienischen Wörterbuch

MUGGIANI EDITORE MILANO

The front cover of Munari's supplement to the Italian Dictionary, on which the hand purse posture is used to epitomize Italian gestures.

It is, of course, only the hand-purse-query that is confined in this way. The basic form of the gesture, the hand purse itself, is common everywhere around Italy, but always with a different meaning. It seems to be this situation that creates such sharp geographic boundaries for the query version of the gesture. It cannot seep over into

nearby territories without causing great confusion, because the
niche is already filled there by some other hand purse meaning.

 Three Italian phrases were employed repeatedly when answering
the question 'what does this gesture mean?'. They were: *Che vuoi?*
and *Cosa vuoi?* (= What do you want?), and *Cosa fai?* (= What are
you doing?). Other phrases can be interpreted as: What is it? What's
the matter? What do you mean? What are you saying? In fact,
almost any query can be signalled with a hand purse, depending on
the context. Lou D'Angelo, in his amusing instruction book *How to
be an Italian*, written to explain the gestures of Italian Americans to
non-Italian Americans, makes the point that the hand-purse-query
can even be used as a greeting signal. Walking in his Italian neigh-
bourhood in New York, he saw two men greet one another. One was
on the sidewalk and the other in a fifth-floor window: 'The man on
the street "spoke" first. He cupped his right hand, palm up, bunch-
ing his fingers and touching them together at the tips to the end of
the thumb. By moving the hand slowly up and down from the wrist,
he asked his friend: "What's new?".' This is the non-irritable use of
the gesture, but more often it is to be seen in a context where one
person has behaved stupidly and the gesturer is saying, 'Why are you
such a fool?' This irritation gesture can almost cease to be a query
and can become a statement: 'You fool!' Changes in the accompany-

The querulous hand purse gesture seen on an Italian street corner.

ing facial expression make it easy to interpret which kind of hand-purse-query you are being offered.

2   The hand purse as a sign of excellence

The island of Corfu is only 110 kilometres east of the heel of Italy, and yet to make this short journey is to experience a gestural switch so complete that it converts a 100 per cent figure for *hand purse = query* in Taranto, to a 97 per cent figure for *hand purse = good* in Corfu. This interpretation of the gesture as a sign of excellence remains at this high level as one moves further east, through mainland Greece to Turkey. The variety of words given to us by Greek and Turkish informants when explaining the local meaning of the hand purse included the following: beautiful, correct, delicious, everything in order, excellent, fine, first class, good, great, nice, precious, quality, success, superb and sweet. Several of them made the point that this gesture for good was less powerful than the fingertips kiss. In other words, if you wished to express very strong praise for something, you would kiss your fingertips, but if you wanted to show moderate praise, you would perform the hand purse, usually with a single down-pull of the pursed hand. William Papas, the Greek artist, in his book *Instant Greek* gives a possible clue as to the relationship between the Italian query and the Greek version of the gesture. He says that the hand purse can be used, not only as a sign for excellence, but also as part of a friendly greeting: 'Are you well?' Here, in a question relating to someone feeling good, we may be seeing the bridge between the two regional versions of the gesture. But for the vast majority of Italians and Greeks today, the predominant message of the hand purse is quite distinct. The first thing a typical Italian thinks of is 'what do you want?' and the first word that comes into a typical Greek's mind is 'good'. So, even though the friendly greeting may explain a possible relationship between these two messages, it must not be assumed that its existence in any way blurs the regional contrast.

The hand purse as a sign for good is not totally confined to the S.E. zone of Europe. A small number of informants in many parts of the continent also recorded this interpretation, with the figure for Portugal rising as high as 30 per cent. A glance at the gesture map reveals one interesting feature of this scatter, namely, that throughout the Italian-speaking zone there was not one single case of this interpretation of the hand purse, the predominant 'query' meaning in that region successfully obliterating the rival message.

3   The hand purse as a criticism

In one small area, the Mediterranean island of Malta, a striking change takes place. The hand purse still occurs in its 'down-pull' form, with the pursed fingers being lowered once through the air, as in Greece, and the message is still sometimes given as 'good', but it is no longer complimentary. The 'good' is always sarcastic and the compliment becomes a sneer. Some informants gave the meaning as: 'He may seem good, but really he is bad', and others went further and said simply, 'He is no good', or 'He is bad'. In this way the message, although related to the Greek signal, has become completely inverted. This particular usage is almost entirely restricted to the small island population on Malta, but there was just a hint of it from the Greek world. Two of our 90 Greek-speaking informants (both from the island of Corfu) said that, although the primary meaning of the gesture for them was 'good', it was also sometimes used sarcastically by local people. This rare Greek usage, which becomes the dominant theme on Malta, suggests an ancient link between the two regions. To explain why the Maltese have converted the gesture from a complimentary to a critical one it is only necessary to look at Malta's geographical position. It is so close to the Italian-speaking world that there are many ties with that region. As we have already pointed out, when used as a query, the Italian hand purse gesture often has a querulous, irritated flavour: 'What are you doing, you fool?' 'You idiot, what are you trying to say?' From there, it is only a short step to 'You fool!' and the gesture can easily become highly critical. If we look upon the Maltese as falling half-way between the Italian and the Greek meanings, then their special use of the gesture makes sense.

4   The hand purse as a sign for slowly

In our one Arab location, Tunisia, another dominant meaning for the gesture emerged. Here most people employ the hand purse as a sign for 'slow down', and it is particularly common in traffic situations. A driver puts his hand out of the window of his car and signals to another driver to 'wait', 'be patient', 'take it slowly' or 'don't go so fast'. The pursed hand may be held still, or slowly raised and lowered. In a sense, this is a request for greater precision in driving, taking the concept of precision from the original hand purse baton signal.

Without studying other Arab cultures we cannot be sure whether this 'slow down' usage is widespread, but it is certainly not confined to Tunisia, having been seen by one of us in the Lebanon.

Several of our Tunisian informants made it clear to us that the exact meaning of the hand purse depended on the way the hand was moved while in the pursed position. There are three local variants and most informants agreed that they had the following meanings:

a   Pursed hand moves slowly up and down . . . . slowly
b   Pursed hand makes single downbeat   . . . . good
c   Pursed hand jerks rapidly up and down . . . . threat

If shown a picture of a pursed hand, with no clue as to any movement it might be making, then the majority of Tunisians interpreted the gesture as meaning 'slowly', revealing this to be the dominant local usage. In other words, if forced to make a choice without the extra information about the nature of the hand movement, they chose the meaning that is presumably most common in Tunisia. A few of them chose instead the interpretations 'good' or 'a threat', but nearly all of them, if pressed, went on to provide the three variant gestures with their three distinct meanings. It seems, therefore, that Tunisia is a 'mixed zone' as far as this particular gesture is concerned. Both the downbeat form and its 'good' message relate to the Greek version of the hand purse; both the rapidly jerked form and its querulous message relate to the Italian version; and the slowly raised and lowered form with its 'slow down' message seems to relate to an Arab usage. The only example of a European using the 'slowly' form of the hand purse was a solitary informant in Central France, whose interpretation of the gesture may well have been the result of France's deep and prolonged involvement as a colonial power in Tunisia and elsewhere in North Africa.

5   The hand purse as a sign of fear
In the Franco-Belgian region the hand purse is predominantly a sign of fear. The messages showed little variation: I'm afraid, I'm scared, I'm anxious, cowardice. So strong was this dominant meaning that, although it is usually performed with a slight opening and closing of the bunched fingertips, the static pursed hand was interpreted in exactly the same way.

The centre of this particular usage seems to be Belgium and the northern half of France. In the extreme south of France the response is weaker. Two curious features of this distribution have emerged. First, up in the north of its range, the Flemish-speaking Belgians contrast strikingly with the Dutch. The figures are: French-speaking

Belgians 63 per cent, Flemish-speaking Belgians 77 per cent, Dutch 0
per cent. This dramatic drop in the hand-purse-fear interpretation is
not the result of some competing usage in Holland. The Dutch are
still using the hand purse predominantly in its primitive baton role
as a way of emphasizing their words. So there is nothing to stop the
'invasion', from the Flemish population in the south, of the symbolic hand purse meaning fear. What factor is keeping it out so
effectively remains to be investigated.

A second odd feature of the hand-purse-fear distribution is its
rather high (37 per cent) occurrence in Portugal, despite a complete
absence in the intervening Spanish region. This can partly be explained by the next meaning:

6   The hand purse as a sign for many
Throughout Spain, the dominant meaning for the hand purse gesture is 'lots' — in particular, lots of people — and it seems to be this
interpretation that is filling the gap, so to speak, between France and
Portugal, and preventing the 'fear' signal from operating in that
region. The strange feature of this situation is that the form of the
gesture does not seem to differ at all. In both the 'French fear'
gesture and the 'Spanish many' gesture, the hand is either held static
or there is a slight opening and closing of the bunched fingertips. In
other instances of 'neighbouring hand purses', there has usually
been a minor variation in the hand movement associated with the
purse gesture, which has helped to distinguish them, if only slightly.
But here there does not appear to be even a slight clue to assist in
separating them. In other words, when Portuguese and Spaniards
meet, they will be using precisely the same gesture to mean two quite
different things. The same confusion must also exist between Spaniards and Frenchmen, and the problem seems to have spread into
southern France, because when we visited that region we were given
both interpretations of the gesture by local informants. One man
would say, on being shown a drawing of the hand purse gesture,
'That means fear, but we usually do it with a slight opening and
closing of the fingers.' The next man interviewed would then say,
'That means lots, but we usually do it with a slight opening and
closing of the fingers.' As far as we can tell, this must lead to local
misunderstandings, and it is surprising that no differentiation has
occurred, creating easily distinguished local variants of the gesture,
one for each of its two local meanings. Our prediction is that this is
likely to take place at some time in the future, or that one or other of

the usages for this gesture will come to dominate the local scene.

For some reason we cannot explain, there is another, isolated centre for the hand-purse-many gesture, further to the east, in Yugoslavia. Why the Yugoslavs should be linked to the Spanish-speaking peoples with regard to this particular gesture-meaning remains a mystery.

Those, then, are the six major meanings for the hand purse gesture that we have encountered in the field. Had we travelled beyond the European–Mediterranean zone, we might have discovered even more. It is clearly a multi-message gesture with a complex cultural history of local specialization and differentiation.

Because the geography of this particular gesture is so complicated, it may help to summarize it in the form of a chart, showing its main zones:

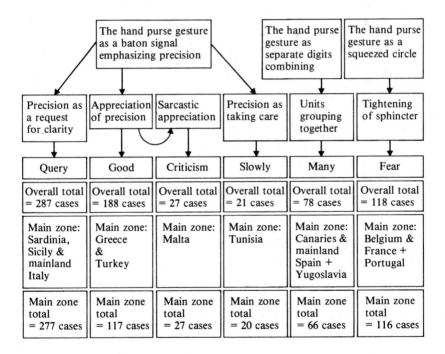

The hand purse gesture as a baton signal emphasizing precision				The hand purse gesture as separate digits combining	The hand purse gesture as a squeezed circle
Precision as a request for clarity	Appreciation of precision	Sarcastic appreciation	Precision as taking care	Units grouping together	Tightening of sphincter
Query	Good	Criticism	Slowly	Many	Fear
Overall total = 287 cases	Overall total = 188 cases	Overall total = 27 cases	Overall total = 21 cases	Overall total = 78 cases	Overall total = 118 cases
Main zone: Sardinia, Sicily & mainland Italy	Main zone: Greece & Turkey	Main zone: Malta	Main zone: Tunisia	Main zone: Canaries & mainland Spain + Yugoslavia	Main zone: Belgium & France + Portugal
Main zone total = 277 cases	Main zone total = 117 cases	Main zone total = 27 cases	Main zone total = 20 cases	Main zone total = 66 cases	Main zone total = 116 cases

Together, these six major meanings accounted for 719 of our 1,200 informants. Of the remainder, 353 did not recognize the gesture at all, 63 identified it in its original baton role, as a way of emphasizing speech, and 65 gave other meanings. Of these 65, most were wild guesses or cases of mistaken identity. For example, 18

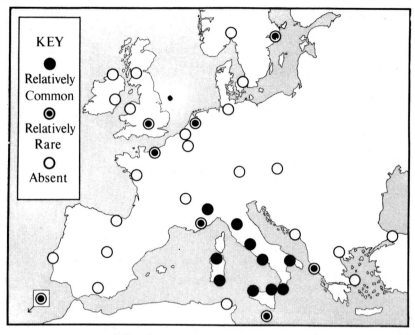

THE HAND PURSE Meaning: query

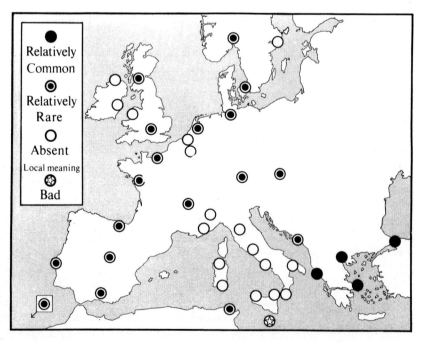

THE HAND PURSE Meaning: good

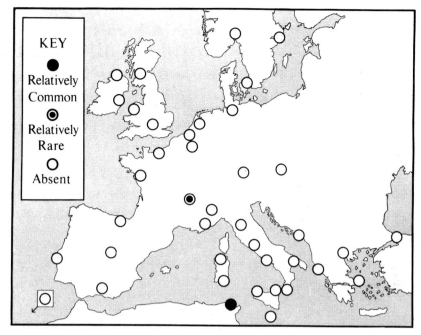

THE HAND PURSE Meaning: slowly

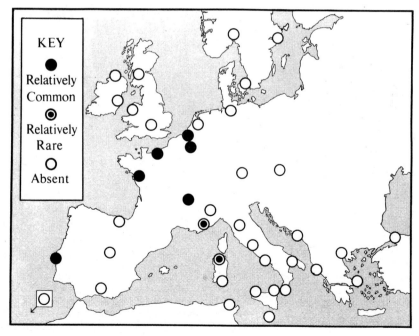

THE HAND PURSE Meaning: fear

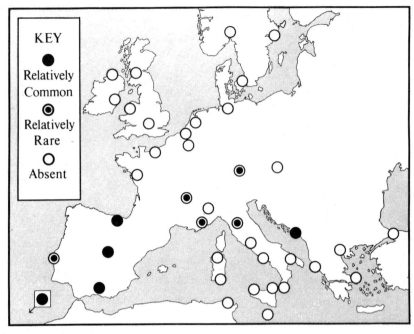

THE HAND PURSE Meaning: lots

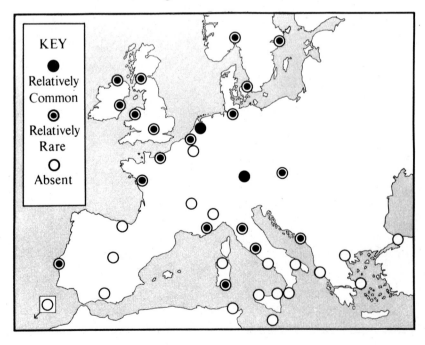

THE HAND PURSE Meaning: emphasis

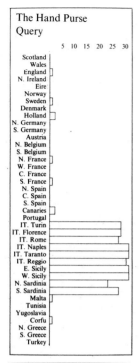

The Hand Purse
Query

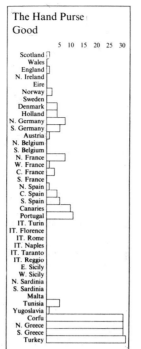

The Hand Purse
Good

The Hand Purse
Slowly

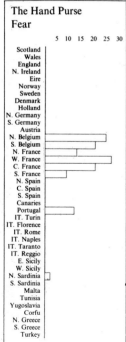

The Hand Purse
Fear

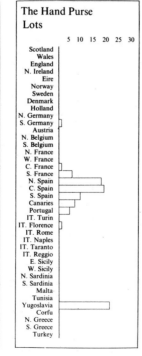

The Hand Purse
Lots

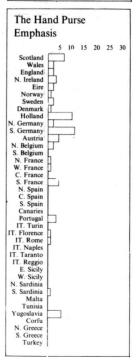

The Hand Purse
Emphasis

informants identified the gesture as an eating sign, confusing it with the mimed act of holding food prior to placing it in the mouth. In the true feeding gesture for 'hunger', the hand is brought right up to the opened mouth. Anyone interpreting the hand purse in this way must obviously be ignorant of its other uses, or no such stretching of the imagination would have occurred. In the same way, 10 informants identified the hand purse as a 'money' gesture, confusing it with the fingers-rubbing action of someone asking for cash.

One final point can be made, concerning those people who still identified the hand purse gesture in its primitive form, as a baton signal to stress speech. The total of 63 seems large, but it was in reality so widely scattered across Europe that no high figures were obtained for it anywhere. The greatest was 33 per cent in Southern Germany. But there is an interesting feature of this wide scatter, namely that it shows a slightly higher level in northern Europe than in the south. If the British, Scandinavian, Dutch and German regions are roughly lumped together as 'North Europe', then it emerges that nearly 70 per cent of all the informants identifying the hand purse as a simple emphasis signal come from that region. The chart giving the main zones of the symbolic uses of the gesture provides the explanation of why this should be, because nearly all the six major symbolic meanings for the gesture are situated in the Latin and Mediterranean countries in the south. In other words, where an advanced local symbolism takes over, the primitive baton-emphasis meaning is overlooked. This does not mean that the gesture ceases to be used as a baton signal while people are talking to one another, but merely that our informants were more readily aware of the special symbolic roles of the gesture, and these then swamped out any other interpretation.

The cheek screw gesture meaning that something is good, seen in a village in the Massico range north of Naples.

5 The Cheek Screw

THE CHEEK SCREW MEANINGS:

1	Good	253
2	Effeminate	32
3	Crazy	25
4	Crafty	18
5	others	58
6	not used	814

(Based on 1,200 informants at 40 locations)

DESCRIPTION

A straightened forefinger is pressed against the centre of the cheek and the hand is then rotated, as if screwing something into the face. The other digits of the hand are kept closed. Occasionally, the thumb and forefinger are used instead of the forefinger alone.

ORIGINS

The cheek screw is primarily an Italian gesture of praise. It is little known elsewhere and is hardly ever mentioned in books dealing with European gestures. Surprisingly, it is seldom included even in publications discussing Italian gestures, although it is common enough in that country. It has three possible origins:

1   Tasty — 'on the tooth'
For many people, this is the gesture to use when praising food. When something is tasty or delicious to eat, the fact is signified by a pleasant expression combined with a screwed cheek. There is an Italian expression '*al dente*', 'on the tooth', which means that some-

thing is 'just right for eating' — crunchy, not soggy, and indicates that the food in question, usually pasta, has been cooked to exactly the right degree. The rotating forefinger draws attention to the important feature of the pasta, namely its texture.

A Frenchman, wishing to praise the taste of a delicious morsel, would almost certainly use the fingertips kiss at precisely the moment his Italian counterpart would perform the cheek screw. This may explain why the fingertips kiss is much less popular in Italy than in France (and many other European regions). Having two gestures available for the same message, the Italian is more likely to use his own local speciality.

If 'on the tooth' is the true origin of the cheek screw gesture, then it is easy to see how it could have developed from a mimic act of crunching food, to a symbolic gesture meaning good food, or tasty. From delicious food it is only a short step to delicious in a general sense, and thence to beauty and a 'delicious girl', finally becoming so generalized as to be useful for anything good, regardless of its specific nature.

2 · A dimpled cheek

A second possible source cannot be overlooked. Dimpled cheeks have often been thought of as beautiful, and pressing the tip of the forefinger into the centre of the soft cheek flesh has the effect of producing a dimple-like indentation. It is possible that this is another source for the cheek screw gesture, leading directly to the symbolic meaning: 'beautiful'. There is no reason why both trends should not have occurred, ultimately becoming confused with one another.

In support of this dimpled origin is the fact that for some people the gesture has a special meaning: pretty, in the sense of being effeminate. It is then used about a man and, in effect, says he has dimpled cheeks like a little girl.

3 A modified moustache twist

Some Europeans respond to the sight of an attractive girl by twiddling the tips of an imaginary, waxed moustache. They are, as it were, symbolically preening themselves, the message being: she is beautiful — she excites me — therefore I must smarten myself up before making an advance. Today, long after the demise of the waxed moustache fashion, the action survives as a relic gesture. Performed at full intensity, the hand movements are a perfect mime of the act of

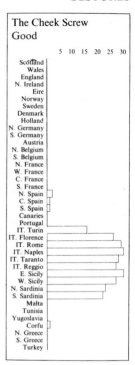

The thumb and forefinger variant of the cheek screw gesture, meaning good, seen in a village north of Naples.

moustache-tip twirling, involving both hands, but at lower intensities only one hand is used and the twirling action may become highly stylized and simplified. The gesture then begins to look rather similar to the cheek screw, and David Efron, in his study of *Gesture, Race and Culture,* depicts an Italian performing it in the middle of his cheek, instead of higher up, where a waxed moustache-tip would be. He also records it as now having a general message of 'good, sweet, pretty'. This means that we cannot, at this stage, eliminate the possibility that the cheek screw is, in reality, a highly modified form of the moustache twist.

DISTRIBUTION

Taking Europe as a whole, the cheek screw is not a common gesture and was totally unknown at many locations. Of our 1,200 informants, 814 had no idea what it meant, and a further 58 gave vague and hesitant answers that were clearly wild guesses, or cases of 'over-helpfulness'. In French-speaking areas it was often confused with 'Le Bidon', an insulting gesture made by inflating the cheek and then

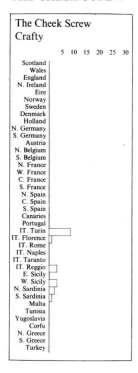

The Cheek Screw
Crafty

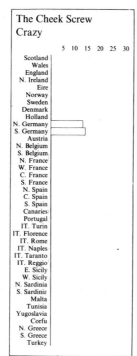

The Cheek Screw
Crazy

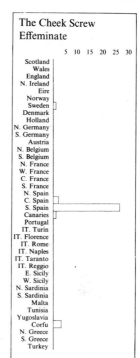

The Cheek Screw
Effeminate

sharply deflating it by prodding it with a stiff forefinger. The essence of 'Le Bidon' is not the touching of the cheek by the forefinger, but the enforced explosion of air from the mouth that results from it. It is a gesture used to indicate that something may seem good but is in reality quite worthless — full of hot air. To confuse this with the true cheek screw gesture can only mean that the latter is unknown locally.

Other informants helpfully suggested that the cheek screw gesture might indicate toothache, or someone being thoughtful, and it soon became clear, from the large number of varying guesses, that this particular gesture has never travelled far across Europe and, furthermore, is not even known about, as a 'foreign gesture', by those who do not employ it themselves.

Once you enter the Italian-speaking world, however, the cheek screw is recognized immediately by nearly everyone. This was true at all ten of our Italian-speaking locations, including both Sicily and Sardinia as well as the mainland. There is hardly any seepage of this gesture across the borders, to neighbouring countries. A journey from Turin in N.W. Italy to Nice in S.E. France sees the figure

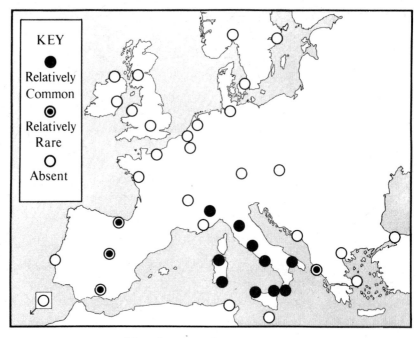

THE CHEEK SCREW Meaning: good

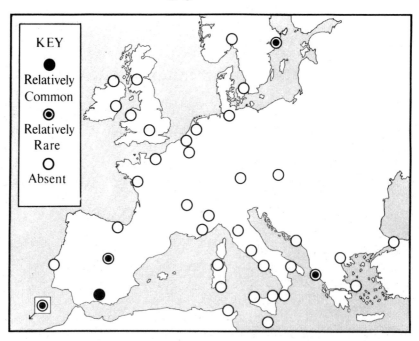

THE CHEEK SCREW Meaning: effeminate

drop to zero, as does the short sea journey from Sicily to Malta.

Inside Italy, the words used to describe the meaning of the gesture included: beautiful, delicious, excellent, good, great, lovely, pleasant and sweet. The most frequently heard Italian words were: *buono, bello, bravo* and *saporito*. In addition to this general kind of praise, there was another, more specialized form of respect. At six of our Italian locations a few people insisted that the gesture specifically meant 'crafty', 'clever', or 'cunning', and they used words such as *furbo, dritto, speculatore, in gamba* and *mafioso*.

A completely different meaning was discovered, centred in southern Spain. There, nearly everyone agreed that the cheek screw is a sign used to indicate that a man is effeminate or a homosexual. This relates to the dimpled cheek symbolism and could lead to considerable confusion if made by a Spaniard to an Italian or vice versa. The effeminate interpretation is rare elsewhere, even in other Spanish-speaking regions. A few examples of it were found in the Canary Islands and central Spain, but by the time one reaches the far north of that country it seems to have disappeared altogether. This implies an Arab influence coming in from the south across the Straits of Gibraltar and, in this connection, it is worth recording that Robert Barakat, in his study of Arab gestures, has listed the cheek screw as a way of commenting on a beautiful woman. Such an Arab gesture, deliberately applied to a male in southern Spain (where there has been a strong Arab influence for centuries) would obviously become an immediate challenge to his masculinity and could quickly grow into a local insult.

In Germany, about half our informants, both in the north and the south, identified the cheek screw as meaning 'he is crazy'. At first, we assumed this was yet another case of mistaken identity. We had met this error elsewhere at locations where a true cheek screw was unknown. Asked the meaning of the gesture, a man would say 'crazy', but when pressed to demonstrate the action would proceed to rotate his forefinger, not against his cheek, but on his temple. The temple screw is, of course, a common and widespread gesture symbolizing a rotating or 'dizzy brain', and such informants would explain their error by saying that 'here we do it on the temple, and I thought that is what you meant'. Such people were merely being over-helpful, but in Germany the situation was clearly different. When asked to demonstrate the 'crazy cheek screw', instead of moving the forefinger up to the temple, the informants proceeded to perform a perfect cheek screw exactly like the Italian gesture of

The German cheek screw gesture meaning that someone is crazy. It is a covert version of the temple screw.

praise (see page 61). Pursuing this further it soon emerged that, far from being an over-helpful error, the German interpretation was based on a special, local use of the cheek screw, common in that region. It appears that, in the past, prosecutions and court convictions have resulted from the use of the familiar temple screw, with the outcome that the cheek screw has been developed as a surreptitious form of insult. For example, if a German driver makes the temple screw at another driver, the police are liable to take action against him, accusing him of insulting behaviour. The driver's solution, on a subsequent occasion, is to shift the gesture down to the cheek region where it is less conspicuous. His victim still gets the message, but the policeman finds it difficult to detect at a distance. Even if the policeman does manage to spot it, and has learnt that it is the new 'secret' way of saying 'crazy', he will have a harder job proving it in a court of law. The man can easily defend himself by claiming that his tooth was hurting. In this valuable new role, the gesture has spread rapidly amongst the German population and was known by 25 of our 60 German informants. It remains to be seen whether, during the course of time, it becomes so notoriously familiar that it, too, like the temple screw, becomes officially condemned and the subject of court prosecutions.

6 The Eyelid Pull

THE EYELID PULL
MEANINGS:

1	I am alert	498
2	Be alert	399
3	Praise	23
4	Complicity	14
5	Boredom	9
6	others	49
7	not used	208

(Based on 1,200 informants
at 40 locations)

DESCRIPTION

The extended forefinger is placed just below the centre of one eye, where it pulls the skin downwards, tugging at the lower eyelid. This has the effect of opening the eye wider, and is performed while looking straight at the companion. The mouth corners are usually lowered, but may be neutral. Sometimes the gesturer points with his free hand in the direction of a third party, indicating that the latter is the cause of the signal. Or he may accompany the gesture with a raised forefinger, indicating a more general, undirected warning.

ORIGINS

The origin of this gesture is obvious enough. Since the eyes are the main channel of input for the human species, it follows that a simple action of widening the eye symbolizes an increase in visual input, and therefore transmits a message of heightened alertness.

This is the only gesture in our study that does have such an obvious derivation, and it might be argued that, as a result, our informants in the field would be able to guess the meaning of this particular action, even if it were not employed in their local community. Were this so, there would be little hope of detecting any pattern emerge when mapping the distribution of the gesture. In reality, this is not the case. It seems that, despite its simple origins, the eye-pull gesture has come to represent different facets of alertness in the various regions. There have been two major trends and three minor ones:

1   Alertness on the part of the gesturer himself

The primary signal 'alert' becomes 'I am alert'. The opened eye of the gesturer symbolizes his own awareness of something. In this symbolic role, the eye-pull gesture has a wide range of related meanings, from a simple 'I have seen it', or 'I am looking', to various denials of gullibility, such as 'Do you think I am stupid?', or 'You can't fool me', and to expressions of disbelief, such as 'You are lying', or 'I don't believe you'. The common factor is always that the gesturer is alert to what is going on, and is not going to miss the point, whether from his own lack of effort, or as a result of some effort to deceive him.

The eyelid pull gesture of a modern German in Munich, meaning: I am alert.

2   Alertness on the part of the companion

Here the primary signal becomes the message 'you be alert'. The opened eye of the gesturer symbolizes the condition he is requesting from someone else. He may do this simply by asking someone to 'look at this', or he may use the gesture as part of a more forceful demand, such as 'pay attention!'. If a third person is involved, he may perform the eye-pull towards his companion as a friendly warning, the message being 'watch out for him' — be alert for danger. This warning often includes an added comment about the third party: 'Be careful, he is crafty.' From there it can extend its range to a simple 'He is crafty' statement. When this happens, an ambiguity creeps in, because the message can now be read either as 'keep *your* eyes open if you wish to avoid his craftiness', or as 'he is crafty and has *his* eyes wide open, so take care.' Even greater ambiguity arises when the message becomes 'he is smart', because this can either be a warning that 'he is smart enough to harm you, so keep your eyes open', or a simple act of praise meaning 'he is very smart and always keeps his eyes open.' In our field studies we have tended to interpret 'smartness', 'craftiness' and 'cunning' as warnings rather than as praise, but we realize the distinction is subtle.

3   Alertness as praise
When we see something we like, we open our eyes wide in admiration. We speak of an attractive girl as 'an eyeful', and the eye-pull gesture has occasionally taken on this symbolic role, although it is not by any means as common as the previous two usages. It could be argued that some of the 'he is smart' messages should be included in this category, but for the reasons already given, we have excluded such comments and confined the praise category to such comments as 'good' and 'beautiful'.

4   Alertness as complicity
For certain people, the eye-pull gesture has the meaning 'You and I see something together', implying something shared to the exclusion of others. This can range from a simple agreement, to a shared secret. The rarity of this usage is related to the existence of another gesture (the nose tap) which is more popular in such contexts, and which we discuss later in the book.

5   Alertness as a struggle against boredom
When we are bored it may make us physically tired, and we often use such expressions as 'I could hardly keep my eyes open'. For some, the eye-pull gesture thus becomes a symbol of extreme boredom. By pulling open his eye, the gesturer is saying 'I must try and stay awake'. The context for this usage is usually a lengthy lecture, or an

The eyelid pull gesture of a modern Neapolitan, meaning be alert.

uninspiring musical or theatrical performance. It is rather surprising, at first glance, that this is such a rare use of the gesture, but this is probably the result of its common employment as a symbolic 'I am alert' message. The boredom version: 'I really ought to be alert, but find it hard' could be confused with the more popular 'I *am* alert' meaning. Performed silently, at a public event, the gesture could therefore be taken as praise instead of criticism.

These are the five major uses of the eye-pull gesture, but before reporting on their present distribution across Europe, it is important to stress that our categories are not as clear-cut in reality as they may appear here. Many of our informants mentioned that they use the gesture in several different ways, according to the context. This is undoubtedly due to the rather obvious derivation mentioned earlier. There is no mystery about the origin of the gesture, so it can be used in a much more variable way than some of the symbolic gestures we discuss, which have more obscure beginnings. The nose-thumb gesture, for example, has many possible origins, heavily shrouded by the passage of time, but has only one, clear, dominant meaning. The eye-pull, by contrast, has only one simple derivation — seeing more of something — but has many different meanings.

DISTRIBUTION

When we first separated the enormous variety of answers we were given in response to the question 'what does this gesture mean locally?', we were not at all sure that the result would create any characteristic pattern of distribution. When we came to map the results, however, a striking pattern did emerge, revealing several major zones of bias.

The gesture was generally less popular in the north of Europe, but was never known to less than a third of our informants at any location. In the south and around the Mediterranean it was known to almost everyone. Altogether it was known to 992 of our 1,200 informants, and the vast majority — 897 — interpreted it in one of its two major meanings, either 'I am alert' or 'be alert'. If these two meanings are mapped, it immediately becomes clear that there are four main zones across Europe, as you travel from west to east. If we over-simplify slightly and label the four major cultural regions of southern Europe as, from west to east: Spain, France, Italy and Greece, then it becomes possible to extract the following pattern by comparing the two gesture maps opposite:

West . . . . *(Southern Europe)* . . . . East			
Spanish zone	French zone	Italian zone	Greek zone
'Be alert'	'I am alert'	'Be alert'	'I am alert'

The Spanish zone excludes Portugal, where there is a mixture of meanings. The French zone includes French-speaking Belgium in the north. The Italian zone shows a lower response in Sardinia, where the gesture is less popular, and in Florence, where there is a competing meaning. (In Florence, 7 informants said that the gesture meant 'something beautiful' and its use as a gesture of praise in that city appears to clash with its use as a 'be alert' signal.) The Greek zone stretched beyond Greece itself to encompass both Yugoslavia and Turkey.

To sum up the situation, crudely, it could be said that, in the French and Greek zones, people use the eye-pull gesture to indicate their superiority or disbelief, while in the Spanish and Italian zones they use it to give a friendly warning. How this major zoning has come about remains to be explained.

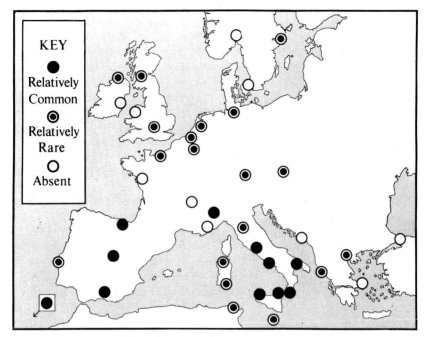

THE EYELID PULL   Meaning: be alert

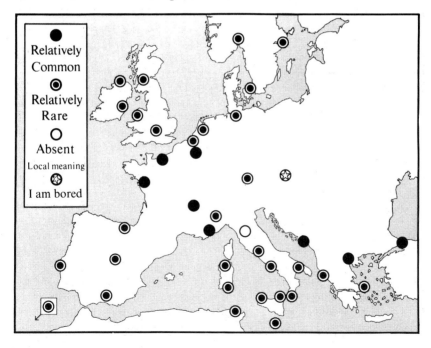

THE EYELID PULL   Meaning: I am alert

The eyelid pull gesture of a
nineteenth-century Neapolitan,
meaning that someone must
be alert. From De Jorio, 1832.

There are a number of special phrases that are used in different
countries when speaking of this gesture. In France, for instance,
almost everyone gives the phrase *mon œil*, literally 'my eye', meaning 'I don't believe you'. In Italy, the most popular words are *furbo*
and *dritto*, meaning, artful, sly, or cunning, and are used in the
context 'watch him, he's wily'.

In particular, there are a number of colloquial phrases which
carry the same basic meaning: 'You can't fool me.' They include the
following:

'*There's no green in my eye*' (British), based on the idea that
green = immature, and that 'my eye' is therefore too mature to be
taken in by you.
'*All my eye and Betty Martin*' (British), based on the name of a
notorious fallen woman of the eighteenth century who managed to
persuade a Mr Martin to marry her. Presumably the phrase means
'you won't fool me like Betty Martin fooled her husband'.
'*In the eye, Karl*', or '*In the eye of Karl XIIth*' are phrases used in
Denmark. The Danes also have a joke phrase employed in the same
way: '*Did you see the train?*' The joke goes: 'Did you see the train?'
'No.' 'Then it must have gone round the corner.' ... In other words,
'I fooled you'.

'*I don't have a wooden eye*' is the German popular phrase, implying that 'my eye is fine and clear and can see what you are up to.' The phrase is usually reduced simply to 'wooden eye' (= *Holzauge*). In addition, Germans may say, '*Someone tried to put a fly in my eye*' as they perform the eye-pull gesture, meaning 'they tried to stop me seeing what was going on, but failed.'

'*If I were four years in the Sahara there would still be no sand in my eye*' is the rather ornate phrasing we encountered in Vienna.

'*Esperteza saloia*' was the popular Portuguese phrase that went with the eye-pull there, meaning, literally, 'peasant cunning'.

'*I gra mi oko*' was the Yugoslav saying meaning, simply, 'my eye is active'.

It is intriguing that so many popular sayings go with the gesture in its 'I am alert' role. The reason seems to be that when a man is driven to asserting that he is no fool, he is likely to have found himself momentarily in a victim role, and needs some sort of colourful retort to counterbalance the situation. The eye-pull gesture may be sufficient by itself, but it often seems necessary to embellish it with a slang expression, which emphasizes his worldliness.

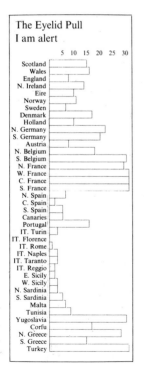

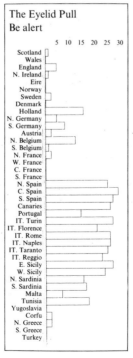

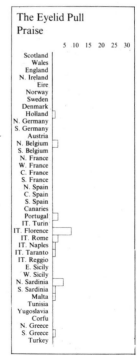

Finally, of the three minor usages of the eye-pull, two show little regional concentration. Both the 'praise' and the 'complicity' meanings (see chart on pp. 272–3) are scattered at very low levels over a wide range. The third usage, as a sign of boredom, does, however, show a remarkable localization, being found by us only at one site, namely Vienna. It is rare to find such a limited distribution for any gesture meaning, and it would be interesting to trace its origins in Austria and to find out why it has not spread elsewhere. Of our 30 informants 9 gave this as the dominant meaning in Vienna, but there was not even a hint of it at other locations. In a sense, it is a variant of the 'I am alert' message, which becomes transformed into 'I must try and be alert'.

The forearm jerk of an Englishman, employed as a sexual comment.

7 The Forearm Jerk

**THE FOREARM
JERK MEANINGS:**

1 Sexual insult   761
2 Sexual comment 144
3 Strength   141
4 others   17
5 not used   137
(Based on 1,200 informants
at 40 locations)

DESCRIPTION

The clenched fist is jerked forcibly upwards. The jerked arm (usually
the right) is bent at the elbow and, as the jerk is performed, the other
(left) hand is slapped down hard on the upper-arm, as if something is
checking the upward movement. There are many minor variations
of this basic pattern.

ORIGINS

The forearm jerk is a phallic gesture. The forearm with its clenched
fist represents a super-normal phallus and its jerking movement
imitates the thrusting of the penis. The slap of the left hand against
the upper-arm seems to indicate that the super-penis has been thrust
into an orifice as far as it will go, and has met resistance which
prevents it from going further. To be specific, therefore, the forearm
jerk gesture represents *maximum intromission*.

The gesture is most often seen in male groups, with one man using
it to insult another. The insult is primarily anal, rather than genital.
Despite this, there is no hint of homosexuality about the use of the
gesture. It is essentially a phallic threat and, as such, is remarkably
similar to certain displays of monkeys and apes. In some species a
male will sit with its legs apart and threaten other males by suddenly

erecting its penis at them. In a few species, the male genitals have become brightly coloured as an enhancement of this display. The origin of phallic threats can be found in the mating actions of primates. During copulation, it is the male that actively mounts and penetrates the female. Since mating males are usually dominant individuals with a high status in the group, the act of mating becomes synonymous with dominance. Mounting and making pelvic thrusts therefore becomes a symbolic way of saying 'I am dominant over you' and can be used by a dominant male towards either a subordinate female *or* a subordinate male. When a male mounts another male as a status display, he usually does no more than position himself, make a few perfunctory pelvic thrusts without anal insertion, and then dismount. It is a token assault — a symbol of his power over the weaker animal. Indeed, so much a token has it become, that a dominant female can be seen to perform it, both towards subordinate females and subordinate males. Gender is no longer important — either sex can go through the motions of mounting or pelvic thrusting. In a similar way, the use of a 'phallic forearm' by a human being does not necessarily require that the gesturer should be the owner of a real penis. The display can be given by a hostile female to either sex, just as it can be given by a hostile male to either sex. All it needs is a momentary state of dominance over another individual. The gesture may appear to be sexual and may have its origins in a sexual act, but it is now largely emancipated from considerations of sexuality and firmly embedded in the world of inter-personal hostility.

The forearm jerk is not the only form of insulting phallic symbolism, though it is perhaps the most impressive. The very size of penis-substitute leaves no doubt about the omnipotence of its owner. This may explain why this gesture has become so popular in recent years and why it seems to have eclipsed — in certain regions, at least — the much more ancient obscene insult, the middle-finger jerk. The size of a finger makes it a poor symbolic substitute for an erect human penis. Perhaps it would be true to say that the forearm jerk has developed as a super-normal version of the earlier middle-finger gesture, with the enlarged size of the token phallus giving it an immediate advantage. But we do not know the early history of the rivalry between these two gestures. All we do know is that the middle-finger jerk was so popular among the Romans that they even gave a special name to the middle digit, calling it the impudent finger: *digitus impudicus*. It was also known as the obscene finger, or the infamous finger, and there are a number of references to its use in the writings of classical authors. For instance, Martial (*Epigrams* VI.LXX): 'he points his finger, and the insulting one at that, towards Alcon, Dasius and Symmachus.' The emperor Caligula is thought to have used the extended middle finger when offering his hand to be kissed, as a deliberately scandalous act. And, according to Suetonius, Pylades was banished from Italy for making the obscene middle-finger gesture at a critical member of an audience who was trying to hiss him from the stage. There were other obscene gestures in use in Ancient Rome, but the forearm jerk does not seem to have been one of them. In fact, we have been unable to find any early references to it. The middle-finger jerk has survived for over 2,000 years and is still current in many parts of the world, especially the United States, so that there has not been a complete replacement of the old, finger-sized symbol with the new, improved, arm-sized symbol. The latter is merely an addition to the potential repertoire of the would-be insulter.

If titles can be used as a guide, it seems possible that the forearm jerk developed first in the French-speaking world, because it is there that it has been given a special name. For the British and the Italians, it has no name, but almost every Frenchman knows it as the '*bras d'honneur*', literally, the 'arm of honour'. This equates male honour with male virility, which is easy enough to understand, bearing in mind the relationship between male sexual displays and high status, discussed earlier, but it is a curiously old-fashioned term which suggests that it has been in use over a long period. Were this not the case, it would be rather strange for a title relating to 'honour' to be used in modern times for a gesture that is, by common knowledge, a gross obscenity. But the exact date of its beginnings remains a mystery.

Today, in addition to its role as a sexual insult, the forearm jerk also appears as a vulgarly complimentary sexual comment. In some countries this has become the dominant theme for the gesture, and it is employed as a signal that a male feels sexually aroused by a particular female. It is not usually performed *to* the female, but *about* her. If a male finds a female sexually attractive he may perform the forearm jerk to indicate to one of his male companions what he would like to do to her. If she is present, this is normally done without her knowledge. Alternatively, it may be done in her absence but when a group of men are debating her sexual qualities. In a sense, it then becomes a gesture of sexual praise with a completely different meaning from the phallic insult. All they have in common is the symbolic erection of the penis. Of course, if the female in question does observe the gesture, she may be insulted by it, but the message is quite distinct. It is a sexual gesture about a sexual feeling, whereas the phallic threat is a sexual gesture about a hostile feeling. The one says, 'I want you', the other, 'get lost'.

A third meaning is often given when people who do not know the sexual connotations of the forearm jerk are asked to explain it. They see the raised, bent arm, with a hand apparently holding the biceps, and assume that it is a display of manly strength — not in the virile sense, but purely as a show of bulging arm muscles. In a way, this is a case of mistaken identity of the kind we have encountered with other gestures, but the difference here is that the mistake is made so frequently that it has to be considered as a major meaning for this gesture.

At sporting events recently, a subtle blend has developed between the phallic erection of the forearm and the simple, muscle display. A triumphant winner, in his moment of elation, can often be seen to bring his bent forearm up into the stiffly bent, muscle-bulging posture, and to do so in such a way that there is something inescapably

The palm-down variant of the Neapolitan forearm jerk, used as a sexual insult.

The British forearm jerk employed as a phallic comment by female
footballers. From a painting by Eric Scott, 1976.

'erectile' about the action. The other hand is not slapped on to the
upper-arm, as in the case of the full-blooded phallic display, but the
way the fist rises up through the air has an unmistakable hint of
sexuality. This puts it into a special category of its own. It is not
directed at the opponents, or defeated rivals, as would be the typical
phallic insult, nor is it a comment on sexual arousal. It is done for the
benefit of the winner's team-mates or his fans, and is in effect a
comment on, or a celebration of, his sudden moment of dominance.

DISTRIBUTION

The forearm jerk as a phallic insult was known by at least someone
at nearly all of our locations (38 out of the 40 sites), but the
distribution was far from even. There were two distinct zones and
these are reflected in our gesture map on page 90. Expressed in
general terms, we can say that this phallic insult was rare in northern
Europe and extremely common in southern Europe and around the

Mediterranean. It would produce little reaction in a Swede, but almost every Latin male would receive the message loud and clear.

To be more specific, if we call the British Isles, Scandinavia, Holland, Germany and Austria 'North Europe', and the rest of our study area 'South Europe', then the gesture was known to only 11 per cent of the northerners, but to a massive 85 per cent of the southerners. We suspect that, in reality, the difference may be even greater, because in certain countries in the south the gesture is considered so obscene that one can be arrested for using it in the street. This meant that at some locations a few of our informants would be too shy to admit knowledge of it. When asked what the forearm jerk meant they would give an embarrassed laugh, or a knowing smile, and then claim that they had never heard of it, never seen it and had no knowledge of it. Although it was tempting to record their answers as positive, we could not do so because we required a specific reply from them as regards the message transmitted by the gesture. But had we included such people in our figures, the already high 85 per cent level would have risen even higher.

If we turn to the use of the forearm jerk as a vulgar sexual compliment or comment, another highly characteristic distribution pattern appears on the gesture map (see page 90). The British have never seen themselves as world leaders in the realm of flamboyant gesticulation, but for once they have no gestural equal. When it comes to paying an obscene compliment, the British region has no rivals. Our impression is that this is a post-war phenomenon and that the 'I am sexually aroused' forearm jerk was the result of a local distortion of the continental phallic insult. This is not a complete switch, but it is a major shift of emphasis. If we average out the British figures against those for all the other localities, the percentages are: obscene compliment in British region: 63 per cent. In all other localities: 5 per cent.

Perhaps the best way to impart the true flavour of these two main meanings of the forearm jerk — the sexual insult and the sexual comment — and to underline the difference between them, is to list a selection of the most popular terms used to describe them by our informants:

The sexual insult. Bugger off!, fuck off!, get lost!, get stuffed, go to hell, go to the devil, I'll get you, piss off!, take this!, up yours.

The sexual comment. A bit of all right, a good bit, a good woman, a nice piece, cor! what a woman, good for a screw, having a woman,

I'd like to do her, I fancy her, I know what I'd do to her, randy, would like to give her one.

For the record, it may be worth adding some of the most popular foreign terms for the sexual insult. For example, in France: *bras de fer, bras d'honneur, faire mâcher les poings, le gros bras, on s'en fout, va chez les Grecques, va te faire foutre*. In Spain: *corte de manga, miau, ¡toma!*. In Portugal: *foda-se, mandar para o caralho, manguito, pataco, vai-te lixar*. In Italy: *cazzo, vai in quel paese, va fan' culo*.

As already mentioned, there was a third major meaning for the forearm jerk, employed by those who did not know of its use as an obscenity — or who perhaps knew, but preferred to ignore it. This was the category that interpreted the gesture as a sign of physical strength. They used such phrases as: holding biceps, I'm strong, look at my muscles, muscle flexing, powerful, strong man, tough guy. As the gesture map for this meaning reveals, the areas where this interpretation was most common were Scandinavia, Germany, Austria and Tunisia. This means that, if the three major meanings are viewed together, one of them is present as a dominant interpretation in almost every location we visited. Only Denmark and Holland are poorly represented.

A variant form of the forearm jerk, by a Frenchman, with the arm swinging across the body; used as a sexual insult.

Variations

Most of the gestures we studied in the field were found to exist in a number of variant forms, but in the case of the forearm jerk there were so many that they deserve special attention. For the purposes of description, we will assume that the gesture is being made by a right-handed person, with the right arm representing the erect phallus. They can be classified as follows:

1 The upward jerk

The bent right arm is jerked upwards, with the clenched fist held palm-up, and the open left hand slapped down simultaneously on to the right upper-arm. This is the common, standard version of the gesture, and is found almost everywhere.

2 The simplified upward jerk

The same, but without the left hand involved. This symbolizes phallic erection, rather than actual intromission, and is found in those areas where the vulgar sexual compliment is dominant.

3 The multiple upward jerk

The same as No. 1, but with the bent forearm repeatedly raised and lowered, as if making a series of pelvic thrusts.

4 The diagonal jerk

The same as No. 1, but with the forearm raised, not vertically, but diagonally up and across the body of the gesturer. This was noted particularly in Sardinia, but also occurs elsewhere.

5 The sideways jerk

A further development of the last variant, in which the jerked forearm moves horizontally across the body of the gesturer. This was recorded especially in France.

6 The forward jerk

The same as No. 1, but with the right arm shot forward stiffly, as the left hand slaps the upper-arm. There are three positions for the right hand with this variant: clenched fist, palm-up; clenched fist, palm-down; flat hand, palm-down. These were observed mostly in Italy.

7 The amplified forearm jerk

For some gesturers, the simple phallic symbol is not enough and they add to it a special finger gesture. As the right hand is jerked into the air, it adopts an obscene finger posture that results in the transmission of a simultaneous, double obscenity. There are four versions of this: (a) forearm jerk + the middle-finger gesture. The middle finger, as already mentioned, is an ancient phallic symbol when stiffly extended from an otherwise clenched fist. So to perform the forearm jerk with the middle finger 'erect' is to offer two phallic insults at once. This was noted particularly in the Canary Islands and Portugal. (b) The forearm jerk + the stiff forefinger. In Spain, the forefinger is sometimes used instead of the middle finger when making a phallic finger gesture, and this, too, was sometimes combined with the forearm jerk. (c) The forearm jerk + the fig-sign. The fig-sign consists of thrusting the thumb between the first and second fingers of a clenched fist. It is a gesture we will be dealing with at length later in the book, and there are differing opinions about its symbolic significance. It is generally accepted, however, as a sexual gesture, so that when it combines with the forearm jerk it increases the intensity of the insult. (d) The forearm jerk + the horn-sign. Again, a gesture we will discuss in detail later, and again a gross insult in its own right. As before, its addition to the forearm jerk doubles the impact. The horn-sign is formed by stiffly extending the forefinger and the little finger from an otherwise clenched fist.

8   The abbreviated forearm jerk
A low intensity version of the gesture consists of a minor jerk, forwards or upwards, of the right forearm, with the left hand slapped down on the jerked forearm itself, instead of the upper-arm.

9   The miniature forearm jerk
In Spain there is a gesture called 'the peseta' (= 'the penny'), in which the two arms of the ordinary gesturer are replaced by his two forefingers. The right forefinger is bent and jerked up into the air, as if it were the right forearm, and at the same time, the left forefinger is slapped down on to it, mimicking the slap of the left hand on the right upper-arm. This miniaturization of the gesture is used in a joking way at close quarters.

10   The cryptic forearm jerk
In some regions, the full-blooded gesture is considered so obscene that it is possible to be arrested for employing it in a public place. This has led to the development of a cryptic version of it, understood by both the gesturer and his victim, but not sufficiently conspicuous

The cryptic upper-arm rub.

to attract attention from outside the group in which it is being used. On the island of Malta, where there is a strong taboo against the full gesture, the cryptic form is no more than a mild rubbing of the left hand on the right upper-arm. In other regions, two fingers of the left hand are slapped on to the right upper-arm. In neither case does the actual forearm jerk occur. These are gestural equivalents of spoken phrases such as 'eff off', or written phrases such as 'f . . . off', which transmit an obscene message without actually saying or writing down the taboo word.

There is one final variation of the forearm jerk, but it does not concern the form of the gesture. Instead it has to do with the strength of its message. Just as swear words vary in their impact as fashions change, with one word becoming gradually 'tamer' and more acceptable in polite company, while another becomes more virulent, so too do obscene gestures. The forearm jerk may be strongly taboo and illegal in Malta, but in other regions it is openly performed at moments of anger, and in still others it is little more than a joke. In Portugal, for instance, the ordinary forearm jerk is done jokingly

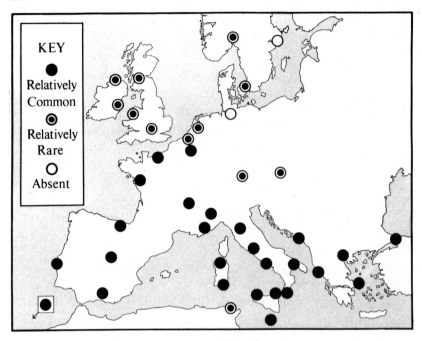

THE FOREARM JERK Meaning: sexual insult

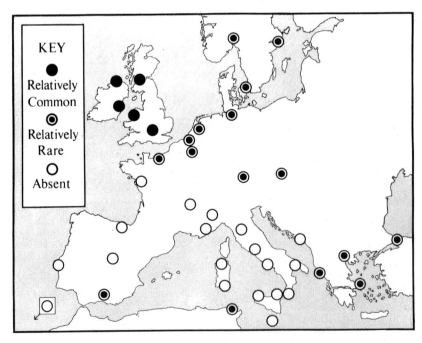

THE FOREARM JERK Meaning: sexual comment

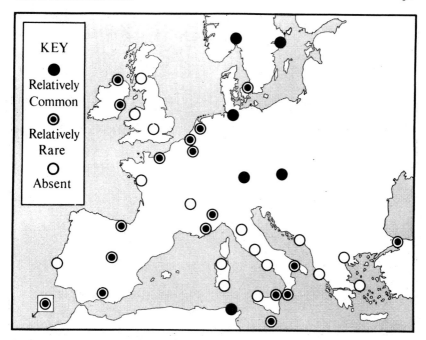

THE FOREARM JERK Meaning: strength

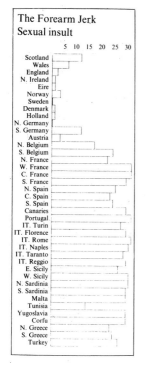

The Forearm Jerk
Sexual insult

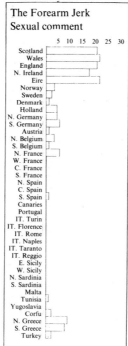

The Forearm Jerk
Sexual comment

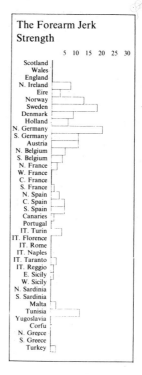

The Forearm Jerk
Strength

between friends and has lost so much of its impact that, if a Portuguese gesturer wishes to be seriously provocative, he has to amplify the gesture by adding the middle-finger jerk to it. When this is done, the gesture is still treated today as a major obscenity. In Greece, on the other hand, the forearm jerk is hardly ever used seriously. There it is nearly always a joke, no matter how it is used. This may be related to the fact that in the Greek-speaking world, there is another obscene gesture   the *moutza* — which takes on the role of *the* taboo obscenity. The *moutza* is performed by pushing an open palm, with fingers stiffly spread, towards the face of the victim. To a non-Greek, it looks similar to an ordinary 'hand-repel' gesture, saying 'go back, go back', but in Greece it has an ancient history dating from Byzantine times, where it originated as a gesture symbolizing the thrusting of faeces into the face of a chained criminal who was being paraded through the streets. For the modern Greek, it has retained its virulent, original meaning and he is therefore less interested in rival obscenities, such as the forearm jerk. A similar situation applies in Britain, where the worst gestural obscenity is the palm-back V-sign (to be discussed later in the book), a gesture that involves jerking forked fingers up into the air. It is probably because of the dominance of this particular sexual insult in Britain, that the forearm jerk has been diverted locally into another role — that of the vulgar sexual compliment. Had the insult V-sign not existed in Britain, the insult forearm jerk might well have crossed the Channel and spread without resistance. This is another case of *gestural niches* being filled and blocking the spread of an invading gesture from foreign parts.

8 The Flat-hand Flick

**THE FLAT HAND
FLICK MEANINGS:**

1 Departure
   demand   412
2 Departure
   description   105
3 Departure request 28
4 others   23
5 not used   632
(Based on 1,200 informants
at 40 locations)

DESCRIPTION

The right hand, held on edge, with the thumb uppermost and all
digits stretched out, is flicked up slightly into the air. This movement
is checked by the left hand, also held with thumb uppermost and
digits stretched, chopping down on to the right wrist.

ORIGINS

There are two elements to this gesture. The flicked right hand
imitates the action of something going away from the gesturer. The
chopping down of the left hand amplifies this by symbolically am-
putating the right hand, to facilitate, as it were, its moving off in the
direction indicated. Together these elements combine to symbolize
some kind of departure. The nature of this departure varies. It can be
a command, such as 'go away', a description, such as 'he's gone
away', or a request, such as 'please move on'.

Because this gesture has such obvious origins, it might be imagined that our informants would be able to guess its significance, but
this was not the case. Since it has become rather stylized in form, it is
not recognized as a departure signal in many regions. The simple act
of waving someone away with a rejecting arm movement would
probably be understood almost anywhere in the world, but the

special chop-and-jerk of the flat-hand flick gesture is sufficiently formalized to puzzle the uninitiated. The result is that it does show a geographical distribution of a limited, zonal type, and justifies an attempt to map its range.

DISTRIBUTION

Recognition of this gesture was non-existent in northern Europe. Not a single informant identified it (with the exception of a few wild guesses) in the British region, Scandinavia, or Holland, and it was also extremely rare in the German-speaking zone. Throughout southern Europe and the Mediterranean it was, however, moderately well known in most places.

There are two dominant zones for the use of this gesture, one in France and the other in Italy, but, as our gesture maps show, the meaning was different in the two cases. In Italy, the gesture is almost exclusively a rejection: buzz off, get lost, go away, push off. In France, this command is also employed, but there it is rivalled by the

The flat-hand flick used by Frenchmen to indicate that someone has departed.

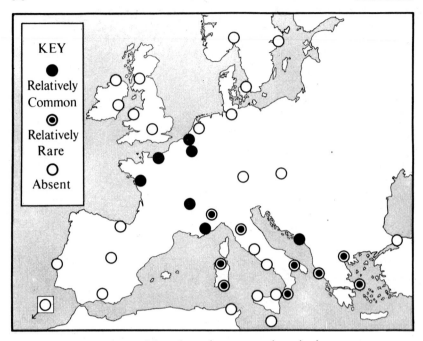

THE FLAT-HAND FLICK Meaning: departure description

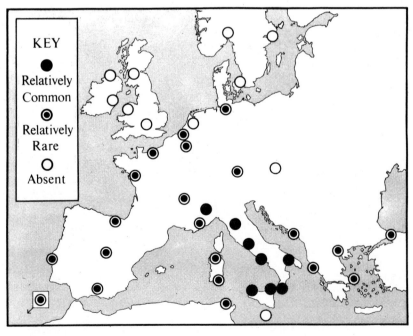

THE FLAT-HAND FLICK Meaning: departure demand

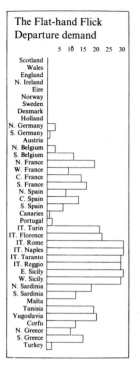

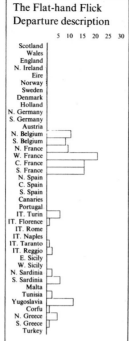

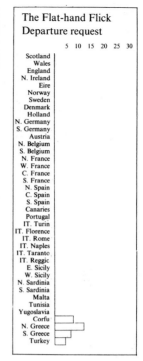

descriptive meaning: he's gone away, I'm going, I'm leaving, I'm off, I've run away, I was gone, they're making off, we're off. There are no sharp borderlines between these two main zones. The secondary meaning seeps over in both cases. There are a few striking changes in other areas, however. The descriptive meaning is strong in southern France, but totally absent in Spain. The rejection meaning is very strong in Sicily, but totally absent in Malta, less than 60 miles south. In fact, Malta was unusual in being the only southern location where the gesture was totally unknown in any of its main meanings, a link with the north that may be explained by Malta's long colonial association with Britain.

In the far south-east, the Greco-Turkish zone, a third main meaning appears. There the flat-hand flick was frequently interpreted as a traffic signal indicating: 'please pass', 'move on', 'pass this way', 'pass by', 'this way', and was essentially a polite request, rather than a command. This specifically directional use of the gesture was not encountered elsewhere.

There are several variants of the flat-hand flick. The flicked right hand may make only one or two jerks, or it may be wagged up and down repeatedly. The chopping left hand may play a rather weak role, barely hitting the right forearm, or conversely it may play an exaggerated role, repeatedly chopping down on to the forearm with each jerk of the right hand. An intense form of the gesture involves a hand-chop down on to the arm-crook, so that the whole forearm jerks forward. In this last variant, the gesture begins to look rather like the phallic forearm jerk, and a few of our informants did, in fact, mistake it for that gesture.

9 The Ring

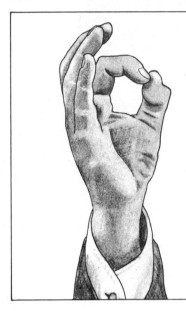

THE RING MEANINGS:

1	O.K. – Good	700
2	Orifice	128
3	Zero	115
4	Threat	16
5	others	27
6	not used	214

(Based on 1,200 informants at 40 locations)

DESCRIPTION

The hand is held up, with the palm facing away from the gesturer, and with the thumb and forefinger touching to form a circle. The other three fingers are extended and slightly spread. Usually, as the hand is brought up into position, it makes a short forward jerk and then freezes for a few moments before being lowered.

ORIGINS — As an O.K. Sign

The dominant meaning for the ring gesture is 'O.K.' In fact, this slang expression has become so closely associated with it, that the action has often been called simply 'The O.K. Gesture'. This is because the verbal term and the physical action embrace the same range of closely related messages. They extend from precision and approval to agreement and praise. When the expression is spoken, or the gesture is made, it can signify that something is correct or exactly right; or that it is highly appropriate or acceptable; or that it is very good or perfect. These are all related terms and yet it is difficult to group them together under one heading, with a single title, without resorting to the use of the colloquial phrase 'O.K.'

Because of this very close relationship between the phrase and the gesture, it has been suggested that perhaps the O formed by the circle of the thumb and forefinger actually stands for the O of the 'O.K.'; in other words, that the ring gesture has developed as a symbolic visual equivalent of the spoken message, and is dependent upon it for its existence. It is certainly true that, where the ring sign is used by non-English speaking people, it is often referred to as the 'American O.K.', even when speaking in their native tongues. If this is the origin of the gesture, then the first task is to establish the derivation of the O.K. expression itself, but this is by no means easy to do.

Etymologists have been arguing over the first use of the term for many years. Linguist Allen Read believes he has pin-pointed its first appearance, which he records as March 23rd, 1839, in an article in the *Boston Morning Post*. It is used there as 'o.k. — all correct', and he points out that, at the time, newspapers were making great play with joke initials, often deliberately based on mis-spellings. Other examples, which did not catch on, were K.G. (for 'no go' = Know Go) and K.Y. (for 'no use' = Know Yuse). By the following year the Boston craze for playful initials had spread to New York, and before the end of 1839 was to be found as far away as New Orleans. The craze eventually lost impetus, but from it the initials O.K. survived, possibly because they had come to stand for a family of closely related meanings that were not capable of grouping under the banner of a more respectable, official English word.

Although this explanation of its survival in everyday speech is almost certainly correct, the Bostonian origin of the expression is hotly contested and rival theories abound. One authority insists that it can be traced back to a nineteenth-century American political figure with the nickname of 'Old Kinderhook'. Another states that it comes from the *accidental* spelling of 'all correct', as 'Oll Korrect'. Yet another claims that it is the opposite of the boxing term 'K.O.' (knocked out). A further interpretation sees it as standing for 'Old Keokuk', an Indian chief who signed his treaties with his initials. Also relating it to the Indian world is the idea that it comes from a Choctaw word *oke*, meaning 'it is so'. Less popular explanations derive it variously from: the initials of Otto Kaiser, a German-born American industrialist; the southern French dialect word *oc* (= *oui*); the French phrase *aux quais* stencilled on the casks of Puerto Rico rum specially selected for export; a place in Haiti called *Aus Cayes*, noted for its excellent rum; the Scots expression *Och Aye*!; the Finnish word *oikea*; the Latin phrase *omnia correcta*; a mis-reading of O.R. (order recorded); and, finally, the letters indicating rank appended to the signature of a German *Ober-kommandant.*

Each protagonist in the debate believes that his particular source is the original one and that all the others are secondary uses. Until an impressively early reference is found to one of these sources, which pre-dates all the others by a wide margin, the matter will never be settled. Whichever candidate is ultimately appointed, it is certain that during the nineteenth century the popularity of the expression spread far and wide. In England it was well known in the 1860s, and a music hall singer by the name of the Great Vance included it in his famous song 'Walking in the Zoo' (which introduced the word 'zoo' into the language, and must therefore have made some impact at the time), using the sentence 'Walking in the the Zoo is the O.K. thing to do.' This dispels any notion that 'O.K.' was a twentieth-century Americanism first imported into Europe by G.I.s during wartime, as has sometimes been claimed. Its widespread usage in the last century and the confusion over its exact site of origin makes it difficult for us to link the history of the expression with the initial development of the ring gesture. As a consolation, it occurred to us that perhaps, in any case, the idea that the gesture was dependent on the rise of the O.K. expression was in itself incorrect. This does not mean that the birth of the 'O.K.' did not act in a supportive role, providing a convenient verbal 'booster' for the gesture. To that extent, the phrase has almost certainly been important in helping to keep the gesture alive and popular, but its sources, we felt, might go back much further, to another derivational root.

The root we had in mind is the same one we encountered before when tracing the origins of the hand purse gesture. That, we saw, could be related to a simple baton signal employed as an 'emphasizer' during animated conversation, the posture of the fingers relating to the characteristic 'precision grip' of the human hand. Just as that gesture could come to stand for something good or precise, so too, we realized, could the thumb-and-forefinger ring. This hand posture, although employing the tips of only two digits, is an action of even greater precision. The essence of the gesture, as a baton, is not, of course, the making of a circular shape with the two digits, but the bringing together of the ends of those digits as if holding an imaginary, minute object. The ring is formed passively, as it were, as a result of this precision hold.

We know that this precision baton is used commonly and unconsciously during modern times, when groups of people gather for conversation. They are not specifically aware that they are employing it at any one moment, and the baton action has been given no special name. But film analysis of the conversation sequences in which it occurs do reveal that it appears at moments where speakers are making some fine point, or requesting greater precision in some way. All that remained was for us to trace ancient examples of this baton, so that we could be sure its baton role was old enough and well established enough to have given rise to a symbolic offshoot — the present-day ring gesture.

We managed to find such a reference in the writings of the first century A.D. Roman teacher Quintilian. In his *Institutio Oratoria* (Book XI, III, 104) he makes the following comment: 'If the first finger touch the middle of the right-hand edge of the thumb-nail with its extremity, the other fingers being relaxed, we shall have a graceful gesture well suited to express approval.' The details of this description are of special interest, because by insisting that the forefinger-tip touches, not merely the end of the thumb, but 'the right-hand edge of the thumb-nail', Quintilian ensures that the precision hold is made in such a way that the two digits are more or less forced to adopt a circular posture. It is possible to bring the fleshy tips together in such a way that the shape created is a 'circle' so squashed as to be hardly circular at all. But the details he gives insist on the ring shape and leave no doubt that he was writing about exactly the same gesture that we see today.

The English gesture student John Bulwer, writing in his *Chirologia* of 1644, makes the same point (perhaps borrowing it from Quintilian) when he says: 'The top of the fore-finger moved to joyne with the naile of the Thumbe that's next to it, the other fingers in remitter, is opportune for those who relate, distinguish, or approve.' These early references clearly show both that the gesture was in common use then, and also that it could signify approval — one of the key qualities of the modern ring sign. So it seems likely that the use of the gesture in this role may well have developed into a fully-fledged symbolic action many years ago, long before the advent of the supportive O.K. expression. But the exact date of this shift, from a baton unconsciously accompanying speech, to a deliberate, specifically recognized symbolic gesture which could act as a substitute for speech, is still not known to us. Frederick Elworthy, in his folklore studies in late Victorian times, came across several amulets of hands displaying the ring gesture, which confirms that by then it was well established as a symbolic gesture of some kind, but this is already very 'modern' in relation to our classical reference.

Another possible source for the O.K. meaning of the ring gesture deserves a brief mention. In France, there is a special, local variant of the fingertips kiss, involving only the thumb and forefinger. The tips of these two digits are brought together and then, after being kissed to the lips, are jerked away and up into the air. As this is done, the tips remain in contact (in contrast to the five fingertips of the typical fingertips kiss, which are fanned out and spread as the hand is jerked away from the lips), so that, at the end of this action, the hand posture is remarkably similar to that of the ring gesture. A typical illustration of this moment in the 'two-tips kiss' shows a French chef extolling the virtues of his art, with his facial expression leaving no doubt about the fact that he considers his food to be 'O.K.' So, here again, is a possible 'parent gesture' carrying basically the same message. But again, we feel that this is a case of a 'supportive role' rather than an originating one. We consider that the early derivation of the ring sign from a precision baton preceded both the linkage with the O.K. phrase and the possible association with the 'chef's

The 'chef's delight' version of the ring gesture related to the French thumb-and-forefinger-tips kiss.

delight' two-digit kiss. The results of our new field studies tend to confirm this, as we shall see in a moment, but first it is necessary to examine the symbolic origins of the ring sign in some of its other major roles, for the O.K. role is only one of several totally distinct capacities enjoyed by this particular hand posture.

ORIGINS — As an Orifice Sign

Even more ancient than the precision baton version of the ring sign, is its use as a symbol of an orifice. Here, the source of the symbolism is obvious enough. The circular shape made by the thumb and forefinger is seen as representing a body orifice, usually the anus, but occasionally the vagina. This usage has been traced back to early vase paintings. One example, according to Andrea de Jorio, shows four athletes bathing outside the gymnasium, with one of them clearly making the orifice gesture. It is always possible that Frederick Elworthy's amulets showing a hand in the ring posture are, in reality, not early O.K. signs, but obscene gestures worn to protect the wearer from the Evil Eye. The theory behind such amuletic use was that, when the Evil Eye saw the obscenity of the gesture, it would be distracted from its more serious business of casting an evil spell on the amulet-owner. Such amulets are still sold today, and we were able to find an example as far away as the Canary Islands, but when asked the meaning of the hand posture, the seller was unable to give an answer, beyond the usual 'it is for good luck'.

The orifice symbolism of the ring gesture has developed a family of related meanings as time has passed, and today, in different regions, as we shall demonstrate in a moment, it can mean '*you* are an orifice', 'you have a large orifice', or 'you are a homosexual' — all used as insults — or 'I want an orifice', 'You have a beautiful orifice', 'Please give me your orifice', or 'Let's go and look for an orifice' — all used as vulgar sexual comments or invitations. The obscene insults are almost always anal, while the comments may be either anal or vaginal. Different regions stress different aspects of this symbolism, but all clearly stem from the same basic symbolic equation: hand ring = hole = body orifice.

ORIGINS — As a Zero Sign

A third, completely distinct symbolism has developed in some regions. There, the ring shape is seen as symbolic of a nought — a numerical O instead of an alphabetical O — and from this starting point, the message becomes zero, worthless, no good. This, of course, is the precise opposite of the dominant use of the ring gesture, as a sign for 'good, great'. Since both often occur in the same districts, it poses some intriguing questions about gesture-confusion. Normally, gesture systems avoid ambiguity, but here the possibilities for error seem to be enormous, and their existence requires explanation. Suffice it to say for the moment that, as far as origins are concerned, there is no mystery about the zero message, except that we have no idea when it first came into use, and we can find no early references to it whatsoever.

The French version of the ring gesture meaning that something is worthless, or zero.

ORIGINS — As a Threat Signal

A small, but significant number of people employ the ring gesture as a threat signal, giving it a fourth basic meaning. This appears to be an extension of the 'zero, worthless' category, the 'no good' message of the zero ring being modified to mean '*you* are no good'. When performed as a threat, the thumb-and-forefinger circle is combined with rather stiffly flattened fingers, and the hand is chopped through the air with short, repeated jerks. Because of the 'karate chop' style of the action, with the middle finger, ring finger and little finger all fully extended, the gesture does not look particularly like the standard version of a ring gesture, to those familiar with it as an O.K.

sign, an obscenity, or a zero. But for people who never use these standard forms of the gesture, there is no problem. Show them a standard ring gesture and they immediately identify it as their own threat signal. They may say 'here, we do it more like this', indicating the more vigorous chopping action of the hand, but they will make the connection none the less. In other words, in terms of inter-cultural confusion, their lack of distinction between the two ring *styles* will mean that there is a danger of misinterpretation when they meet 'O.K. ring' visitors or foreigners.

The derivation of the threat ring from the zero ring is an interesting one, because it seems to involve a gestural rarity, namely a hybrid action. One of the main characteristics of gestures is that, unlike words, they seldom combine to form new patterns out of a mixture of old ones. This does occur, of course, with formalized, coded deaf-and-dumb sign language, which sets out to copy speech, but it is largely absent with ordinary, colloquial gesturing. The ring threat is an exception to this rule because it is essentially a combination of the ring (meaning 'you are so worthless') and the hand chop (meaning 'I will kill you'). It occurs most commonly in a culture where the ordinary version of the ring gesture nearly always means zero, which helps to confirm this interpretation, and it is intriguing that the verbal equivalent of the threat gesture is usually given as 'I will kill you tomorrow', thereby implying that the victim is so worthless that he is not even sufficiently challenging to require despatching immediately. He is such a zero that his demise can safely be postponed to a more convenient time.

OTHER ORIGINS

Two rare usages deserve a brief mention, one because it is so puzzling and the other because, although rare in European and Mediterranean regions, it is extremely common elsewhere.

The puzzling example concerns the use of the ring gesture as meaning 'Thursday'. At first sight this seems either like a wild guess, or like some fragment of a completely arbitrary sign language code. It is neither, but simply the result of counting the days of the week on the fingers of the hand, employing the thumb as the counting digit. The thumb is pressed first to the little finger ($=$ Monday), then the ring finger ($=$ Tuesday), then the middle finger ($=$ Wednesday) and finally the forefinger ($=$ Thursday). At the moment when Thursday is being counted off, the hand posture momentarily looks like the ring gesture, and a few of the many people we interviewed, not knowing any dominant meaning for the gesture, gave this interpretation.

The final example, which we hardly encountered at all in Europe, sees the ring as a symbol of money. Because the fingers make a circular shape and because coins are circular, another symbolic equation is born, and in the Far East, at least, has taken a firm hold. To the Japanese, it seems, the money signal is widespread and popular, but in Europe there were already too many rival claims on the gesture for yet another meaning to establish itself, and we have only found the 'money ring' gesture in one or two isolated cases.

DISTRIBUTION

In each of its four main meanings — O.K., Orifice, Zero, and Threat — the ring gesture showed a characteristic distribution with special zonal concentrations. In its dominant usage, as an O.K. sign, it was found scattered over the whole of the European and Mediterranean range of our field study, with the single exception of Tunisia. But, despite this wide scatter, there were nevertheless three areas of peak popularity. These were (1) northern Europe, from the British Isles, through Scandinavia, to Germany and Austria; (2) south central Europe, from Yugoslavia, through southern Italy to Sicily, and (3) central Spain, through southern Spain, down to the Canaries. There was no dramatic, sharp fall-off in popularity at the edges of the zones, as occurs with some other gestures. Nearly always, the neighbouring regions showed the O.K. ring usage at only a slightly reduced level. Only in the special case of Tunisia was there anything approaching a 'gesture frontier', and with the major sea separation between North Africa and southern Europe, this hardly rates as a neighbouring zone. West Sicily is about 160 kilometres across the Mediterranean from the tip of Tunisia, and culturally the distance is much greater, so that the fall from 77 per cent to 0 per cent for the use of the O.K. ring is not surprising. Excluding this one Arab culture, however, the gesture could be said to have become truly European, understood everywhere by at least a section of the population. Because of this there are no clues in the present-day distribution of the O.K. ring to help us decide about its possible origins. It could have begun almost anywhere and spread in almost any direction.

The zero ring gesture has a much more restricted distribution, being firmly centred on the Franco-Belgian region. An average of 48 per cent of our French and Belgian informants interpreted it this way, compared with an average of less than 2 per cent for the rest of Europe. The really surprising feature of this distribution is its relation to the scatter of the O.K. ring sign. Instead of fading out in the Franco-Belgian zone, in competition with the zero ring, it survives there at a remarkably high level, averaging an overall 39 per cent. What makes this strange is that the two meanings for the same gesture are in complete opposition to one another. The O.K. ring basically means that something is *good*, the zero ring that it is worthless, or *no good*. Since 48 per cent see it one way, and 39 per cent see it the other, how does it happen that there is no confusion? Every one of our six Franco-Belgian locations revealed a significant use of both gesture meanings and this posed us a problem we had not met elsewhere with other gestures.

The first question to ask was whether the ring gesture had a slightly different, but crucial variation in form, according to the meaning being given it. Was the O.K. ring rounder, flatter, or stiffer than the zero ring, or vice versa? If so, then to the trained eye of the local population, there would appear to be two gestures, rather than a single one. To an outsider, familiar only with one interpretation, a subtle difference might easily be overlooked, but to a Frenchman or a Belgian, tuned in to the double usage, the small distinction might be obvious. The facts did not support this. True, there were variants of the basic hand posture, but these were far from consistent and appeared to be little more than individual idiosyncrasies. One informant told us that with the O.K. ring, the fingers not forming the ring were flatter; another assured us that with the zero ring, the fingers were flatter, and that with the O.K. ring, they were slightly curled; yet another informed us that for the zero signal it was necessary to curl all the fingers tightly, making a cylinder shape with the hand. We were also told that the O.K. gesture was done by using the thumb and third finger, instead of the first. Another informant said that this was precisely the way to make the zero sign. Yet another claimed it was the second finger that was used for the zero sign, and so on. It was impossible to make any sense out of these variations and, in any case, the vast majority of informants told us there was no difference at all between the two actions.

This meant that the form of the gesture itself could not be providing a major clue as to its meaning. Some informants who knew both meanings said that it was all a matter of the verbal utterance accompanying the gesture — if you meant zero when you made the gesture, you said '*zéro*', if you meant good, you said '*c'est bon*'. In this way there was no confusion. Unfortunately, the gesture is often used silently or at a distance, so this explanation is insufficient. French fishermen told us that when the boats are returning with the catch, the men on board often give the ring gesture to tell those on shore whether their catch has been good or bad. On our evidence, we would expect this to create total confusion on shore, with 48 per cent of those watching imagining that the catch had been no good, while 39 per cent were convinced that it had been extremely good. The fisherman in question denied this hotly, saying that the gesture *always* meant zero and that nobody ever used it to mean that something was good. This gave rise to a new thought, that perhaps there were two distinct social groups in France — the zero-ringers

The ring gesture employed as a lucky charm.

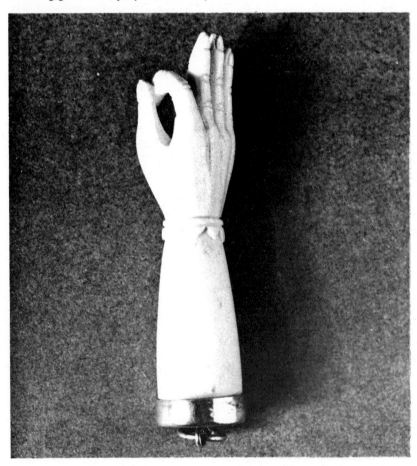

and the O.K.-ringers — and that they moved in different circles and never encountered one another's gesture-meanings. It was certainly true that a number of our informants seemed to agree with this idea, since they always insisted that their own interpretation was the only one, and that the other meaning simply did not exist. But again there was plenty of evidence to counter this. Many of our other informants insisted that both meanings were used locally and that there was no difference between the actions used. Asked how they could tell between them if the ring was made silently, some of them reported that it was a matter of context. If they were making the O.K. gesture they had a happy face, while if they were using the zero meaning they looked sad.

It seemed as if this, at last, was the true explanation. In England, there is only one dominant meaning for the ring gesture. The message it transmits is so strong that, even if done with a glum facial expression accompanying it, the O.K. significance of the hand posture is strong enough to send out its signal. The message *overrides* the context. In France, where there are the two rival meanings, this context-override is replaced by context-dependency, and the significance of the hand action is judged accordingly. However, even this solution met an objection. For instance, two French anglers, sitting side by side watching their fishing rods, were asked about the meaning of the ring gesture. They gave their answers simultaneously. One said '*c'est bon*' and the other said '*zéro*'. They turned to look at one another in astonishment, and began to argue. After some time, they were clearly unable to settle their dispute and looked extremely puzzled. They were friends, so that it was impossible to explain their difference on the basis of the idea that there were two separate social groups involved, groups that never met and which kept alive the two meanings in distinct social compartments. Another example was of a man who was seen to make the ring gesture when talking about wine. He was smiling and his face gave the definite impression that he was saying the wine was 'O.K.', but in fact he was grinning at a friend who thought the wine was good, and the gesture meant that the wine was worthless. The smile on his face was there because he thought his friend was foolish to like such a poor wine.

Taken together, these arguments leave us in something of a dilemma. The O.K. ring and the zero ring may look the same or different. They may be known only as having one meaning, with the other denied, or as both meanings by the same person. They may be dependent on the verbal or non-verbal context, or they may be performed silently, and without a special accompanying expression. In short, there seems to be no general rule that separates them in such a way that all confusion could be avoided. It is hardly surprising that the two French anglers were left arguing over this mystery, as they sat by their fishing rods. What puzzled us was how such a state of affairs could have survived right across the Franco-Belgian area. We might have expected to find small, occasional overlap zones, where the ranges of two gestures met and where, at the boundary between them, people were making errors of interpretation. But even in such limited cases, we would have expected the populations to be *aware* of the problem and to have adapted to it in some way. We can only suppose that the Franco-Belgian situation is unstable and the result of a recent invasion by the O.K. ring, into an ancestral zero-ring zone. If the O.K. version was brought in by visiting Americans and Englishmen, and their films and TV programmes, during comparatively recent times, then we might expect to see some changes in the near future, with one or other meaning gradually coming to dominate the scene. A Parisian we talked to said that, when he moved from his home in the south of France, to live in the big city, he found he had to re-learn his ring gesture, changing from the zero version to the O.K. He saw the latter as the sophisticated, international way of using the sign, and considered the zero meaning to be rather old-fashioned and rural. This is not strictly true, as our subsequent field studies revealed, but it may well be that, in France, the O.K. meaning is a newer one, and is slowly supplanting the older zero meaning.

The real mystery that remained was the slow speed at which this process is taking place. Some factor had to be at work to enable such a strange, contradictory gestural situation to survive at all, even as a transitional phase. The answer appears to be the existence of a blindness to certain kinds of gestural-input. But how can this come about? If someone shakes a fist in front of your face, it is hard to ignore. What is it about the ring gesture that renders it so easily ignorable? The answer seems to be the existence alongside the symbolic ring sign of the original primitive baton gesture. When people talk they frequently adopt a finger posture almost identical to that used in the ring sign. As explained earlier, this looks the most likely candidate for the primary derivation of the O.K. ring. The Frenchman, seeing a symbolic ring gesture which is not the type he uses himself, can perhaps ignore it by transforming it, in his mind, into a simple baton that is doing no more than beat time to words.

Aiding this process is the fact that the most popular way of saying 'everything is fine' in France is not to use the ring gesture, but instead the familiar 'thumbs up'. In the same way, the 'thumbs down' can be used for the opposite signal, in place of the zero ring. This means that, although most people know about, and sometimes use, the ring gesture, it is a rather infrequent gesture — a commonly known gesture, but uncommon in actual use. This means that neither of the ring usages is particularly vital as part of the gestural communication system of the Franco-Belgian region. This, coupled with the presence of a ring-baton, could well make it possible for French gesturers to develop a 'blind eye' when encountering a ring-meaning unfamiliar to them.

We admit that this is not an entirely satisfactory explanation, and suspect that there is still much to be learnt about the way this gesture is employed in the everyday life of the Franco-Belgian zone of Europe. Two clues emerge from our field studies that may be helpful. The first concerns the shifting dominance of the two ring-meanings, as one travels from north to south. In Belgium and the northern parts of France, the O.K. meaning seems to be stronger than the zero. In the southern parts of France, this is reversed. To be more specific, if we lump together our three northern sites for the Franco-Belgian region (N. Belgium, S. Belgium and N. France) and call them 'north', and lump together our three southern sites (W. France, Central France and S. France) and call them 'south', then we can express the change in the zero/O.K. ratio in these two subzones. Our figures show that in the north, there are 7 zero-rings for every 10 O.K.-rings, while in the south there are 22 zero-rings for every 10 O.K.-rings. So the zero meaning is three times stronger in relation to the O.K.-ring, if you move from the northern part of the Franco-Belgian zone to the southern.

This north south difference is not enough to enable us to label the zero-ring as a southern French gesture. That would be putting it too strongly. But there is clearly some social factor at work that is influencing the northern population differently from the south. Perhaps we are witnessing the demise of the zero-ring gesture, with its decay moving faster in the more cosmopolitan northern areas. Perhaps this zero meaning once dominated the whole French-speaking region and then began to clash with, and eventually succumb to, the invading O.K. sign. We cannot be sure, but this seems to us the most likely explanation.

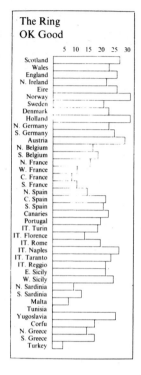

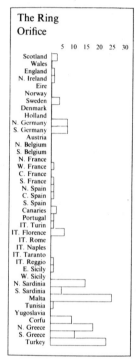

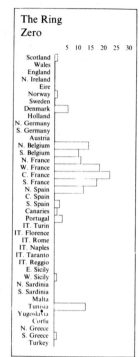

A second clue comes from our field work in Tunisia. There the zero meaning is strong (40 per cent), but the O.K. meaning is absent. The most common interpretation of the ring gesture is as a threat (43 per cent), but even this seems to stem from the zero usage, as already explained (= you are a big zero!). Tunisians, belonging to an ex-French colony, have almost certainly acquired their ring gesture from their ex-colonial masters, and it may be significant that, although they borrowed the French zero sign, they did not borrow the equally French O.K. sign. The suggestion here, and it must be admitted that it is no more than a suggestion, is that at the time when the French colonists were influencing Tunisian culture, they were only using the zero version of the ring gesture. If they had taken both with them, it seems reasonable to suppose that the O.K. version would have been borrowed just as readily (perhaps more so, since there are plenty of Arab insult gestures and threat gestures, and the 'worthless' message of the ring sign would have been the less useful of the two, as an addition to the existing gesture repertoire). This makes us speculate that perhaps the French, when they took over the country in 1881, were familiar with the zero-ring gesture and passed

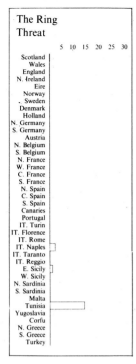

The Ring
Threat

	5	10	15	20	25	30
Scotland						
Wales						
England						
N. Ireland						
Eire						
Norway						
Sweden						
Denmark						
Holland						
N. Germany						
S. Germany						
Austria						
N. Belgium						
S. Belgium						
N. France						
W. France						
C. France						
S. France						
N. Spain						
C. Spain						
S. Spain						
Canaries						
Portugal						
IT. Turin						
IT. Florence						
IT. Rome						
IT. Naples						
IT. Taranto						
IT. Reggio						
E. Sicily						
W. Sicily						
N. Sardinia						
S. Sardinia						
Malta						
Tunisia						
Yugoslavia						
Corfu						
N. Greece						
S. Greece						
Turkey						

The ring gesture as a sign of precision, from a watercolour series on Italian gestures, 1820 (Mansell Collection).

it on, but had yet to start using the O.K. version sufficiently for it to be transferred to the Tunisian population. To confirm this, we need to know more about nineteenth-century French gestures, but the literature is weak in this area.

Turning now to a third meaning for the ring gesture — that of a threat — it is significant that we found this almost entirely confined to Tunisia. Since in this role it seems to be a modified form of the zero gesture, meaning 'you are a zero', its appearance in the ex-French colony supports the idea that the zero was the only ring-meaning imported by the early French colonists.

Finally, there is the completely separate use of the ring gesture as an orifice symbol. The earliest example of this, as we mentioned before, was on an ancient Greek vase, and our field studies revealed that, even today, it remains a predominantly Greek-centred usage. As our gesture map shows, it has a wide scatter across Europe, but it is rare almost everywhere except in the S.E. of the continent.

It is possible to separate the interpretations of our 128 informants who regard the gesture as an orifice symbol, according to the orifice indicated (anal or vaginal), the function of the signal (insult or

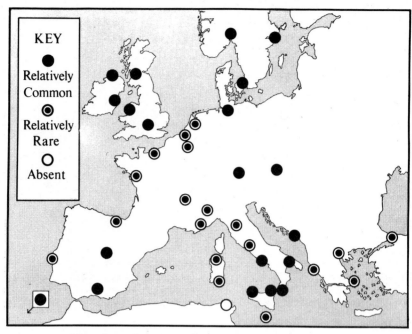

THE RING Meaning: O.K./good

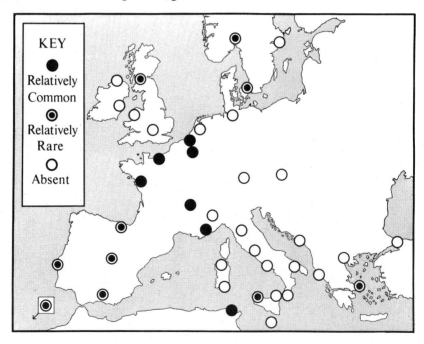

THE RING Meaning: zero

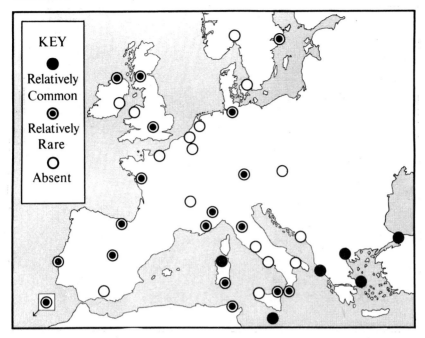

THE RING Meaning: orifice

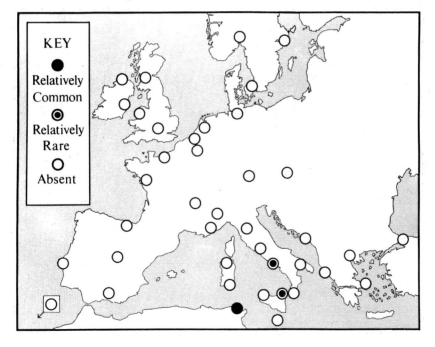

THE RING Meaning: threat

comment), and the gender of the orifice-owner (male or female). When this is done, we find the following figures:

Orifice	ANAL	103
	VAGINAL	13
	Unspecified	12
Function	INSULT	39
	COMMENT or INVITATION	89
Gender	REFERENCE TO MALE	59
	REFERENCE TO FEMALE	15
	Unspecified	54

It is clear from this that the orifice-ring gesture is used primarily as an anal comment about a male. However, this dominant use is confined to the S.E. region of Europe. It occurs only in Turkey, Greece and Malta, where it is either a homosexual invitation, such as 'take my arse', or, more frequently, a homosexual comment, such as 'I need a man', or 'he is a boy-chaser'. Throughout the rest of Europe, it is either a vague, unspecified obscenity, or a lewd comment about a female, or an anal insult.

To sum up, the ring is another example of a multi-message gesture, with several distinct, major meanings, as you travel from place to place. It carries an O.K. message everywhere except Tunisia, a zero message in Belgium, France and Tunisia, an orifice message in Turkey, Greece and Malta, and a threat message in Tunisia. There is considerable, low-level scatter, but these are the main zones for the different meanings, and it is true to say that nowhere was the gesture uncommon in at least one of its meanings. Fifty per cent was the lowest score we recorded anywhere, and usually it was much higher, the average for our entire range being 82 per cent.

This was not exactly what we expected when we began the field study. We had imagined that a particular gesture would be popular in one region and rare, or non-existent in others. What we found, not only with the ring gesture, but also with many of the others we investigated, was that the gesture was well known almost everywhere, and it was the specific gesture-*meanings* that showed regional restrictions. Far from making matters easier for the traveller or foreign visitor, this makes his situation doubly difficult. Not only is his own gesture meaning unknown in many a foreign land, but he will encounter the same gesture there with a totally different meaning. How many times this must have led to misunderstandings, it is hard to guess.

10 The Vertical Horn-sign

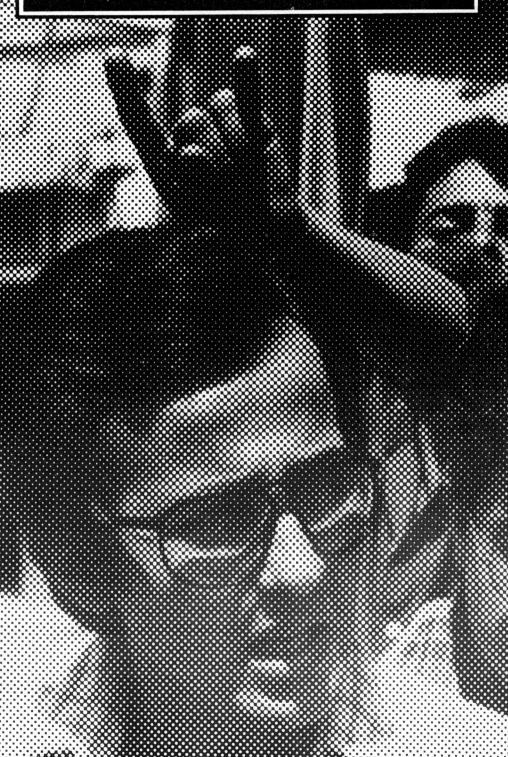

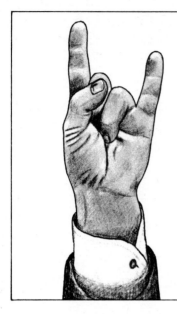

**THE VERTICAL
HORN-SIGN
MEANINGS:**

1	Cuckold	515
2	General insult	29
3	Protection	10
4	Curse	6
5	others	16
6	not used	624

(Based on 1,200 informants
at 40 locations)

DESCRIPTION

The hand is held up with the forefinger and the little finger extended vertically. The other two fingers are held down in a bent position by the thumb, giving the hand the crude shape of an animal's horned head.

ORIGINS

This gesture is a gross insult of a special kind, with a long and ancient history. Its true origins are shrouded in the past, and remain a subject of great controversy. Many explanations have been put forward, each convincing in its own way, but each conflicting strongly with the others. Its dominant meaning, however, is quite specific: it is the sign for a cuckold. Its message is: your wife has been unfaithful to you and has given you the horns of a cuckold. Generalizing from this it becomes a taunt of impotence and stupidity. It implies that a man is either too feeble to satisfy his wife sexually, so that she seeks stimulation elsewhere, or that he is too stupid to realize that she is betraying him with another man. It is often used jokingly as an anti-virility insult, but in the past it has sometimes been taken so seriously that its use has led to feuds, fights and murder. There are even cases recorded in the present century, where

---

on previous page When used in jest, the insulting horn-sign may be displayed behind the victim's head. He is made to 'wear the horns' without his knowledge.

a gesturer has been killed for making the horn-sign as an accusation of cuckoldry. More cautious gesturers usually make the sign secretly behind the victim's back, when the message becomes not 'you are a cuckold', but 'he is a cuckold'.

The great problem with the horn-sign is to decide precisely how the symbolic equation: horns = cuckold, could have arisen. A pair of horns is usually envisaged, in a symbolic sense, as representing the great strength, power and fierceness of a male beast, usually a bull. The horned helmet of the warrior epitomizes his masculinity and virility, so by what possible means could they come to stand for the exact opposite: impotency and cuckoldom? Even a single horn is looked upon as a phallic symbol and the slang term 'horn' has often been used to describe the erect human penis.

Somehow, in finding the link between a pair of horns and the act of sexual betrayal, it is necessary to overcome this much more obvious relationship between horns and virility. Different authorities have proposed strikingly different solutions. Some of these seem to be little more than ingenious guesswork, but since the original connection is lost to us, we can do no more than list the various theories that have been put forward, in the hope that, one day, some new evidence will come to light that will favour one above the rest:

1   The sarcasm theory
This sees the horned hand gesture as symbolizing the head of a fierce, rutting bull. The horns are those of great virility, but the message is heavily sarcastic. The taunting gesture says to the pathetic cuckold *'What* a great bull you are!', but means the exact opposite. This is the explanation given by John Bulwer in his *Chirologia* of 1644, when he says: 'The gesture ... is used in our nimble-fingered times to call one cuckold, and to present the badge of cuckoldry, that mental and imaginary horn; seeming to cry, O man of happy note, whom fortune meaning highly to promote, hath stuck on thy forehead the earnest-penny of succeeding good luck; all of which upbraiding terms many understand by this gesture only of the fingers; for in this sense the common use hath made it the known signal of disparagement, so naturally apt are the fingers to speak scoffs ... which cunning game is received into rhetoric, and called an irony ...' This ironic or sarcastic explanation is the simplest one we have been able to find. It is simple because it sees the horns in their more usual role as symbols of male power, while all the others involve some other, more complicated starting point.

2   The castrated bull theory

Here it is argued that, because domestic bulls are frequently castrated to render them more docile and easy to handle for beef production, the 'typical' bull is not a fierce, rutting beast, but a sexually useless, impotent male. A good, uncastrated bull can serve between 50 and 100 cows a year, so the farmer needs very few of them. All the rest must stand around like helpless 'cuckolds' while the uncastrated bull 'steals' their females, hence the symbolism of horns = cuckold. This is an ingenious idea, but it overlooks the fact that, symbolically, when one thinks of a bull, it is always the great charging monster, the epitome of power and aggression, and not the docile castrates, even though the latter may be far more numerous.

3   The mad bull theory

This idea returns to the concept of a bull as a fierce beast, specifically one driven mad with rage as a result of violent provocation — like a Spanish fighting bull. It is argued that when a man discovers he has been cuckolded he becomes so enraged that he bellows and charges about seeking violent revenge, and therefore acts like a 'mad bull'. The making of the horned hand gesture says, not 'you are a strong, virile bull', but 'what has happened to you will make you like a crazy bull'. In support of this, there was a common term 'horn-mad' in use from the sixteenth to the nineteenth century. In a *Cant Dictionary* of 1690, there is the following definition: Horn-mad — stark staring mad, because cuckolded.

4   The promiscuous cow theory

In this case, the male is accused of wearing horns because his wife is behaving like a cow. The taunt is 'your wife is promiscuous like a cow', therefore you must be a poor, deceived bull. This explanation is one we encountered several times in present-day Europe when talking to people about the possible meaning of the gesture. We found it as far apart as Portugal and Sardinia, but we have no idea how ancient it is.

5   The stag theory

This sees the horns as antlers. The symbolism is based on the fact that, with many deer, there is one dominant male who herds together nearly all the females, and who, by combat, repels all the other males. The latter are forced to gather in a bachelor herd nearby and can only watch helplessly as the top stag mates with all the females.

This is similar to the castrated bull theory, except that here it is based on a natural process, rather than an imposed farming practice. The bachelor males are psychologically, rather than physically, castrated. In support of this idea are a number of early references to men wearing antlers, rather than horns. Even the 'horn' references themselves do not contradict the idea as strongly as might appear, because in the past the word 'horn' was often applied to the antlers of deer. Supporting this line of thought is the fact that 'buck-face' was an early slang term for a cuckold, the name 'buck' referring to the male of the fallow deer. Also, it is possible to find old quotations that clearly indicate that the horns of the cuckold were branching, and must therefore have been seen, at least by some, as being antlers of deer, rather than bull's horns. For example, in Butler's *Remains* of 1680: 'His own branches, his horns, are as mystical as the Whore of Babylon's Palfreys, not to be seen but in a vision.'

6 The Diana theory

Continuing with the idea of a stag, there is a classical legend that has been seen as the starting point for the horns = cuckold equation. This is the story in which Diana the huntress made horns into the symbol of male downfall. Actaeon, another legendary hunter, was supposed to have sneaked a look at her naked body when she was bathing. This so angered her that she turned him into a stag and set his own hounds upon him, which promptly killed and ate him. It could be argued that this hardly made him a cuckold in the strict sense – he was not merely castrated, but totally devoured. And yet, the equation Actaeon = cuckold was certainly made in earlier times, and can be found in quotations from Shakespeare right through to the nineteenth century. Burton, in his *Anatomy of Melancholy* of 1621, says: 'husband and cuckold in that age, it seems, were reciprocal terms; the Emperors themselves did wear Actaeon's Badge', and Farmer and Henley in their *Slang Dictionary* of 1909 give the slang definition of Actaeon simply as 'a cuckold'.

7 The devil's hexing theory

To 'hex' someone is to bewitch or cast a spell on them. G. Legman, an authority on erotic folklore, tells us that, in his opinion, the horns of the horn-sign are those of the devil, and that they relate to the gesturer rather than the victim. It is the gesturer who, summoning up the devil's aid by making the sign of his horns, *causes* the cuckoldry of the victim. Legman explains: 'The horn-shaped gesture of hexing causes impotence in the person so mocked: thus cuckoldry will follow, since he can no longer satisfy his wife.' This works well enough where the message of the gesture is 'you will become a cuckold', but is less satisfactory when it is 'you have been cuckolded' or 'you are wearing a cuckold's horns'. In fact, most references to the gesture see it as mimicking the imaginary horns worn by the cuckold himself, rather than as the devil's horns that are causing the cuckold-to-be. But symbolic equations make strange leaps, and it may well be that the cuckold, in wearing horns, was seen as someone who had been recently 'horned by the devil'.

8   The sacred prostitute theory

Ancient gods wore horns in their original role, as signs of power and masculinity, and certain religious practices involving temple pro-stitutes have been seen as explaining the way in which these horns could become transformed into horns of cuckoldom. Captain Bourke, writing in Victorian times, has this to say: 'The horns of honour of the deities worshipped by women who were ordered by their husbands to become religious prostitutes were transferred to the husband: what had been the outward sign of extreme devotion and self-abnegation was turned into ridicule and opprobrium.' This is basically similar to the sarcasm theory mentioned earlier, with 'good' horns being transformed into 'bad' horns, and it provides a possible reason for the switch from honour to ridicule.

9   The capon theory

One of the strangest explanations concerns the early practice of grafting the spurs of a castrated cockerel on to the root of its excised comb, where they apparently grew and became 'horns'. This claim is backed up by the fact that the German equivalent word for cuckold (*Hahnrei*) originally meant 'capon'.

10   The two-penis theory

Here the two horns are seen as symbolizing two penises. A single horn is a well-known phallic symbol, as already mentioned, and the cuckold's horns are interpreted, not as a pair of horns from a bull's head, but as two phallic symbols, side by side. The horned-hand gesture then becomes a statement to the effect that 'there are two penises in your life, your own and your wife's lover's.' If this seems far-fetched, it should be pointed out that Andrea de Jorio, writing in Naples in 1832, records a slang phrase which was sometimes added to the making of the horned-hand gesture, namely: 'He [the cuckold] is a candle with two wicks.' This explanation has certainly survived to the present day, because we came across it in Northern Sardinia, where it was explained to us that the two horns of the cuckold represented the two penises in the love-life of his adulterous wife.

11   The substitute-penis theory

This is a variant of the last explanation, which was given to us by a Bostonian who suggested that the old European tradition of making a horned hand was based on the idea that the cuckold had to make do with merely symbolic phallic structures, because he lacked the real thing. In other words, because he lacked a functional penis (hence his wife's unfaithfulness) he had to compensate by putting on a show of substitute phalluses (the horns on his head). Psychologically, this relates to the way in which a naturally timid man may sometimes act brashly in an attempt to conceal his shyness.

12   The wife's-legs theory

Next, there is the totally different approach, which interprets the horned-hand gesture as having nothing whatsoever to do with horn-symbolism, but sees the two erect fingers as representing the legs of the cuckold's erring wife. The gesturer is supposed to be saying: 'Your wife is promiscuous, she will spread her legs for anyone, and you, the cuckold, must wear on your head the symbol of her open legs.' Again, this might seem far-fetched, but there is some evidence to support it. A common variant of the horn gesture is one in which the first and second fingers, widely spread apart, are jerked upwards into the air, instead of the usual first and fourth fingers. This forked-fingers gesture is the most popular one for present-day Spaniards, and we also encountered it elsewhere. Furthermore, in earlier centuries in England, the cuckold gesture was often referred to as 'forking the fingers in derision'. James Halliwell, in his *Dictionary of Archaic and Provincial Words*, published in 1881, makes this variant of the gesture more explicit, when he defines the word HORNS as: 'To make horns at a person, to put the forefinger of one hand between the first and second finger of the other.' Here, the forefinger symbolizes a penis entering between the spread legs of the forked hand. The insulting message, quite clearly, is 'Someone else's penis is going between the open legs of your wife', hence, you are a cuckold. This seems very convincing, except for the fact that the typical horn-sign in most regions remains today the erected first and *fourth* fingers, which look much more like a mimic of a pair of animal horns than a pair of spread, female legs. It could be argued that the erect fingers are 'as far apart as possible' and therefore symbolize a female with her legs far apart, inviting copulation, but this seems like special pleading. It is more likely that Halliwell is describing a completely distinct, obscene gesture of copulation which he, or someone else, wrongly labelled the 'horns', confusing it with the main cuckold gesture.

13   The lover's-horns theory

This involves the suggestion that when the gesturer makes the sign of the horned-hand at the cuckold, he is saying: 'these are the horns (virility) of your wife's lover, and you will have to wear (tolerate) them.' In English today, the phrase 'will he wear it' can mean 'will he put up with it', and the idea of a cuckold wearing or carrying a pair of horns can be interpreted as a way of saying that he must accept or carry the burden of the horns with which his wife is betraying him. This explanation does not seem to us to clarify the repeatedly used image of the horned cuckold. Over and over again, as one examines early examples of the hapless cuckold image, it is he who is the horn-*owner*, not merely the horn-tolerator, and any explanation that overlooks this is forced to postulate a major symbolic distortion or misunderstanding.

The two-handed version of the vertical horn-sign, meaning cuckold, in Naples.

14 The absent-warrior theory

A final explanation that neatly overcomes this problem sees the cuckold as an early warrior who has donned a horned helmet and gone off to the wars, leaving behind a lonely wife whose isolation may soon lead to her taking a lover. In other words, the man who wears the horns (= .horned helmet) is most likely to become a cuckold. The simplicity of this explanation makes it most attractive.

There can only be two reasons for this surfeit of explanations for the origin of this particular gesture. Either we are faced with an array of ingenious, scholarly inventions, or the gesture was *initiated* by one of these symbolic equations, and then kept alive by subsequent, *supportive* explanations. The difference between an invented explanation and a supportive one is important to recognize, when considering the history of any symbolic gesture. An invented explanation is an arm-chair rationalization, academically concocted, and remaining trapped on the written page. Transmitted from publication to publication over the years, quoted and re-quoted, it may gain in credence until it becomes authoritative, and yet it may never once feed back into social life, or influence the survival of the gesture concerned. A supportive explanation is similar, but is invented by the people who actually employ the gesture. They have lost touch with the true, original symbolic equation and feel the need for some sort of explanatory idea as a 'back-up' for their use of the gesture. Their new idea, once expressed, spreads through the culture and becomes known to other gesture-users. Because it helps them to understand the nature of the sign they are making, it supports the sign and encourages its continued and even increased use. It therefore acts as a supportive explanation, more important now, in reality, than the true, original explanation.

It is this supportive process that we believe has been largely responsible for the plethora of interpretations of the cuckold horn-sign. A few of the examples we have listed may, of course, be no more than scholars' whims, but the majority of them do seem to be backed up by references and instances of actual usage.

Leaving the cuckold theme now, there are three other minor roles played by the vertical-horns gesture, but these only require brief mention. A small number of people insist that the gesture is merely a generalized insult and that it has nothing to do with cuckoldry. This is almost certainly a case of the origins being forgotten, rather than a separate development. Another group sees the gesture as a protective device used to ward off the evil eye. This is not a common usage, but appears to be even more ancient than the cuckold insult. Examples of the protective horned hand have been found which are well over 2,000 years old. An Etruscan wall painting dating from 520 B.C., at Tarquinia, shows a group of musicians and dancers, one of whom appears to be making the vertical horn-sign as he prances to the music. Vertical, horned hands also appear on ancient pottery from the Daunian culture in east central Italy, dating from the fifth

The ancient use of the vertical horn-sign. This Etruscan wall-painting at Tarquinia dates from 520 B.C.

century B.C. It is always possible, of course, that such hands are making cuckold signs, but this seems an odd gesture to entomb with a man's mortal remains, even if its comment were justified. It is much more likely to be the protective horned hand that would help to guard the tomb against evil influences.

This protective role for the horned hand is much easier to understand symbolically than the cuckold role. Here the horns are protecting the gesturer in their primary capacity as symbols of power and aggression. In fact, this seems a much more obvious and reasonable way of employing the gesture, and the fact that it is used at all in this manner, makes the predominance of the cuckold usage even harder to understand.

There is one final use for the horned hand and that is as a curse. Usually, this is a curse against God, and the gesturer, as he curses the deity for his ill-fortune, makes the horn-sign upwards to the sky. This is essentially a special form of the protective hand, with the curser saying either 'may I be protected from God's stupidity in allowing me to suffer like this', or alternatively, 'may I be protected from the wrath of God for swearing at him like this'.

DISTRIBUTION

The distribution of the vertical horn-sign today surprised us. We expected a very wide range, but did not find it. The reason for our expectation was the great frequency of references to the gesture in the English literature and elsewhere. We knew it was common in Latin countries and so we assumed that it would be spread right across Europe, from the N.W. to the S.E. But this was not the case. Despite endless comments on the 'cuckold's horns' from Shakespeare's time up to the beginning of the nineteenth century, we were to draw a complete blank in our search for the gesture in the British Isles today. Nor did we find it in Scandinavia or Germany. In Holland, Belgium and Austria and even in parts of France, it was extremely rare. As a commonly used gesture, we found it restricted today largely to Portugal, Spain and Italy. This means that we are dealing with a gesture of declining popularity, and it is worth asking why such a distinctive sign should be on the wane, with its geographical range shrinking so dramatically.

The answer appears to lie in the changing attitude towards the act of adultery. Ask anyone today which is the more serious offence — adultery or rape — and they will inevitably answer, rape. But this was not always the case. In ancient times, according to Francis Rous and Zachary Bogan, in their *Attick Antiquities* published in 1685, the situation was reversed, with adultery being the much more savagely punished of the two. They write: 'The ordinary manner of punishing an adulterer has as little modesty as the crime itself ... for having plucked off the hair of his privities, they threw hot ashes in the place, and thrust up a radish or a mullet into his fundament ... A punishment little enough for so great a vice ... On the other side, if

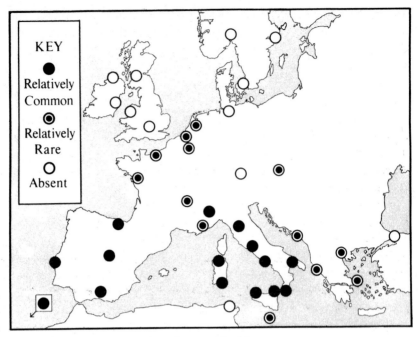

VERTICAL HORN-SIGN Meaning: cuckold

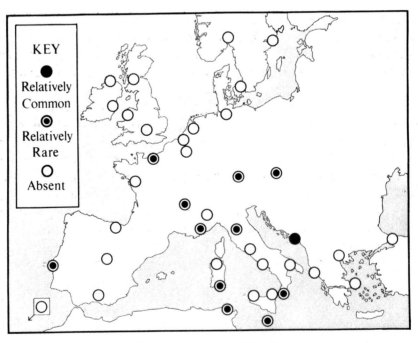

VERTICAL HORN-SIGN Meaning: general insult

the women were forced, and openly abused, the punishment then was no more than a fine.' The reason for being more lenient with the rapist was that he had only stolen the woman's body, while the adulterous seducer had stolen both her body and her mind. This attitude is based on the theft of the husband's property — his wife — rather than on any consideration of the woman's feelings. Given this social climate, it is clear that it was worse for a man to be called a cuckold than to have his wife ravished. Over the centuries, the European scene gradually changed, until today it has become completely reversed. Adultery may still be grounds for divorce, but compared with rape it is a mild offence and, with this shift, the accusation of cuckoldry has lost much of its sting. Alongside this loss has been the loss of the horned-hand gesture. It has only survived as a commonly used insult in those regions where divorce remains illegal or is strongly condemned — in other words, in strongly Catholic countries such as Portugal, Spain and Italy. It is this differential decline in the condemnation of the act of adultery that explains our present gesture map distribution for this gesture, and its shrinkage from a once much wider range across virtually the whole of Europe.

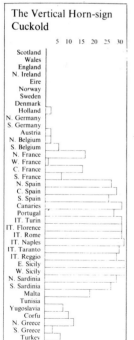

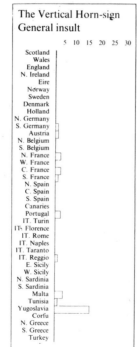

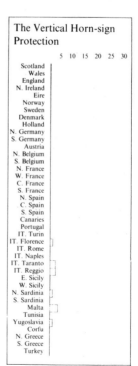

We said earlier that we were unable to find examples of the vertical horn-sign in the British Isles, but we must qualify this comment slightly. We knew from the literature that the gesture arrived in England, probably from Italy, in the sixteenth century. Comments in Shakespeare's plays reveal that the attitude to wearing horns was in a state of flux. It was necessary for the plays to reflect both the old attitude (horns of honour) and the new one (horns of dishonour), where mention was made of them. To give one example, in *As You Like It*, there are the lines: 'Take no scorn, to wear the horn; It was a crest ere thou wast born; Thy father's father wore it, And thy father bore it. The horn, the horn, the lusty horn, Is not a thing to laugh and scorn.' By the seventeenth century there was no longer any doubt left — to wear the horns meant only one thing — ridicule and cuckoldry, and a great deal of the humour of Restoration comedies was based on this concept. A play without a pathetic cuckold became almost a rarity. The gesture was common then, throughout the land, and survived right through until the early part of the nineteenth century, when, in Victorian times, it lost ground and eventually disappeared. Or did it? We had failed to find any knowledge of it when interviewing our standard samples of thirty informants at locations in England, Wales, Scotland and Ireland, but we were keen to know whether, perhaps, at a very low density indeed it did survive in some corners of the British Isles. To find out whether this was so we broadcast an appeal both in Cornwall and in Wales, two areas where we felt it might still be lingering, and we were rewarded with some most interesting correspondence. A number of people wrote to us to say that they recalled the gesture being used in their childhood, or by one particular person in their district, and it was clear that remnants of it did still survive from its once glorious past. When we read the details, however, we discovered that in all cases, the gesture was being used in its protective role, to ward off evil, and never as an insult against a cuckold. Here we must anticipate for a moment the next gesture in our survey. Gesture No. 11 is the horizontal horn-sign — the same hand posture but directed *at* someone, or even slightly downwards. It is a quite distinct gesture, with a different history, and must not be confused with the present one, the vertical horn-sign. So, although the gesture in a crude sense is still clinging on in corners of the British Isles, the cuckold sign in the strict sense can now be said to be dead, except when it re-surfaces artificially in the revivals of Elizabethan or Restoration plays in the theatre.

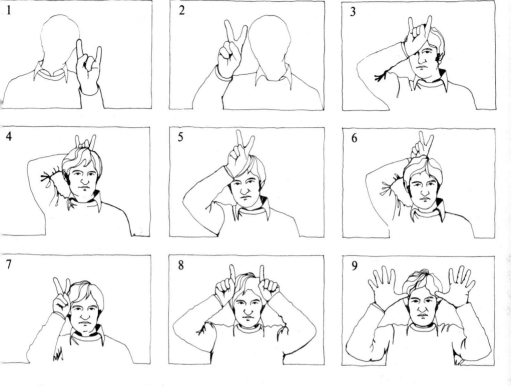

Before leaving the cuckold sign, it is worth recording some of its local names and its local variants. In France it is called: *les cornes, cocu, cornard*; in Portugal it becomes *corno, cornos, cornudo, cabrão*, or *calão*; in Italy it is the *cornuto*, or the *mano cornuta*; and in Malta, the *kurnut*.

There are nine local variants. They are: 1 The standard form, as already described, with the hand held aloft with forefinger and little finger erect. 2 The same, but with first and second fingers erect and forked widely apart. 3 The same as No. 1, but with the hand held up to the centre of the forehead. 4 The same as No. 1, but with the hand held up behind the back of the head. 5 The same as No. 2, but with the hand held up to the forehead. 6 The same as No. 2, but with the hand held up to the back of the head. 7 The same as No. 2, but with the hand held up to the temple. 8 The two hands held up to the temples, with the forefinger of each hand erect, making a pair of horns with one horn on either side of the head. 9 The same as No. 8, but with the thumbs touching the temples and all the fingers splayed out like antlers.

Our second gesture map shows the distribution of the non-cuckold insult. This is rare (only 29 informants out of 1,200, compared with 515 for the cuckold sign), but we have included a map of it because there is one site — Yugoslavia — where it becomes the dominant meaning. Thirteen people there were quite explicit in denying that the insulting nature of the gesture had anything to do with adultery or cuckoldry. Only seven interpreted it as the cuckold gesture. The latter called it by its familiar name: *cornuto*, but the non-cuckold insulters used a completely different name: *rogonja*. This may have a distinct and separate history of its own, but at present we tend to think of it as an 'abstracted' version of the cuckold sign that has lost its roots, retaining only the generalized meaning of an insult.

A final, light-hearted comment on the vertical horn-sign gesture deserves a few lines, if only to illustrate the way in which a gesture can be turned into a joke. In Holland an informant puzzled our interpreter by saying that the gesture meant something he translated as 'pills for the mills'. We asked him to persist and question the man further. It emerged that pills meant Pils, a kind of beer, and the mills was short for the man from the saw-mills. The full answer we finally extracted was that the gesture of holding up two fingers was the way in which the worker from the saw-mills would order four beers. To our surprise the same joke turned up again in England, Denmark, North Germany, South Germany, and the United States. All that changed was the occupation of the supposed gesturer, who variously became a butcher, a carpenter, or any other line of work where finger amputation was considered to be an occupational hazard.

11 The Horizontal Horn-sign

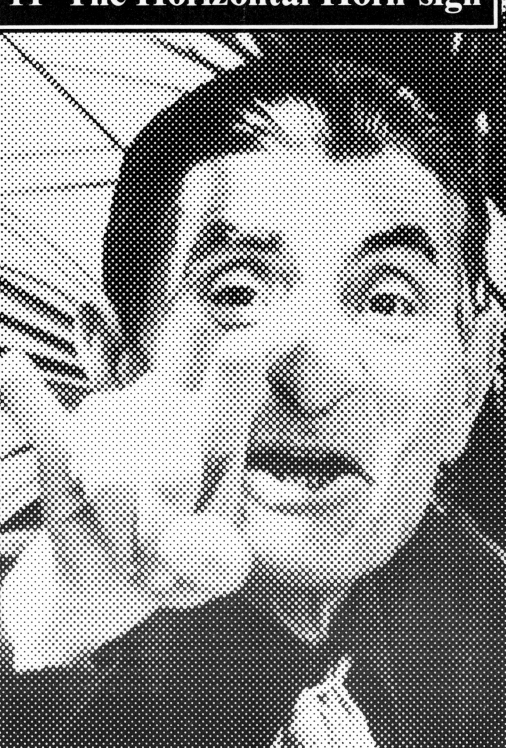

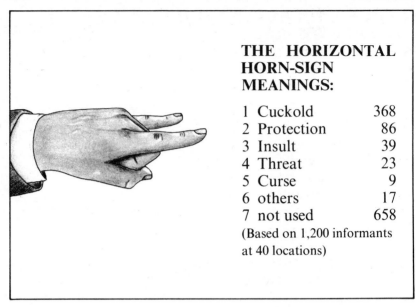

THE HORIZONTAL HORN-SIGN MEANINGS:

1	Cuckold	368
2	Protection	86
3	Insult	39
4	Threat	23
5	Curse	9
6	others	17
7	not used	658

(Based on 1,200 informants at 40 locations)

DESCRIPTION

The hand is pointed forward, with the forefinger and the little finger extended horizontally. The other two fingers are held down in a bent position by the thumb, giving the hand the crude shape of an animal's horned head, lowered as if to charge. This is basically the same gesture as No. 10, except that here it is aimed *at* someone or something. Sometimes the hand is held still and sometimes it is jabbed forward in the air. Occasionally, the forefinger and the second finger are used, when they are widely spread out away from one another. Also, if the gesturer wants to hide his action from the person at which it is aimed, he may keep his hand down by his side, or even in his pocket, when the fingers tend to point more downward than forward.

ORIGINS

This gesture originated long ago, in pre-Roman times, and is more than two and a half thousand years old. It is known from wall-paintings in ancient Etruscan tombs, and from early pottery of the Daunian culture which flourished in east central Italy around the middle of the first millennium B.C. It appears again on an Apulian vase dating from 350 B.C. and is found several times on the sixth-century A.D. mosaics at Ravenna. In fact, if a detailed search were to be made, it is probable that large numbers of examples could be assembled, revealing a common usage of the gesture over many centuries.

In its earliest role, the gesture was essentially a device for self-protection. By making the sign of the horns, the gesturer was supposed to be able to defend himself against evil spirits, the evil eye, or any other form of misfortune that might seem to be threatening him. In this capacity, the horns were being used in their primary symbolic role as representing the defensive power of a great horned animal, almost certainly the bull. The use of the gesture in this way reflects an even older practice, that of placing a pair of horns on the wall of a building, to protect it and its occupants from evil forces. Such horns can be seen to this day on the island of Malta, where many of the old farmhouses are adorned with one or more pairs, either real or sculptured. This practice can be traced back at least 8,000 years to the Neolithic period. One of the earliest towns known to archaeology, Catal Huyuk in Anatolia (part of modern Turkey), was found to contain horn-decorated rooms, and horned artefacts appear repeatedly right through the Bronze Age and the Iron Age in many places in the Middle East and around the Mediterranean.

The horizontal horn-sign depicted on a wall-painting at ancient Pompeii. First century A.D.

From the early bull divinity, there developed a horned god which, with the rise of Christianity, eventually became converted into the horned devil-figure. Today, people often refer to the horn gesture as 'making the sign of the Devil's horns', and when they use it protectively they are, in effect, reinstating the Devil in his earlier, beneficial role as a defending deity. It is amusing that modern-day, devout Christians in Italy will, with one breath, curse the Devil as the great enemy and Prince of Darkness, and with the next breath will proceed to make his sign with their fingers to protect themselves from bad luck.

De Jorio, writing in Naples in 1832, gives some vivid examples of the way in which the protective-horns gesture was used in the nineteenth century. Commenting on the reaction to a *jettatrice* (a woman thought to possess the evil eye), he says:

> Observing that another lady whom she believed to be a *jettatrice* was highly praising the beauty of her husband, and especially of his well-formed thighs and legs, she wished to have recourse to the horn. Not having at hand the grand preservative, not being able to supply it openly by a gesture, and what is more, not believing the repetition by her lips of the word *corno, corno, corno* to be sufficient, she pretended to have need of a handkerchief. She therefore put her hand into her husband's pocket, and there made the *mano cornuta*. Then, with the points of her index and little fingers well extended, began to stab the thigh bone of her husband with such force, as if she wanted to pierce through it; indeed, if she did not pierce it, it was only because she could not. Nor did she leave off her preventive operation until the believed *jettatrice* turned her talk in another direction.

This concealed use of the gesture is common whenever the gesturer suspects an evil influence but for reasons of etiquette does not wish to bring the matter out into the open. If such caution is abandoned, then the hand is whipped up into a directed pointing posture, aiming straight at the face of the person thought to possess the evil eye. Alternatively, if the evil force is considered to be a generalized, diffuse emanation of some kind — 'evil spirits in the air', then the gesture may be made by waving the hand around in all directions.

If this seems archaically superstitious, it should be remembered that the situation has altered little in modern Italy. As recently as 1966, there was a press report to the effect that a butcher in Rome

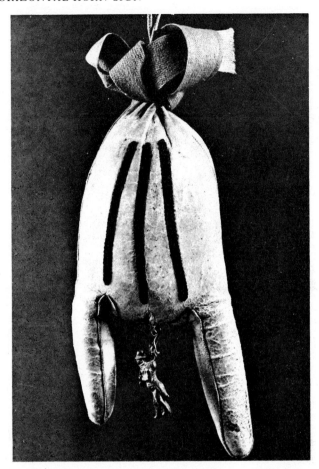

The protective horn-sign in the form of a stuffed glove hung in an Italian shop window to protect the owners from the Evil Eye. Elworthy Collection, Pitt Rivers Museum, Oxford.

had been forced to festoon his shop with protective pairs of horns because of the arrival of a funeral parlour next door to his premises. His customers had refused to enter his shop because, as he put it, they 'thought that the dead bodies were casting an evil eye on my veal chops', and only 'an arena of horns from the Rome abattoir' which effectively turned his shop into 'one giant amulet' was sufficient to combat this malevolent influence.

The wearing of amulets depicting the horned hand has been commonplace for at least 2,000 years, and examples are still sold today in everything from gold to plastic. We have come across them in curio shops all over Europe, from London in the north, to the

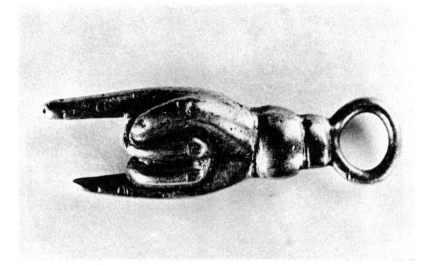

The protective horn-sign employed as an amulet or lucky charm.

Canary Islands in the south. They are referred to simply as 'lucky charms' and it is doubtful whether, in many cases, either the sellers or the buyers are aware of their long and ancient history. During the last century, Neapolitan amulets of the horned hand were usually made of ivory and worn by ladies, according to De Jorio, 'suspended at the end of a necklace, which is ordinarily hidden in the breast; but whenever a person appears who is suspected of being a *jettatore*, the hand quickly goes to the necklace, and the amulet is brought out, dangling in the direction considered necessary. As etiquette does not permit this to be done openly in society, they pretend to be adjusting the kerchief, but the fact remains that they seek to make sure of, and to touch if possible, the *gran preservativo del fascino.*'

In this way the horn-sign can be made, either by erecting a pair of real horns, or by displaying a sculpture or model of horns, or by wearing a 'frozen gesture' in the form of an amulet of a horned hand, or, finally, by making the actual gesture itself.

When we originally selected this gesture as one of our twenty key signs, we did so because we expected to find a completely different meaning from that given for the vertical horns. We expected to find all vertical horn-sign gestures to mean *cuckold*, and all horizontal horn-signs to mean *protection against the evil eye*. This idea stemmed from the earlier literature on the subject, but we soon discovered that it is now sadly out of date. The following comparative table gives the true facts as they are today:

Gesture	Cuckold	Protection
Vertical horns	515	10
Horizontal horns	368	86

In other words, although the horizontal horns are certainly more protective in their modern usage than the vertical horns, it is only a matter of degree. The cuckold meaning dominates in both cases. This reflects an impressive take-over by the cuckold insult during recent centuries.

A rare variant of the protective usage which we encountered is its employment as a curse. Instead of protecting the gesturer, it does direct harm (supposedly) to the victim at which it is aimed. The message then becomes 'I am putting the evil eye on you' or 'I am wishing you bad luck'.

The gesture also becomes a simple act of mockery in certain regions, with no relation, apparently, to any concept of protection or cuckoldry. In such instances it is used in the same way as the more familiar thumbing-a-nose gesture.

The horizontal horn-sign used by angry Italian football fans when their national team lost an important game (Politikens Presse Foto).

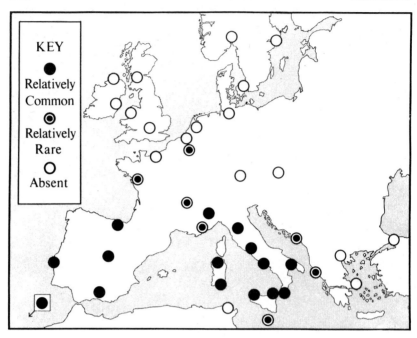

HORIZONTAL HORNS Meaning: cuckold

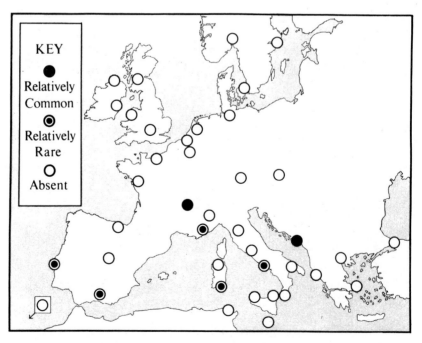

HORIZONTAL HORNS Meaning: general insult

Finally, it is also employed as a savage threat, with the meaning 'I will poke your eyes out'. Here it is no more than a mimed intention movement of the act of prodding the enemy's eyes with the stiffly extended fingers. In this form the forked fingers (first and second) are more popular than the first and fourth.

DISTRIBUTION

Like the vertical-horns gesture, the horizontal horn-sign has lost ground in recent years. It was clear from correspondents in the British Isles that, until comparatively recent times, it was employed as a protective gesture in both Cornwall and Wales, but is now so rare that it does not show up at all on our histograms or gesture maps for those regions. Martin Verity, a solicitor living in Glamorgan, writes of his childhood: 'I am a boy of 4 years of age. I am walking down the road with my nurse. Towards us is coming a woman. My nurse told me to "make horns" to keep off the evil eye. She showed me how to do it, but she told me to put my hand in my pocket, so that the person would not see it. Whether this was part of

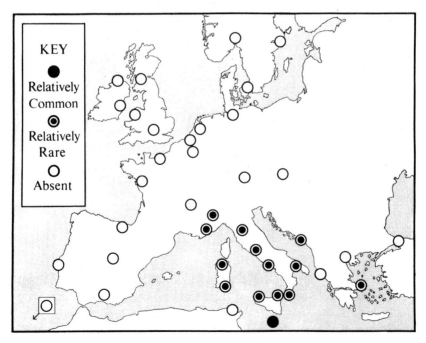

HORIZONTAL HORNS Meaning: protection

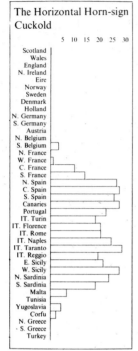

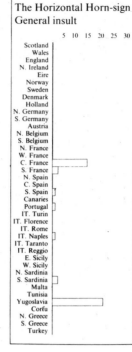

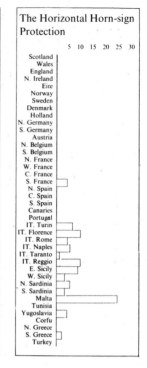

the magic or good manners I do not know. When the woman reached us I saw that she had dreadful cross-eyes. The whole incident so frightened me that I remember it vividly as if it was yesterday. Actually it "worked", as I suffered no ill-effects.' Another correspondent, Brian Stephens, also from Glamorgan, reports that, 'I have only seen it used by my brother, and it was used when he entered a room to cleanse it, as it were.' A third letter, also from Glamorgan, from Bryn Morgan, says: 'Our college warden does this when wishing people or teams good luck before rugby or sports fixtures. But even more interesting is that when talking with a girl, from Swansea, she said she made the sign when a hay lorry went past in the street. Apparently a hay lorry is full of bad luck and it is unlucky to see one. This sign therefore wards off evil and also brings good luck.'

Scanning this correspondence from South Wales, it is almost as if one is reading about nineteenth-century Naples. Clearly the use of the protective horns is not unknown in the British Isles, even today, but it is obviously a rare and vanishing gesture, soon to become extinct. In Ireland, Scotland, Wales and England, not one of our 150

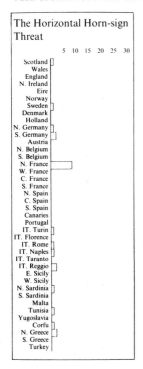

The Horizontal Horn-sign
Threat

	5	10	15	20	25	30
Scotland						
Wales						
England						
N. Ireland						
Eire						
Norway						
Sweden						
Denmark						
Holland						
N. Germany						
S. Germany						
Austria						
N. Belgium						
S. Belgium						
N. France						
W. France						
C. France						
S. France						
N. Spain						
C. Spain						
S. Spain						
Canaries						
Portugal						
IT. Turin						
IT. Florence						
IT. Rome						
IT. Naples						
IT. Taranto						
IT. Reggio						
E. Sicily						
W. Sicily						
N. Sardinia						
S. Sardinia						
Malta						
Tunisia						
Yugoslavia						
Corfu						
N. Greece						
S. Greece						
Turkey						

The protective horn-sign painted on the side
of a modern Maltese water-taxi boat.

randomly selected informants knew what it meant and none had
seen it used locally. Like the vertical horn-sign its range is shrinking,
along with a reduction both in superstitions about evil influences
and strong attitudes towards cuckoldry. But, also like the vertical
horn-sign, it does survive reasonably well in the Mediterranean
regions, as our three gesture maps show. The cuckold map is almost
identical to that for the vertical gesture, with Portugal, Spain and
Italy as the three main centres. The insult map also follows the same
lines as before, with Yugoslavia as the main zone. The protective
map is more interesting because it shows one very strong centre —
the small island of Malta. There, it seems, we are seeing the horizontal horns gesture used today as it once was over much of its range,
predominantly as a protective device. It looks as if Malta, populated
by a small, isolated and still very superstitious people, is clinging to
its ancient gesture more tenaciously than any of its larger neighbours. It is the only country we have found where even boats and
motor cars are adorned with protective horn-signs, and it is possible
to buy plastic horn-sign stickers there to fix on to windscreens or car-
bumpers. This does not mean that the Maltese lack a cuckold

gesture. They employ the vertical sign for this purpose. Indeed, with the modern Maltese we encountered the very reversal pattern for the two gestures that we expected at the outset of our field work, as the following table shows:

Maltese gesture	Cuckold	Protection
Vertical horns	17	3
Horizontal horns	6	23

Of course, we cannot prove that this is typical of the ancient usage-split between the two gestures, but all the early records and artefacts seem to indicate that this was the case and Malta, in this one respect at least, is behaving in a deeply conservative way.

12 The Fig

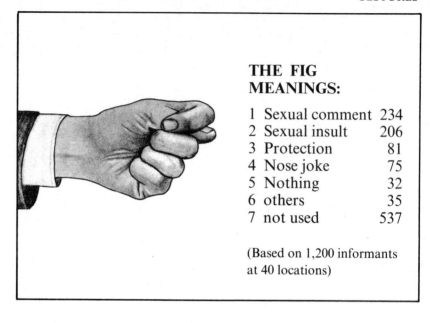

THE FIG MEANINGS:

1	Sexual comment	234
2	Sexual insult	206
3	Protection	81
4	Nose joke	75
5	Nothing	32
6	others	35
7	not used	537

(Based on 1,200 informants at 40 locations)

DESCRIPTION

The hand is closed so that the tip of the thumb protrudes from between the first and second fingers.

ORIGINS

The fig-sign is another ancient gesture with a long and confusing history. Like the horn-sign it occurs in the form of carved amulets dating back to antiquity and still in use today. Like the horn-sign it has two contrasting major roles — as an insult and as a protective device — which rob it of any simple, unified interpretation. It also has other meanings, and if we are to understand its use today we must first look back at the eight possible derivations that have been suggested by various authorities in the past. They are:

1   The fig as female genitals
The thrusting of the thumb between the bent fingers provides a basic sexual symbolism in which the thumb becomes the penis inserted into the vagina, with the bent fingers as the female labia. According to one view, the thumb is only secondary in this symbolism and is there merely to indicate the presence of the female genitals. To display the fig gesture is therefore to make some comment about

female sexuality, without reference to the male element. This can lead to three types of message. First, there is the obscene insult, in which, by thrusting symbolic female genitals at a male victim one is saying that he is less than a man. Second, there is the sexual comment which says, 'I want these (female genitals)', or 'I need a woman'. Alternatively, it can say, 'She is sexy', or 'She is an easy lay', or 'It was good last night'. Third, there is the protective message, based on the idea of diverting the evil eye. When threatened by some supernatural force, the gesturer makes the sign of female genitals with his hand and this so absorbs the evil spirit, that it is distracted from its malevolent purpose and the gesturer escapes damage. Hans Licht, in his study of *Sexual Life in Ancient Greece*, makes the following comment:

> The exposure by a woman of her organ of generation — with which action the gesture of the 'fico' (fig) is associated — broke magic spells, and consequently its image or symbol was carried as an amulet. The exposure of the organs was especially efficacious against hail, bad weather, and storms at sea ...
>
> In antiquity the amulet in the form of the female sexual organ is far less common (than the male), but this can readily be explained. The Greeks ascribed greater power to the man, and therefore his genitals would have the greater effect in averting the evil eye. Instead of representing the actual female organ on amulets it was suggested by symbolism, and usually in the guise of the fico (fig), which often occurs in the specimens extant. These amulets were made of very different sizes and of every kind of material; they were carried singly or in batches strung together, for it was even then believed that 'many a mickle makes a muckle'. They could be carried openly or secretly, and so convinced were people of their power that their mere possession was considered sufficiently effective.

Strangely, these amulets are extremely popular in many places today as 'lucky charms' and they can be seen in their hundreds in curio shops in cities such as London, where the fig gesture itself, made with a living hand, as opposed to a carved one, has been absent for many years and was probably never well known at any time. It is doubtful whether any of the people who buy these little ivory, stone or wooden hands have the slightest notion that they are purchasing and then boldly wearing a symbolic set of female genitals.

Fig-sign amulets collected in Europe in the 1970s. They are sold as lucky charms to people who are usually ignorant of their ancient history or their symbolic significance.

2   The fig as a symbol of virginity

During our field work we located one isolated interpretation of the fig-sign (in Wales) which saw it as a symbol of the female genitals of a virgin. It was explained to us that in the Welsh mountains, many men used this as a sign to indicate that a girl was innocent or virginal. It was appropriate because the thumb thrusting between the bent fingers was so tightly inserted. The 'tight' quality of the gesture meant that the entrance to the symbolic vagina was small and that it was difficult to penetrate — hence its virginal condition. B. Z. Goldberg, in his study of sex in religion, *The Sacred Fire*, supports

this view, pointing out that in some traditions, the Tree of Knowledge in the Garden of Eden ...

> was not an apple tree but a fig tree ... It was the triangular fig-
> leaf that covered the nakedness of Eve, the triangular form
> being itself the symbol of the nakedness of all her daughters.
> The fig, universally considered a symbol of the virgin yoni (the
> female genitals), was the appropriate fruit for the lingam-tree to
> bear. How much more significant is now the seduction of Adam
> by Eve in getting him to partake of the fig-yoni she offered
> him? ... The idol of Bacchus was always made of the wood of
> the ficus and the most sacred object in the Bacchanalian
> procession was a basket of figs.

It is certainly no longer true to say that the fig is universally considered a symbol of virginity, in the way Goldberg suggests. Our
field-trips were only able to discover one man out of the grand total
of 1,200 informants who was convinced that this was the specific
meaning of the gesture. By contrast, several hundred saw it as
sexually active genitals, and the phrases already mentioned, such as
'an easy lay', make it clear that the idea of innocent virginity is far
from their minds when they perform the action.

3   The fig as a symbol of female arousal
Another interpretation which, like the last one, starts from the basic
idea of the fig-sign as representing female genitals, but then goes on
to be more specific, is the one that sees the protruding thumb-tip, not
as the head of an inserted penis, but as an enlarged clitoris. During
sexual arousal the clitoris becomes engorged with blood and in the
process becomes much more sensitive. Certain authorities have seen
the gesture as reflecting this arousal process. Jean Marcadé, in his
essay on the erotic elements in Etruscan and Roman art, *Roma
Amor*, follows this line of argument with the words:

> The gesture of the *fica* or fig is also very old. It consists in
> inserting the tip of the thumb between the index and middle
> fingers, while keeping the hand clenched; originally it must
> certainly have represented the penetration of the phallus into
> the female organ, or feminine erection. I myself favour the latter
> interpretation ...

In our field studies we found nobody who volunteered this specific
interpretation.

4   The fig as a symbol of copulation

In a way, this is the most obvious interpretation, because of the act
of insertion by the thumb. Some of our informants explained the
gesture to us as this, openly naming the thumb as a penis-symbol, or
using phrases such as 'Man and woman making love', when asked
what the fig gesture meant to them.

5   The fig as a phallic gesture

More surprising to us was the discovery that for some people the
gesture is seen essentially as a male sign, depicting the phallus, rather
than the female genitals. Some of our informants described the
gesture as meaning 'I've got this (penis) for you', and the Danish
psychiatrist, Thorkil Vanggaard, in his study of phallic symbolism,
called *Phallos*, has this to say: '... the *fica* — a gesture made by
extending the fist with the thumb protruding between the second and
third fingers — is a phallic representation used as a magic defence
against the evil eye and other dangers.' Another book on *Phallic
Worship*, by George Ryley Scott, makes a similar point. He says
that, apart from obvious phallic images, the ancient world used
'many in the form of a hand which is closed with the thumb protruding between the fore and middle fingers. There are grounds for the
supposition that this represented the *digitus infamis*, which was
supposed to be inimical to the evil eye.' This is an odd statement,
because the *digitus infamis* is the ancient obscenity employing an
erect middle finger as a thrusting phallic symbol, and there is no case
for calling the inserted thumb by this special name. However, some
of our informants did clearly envisage the gesture as essentially
male, with the inserted thumb as the dominant element, so that this
male derivation cannot be entirely rejected.

6   The fig as a worthless object

An entirely different derivation, which removes the gesture altogether from the sexual sphere, is the one that sees the hand posture as
representative of a fruit, the fig, which is proverbially worthless, or
of very low value. Related to this is the phrase, 'I don't care a fig for
him', which has been current in English for at least 400 years.
However, according to Charles Mackay, in his *Greek Etymology*,
this phrase is based, not on the word 'fig', but on the Gaelic word
fuigh, which means a remnant, a paring, refuse or rubbish. So, to
say, 'I don't give a fig for him' really means that he is not worth
giving even the left-over scraps. Be that as it may, the fact remains

A modern German sticker employing the fig gesture, the essential
message being that if you are good at sport, you will also be good at sex.

that the gesture and the saying have become closely linked over the
years and the fig itself *has* been viewed as a low-value fruit. This may
account for the use of the title of the gesture as an insult, but it fails to
explain the link between the form of the gesture and the word 'fig'.
There is nothing particularly fig-like about the inserted-thumb posture of the hand, unless one links it back to a sexual symbolism and
from there to a connection between the fruit and the human genitals.
On this basis it would seem to be reasonable to reject this derivation
altogether, but, as one of the gesture maps will show in a moment,
there is one location where every single informant said that the
gesture meant 'I'll give you nothing'. Significantly, they referred to it
in almost every instance as the 'pomegranate gesture', rather than
the fig. Commenting on this, they said that the pomegranate is
another useless fruit: 'lots of seeds and nothing to eat'. But again,
one has to find a link between the hand posture and the idea of this
other fruit, and again there does not seem to be one, unless the

thumb is seen as 'splitting' the hand like a 'splitting pomegranate'.
But whatever the derivational link, the fact remains that for some
people, at least, the gesture has come to mean 'no worth — nothing
doing.'

7   The fig as a nose joke

A surprisingly large number of people interpreted the fig-sign as a
joke action meaning 'Look, I have stolen your nose', directed towards a young child. The adult playfully grabs the small child's nose
and pretends to pull it off the face, then shows it to the child in the
form of the thumb-tip sticking out through the closed fist. This little
game is common right across Europe and for anyone ignorant of the
more ancient usages of the gesture, it provides the most obvious
explanation of the hand posture.

8   The fig as the Barbarossa insult

Several authorities insist that the fig gesture is derived from a
historical incident that took place in Milan in the twelfth century
A.D. We find this hard to take seriously, when there are so many
ancient examples of fig-signs that pre-date the incident by more than
1,000 years. However, it is entirely possible that the incident has
acted in a supportive role, helping to keep the gesture alive and
thriving. The incident in question concerns an act of humiliation
imposed on the Milanese by the Emperor Frederick Barbarossa.
They had grossly insulted his wife by forcing her to ride out of the
city on a mule, facing backwards. He was so angered by this that
when he besieged and took the city in 1162 he forced his prisoners to
extract a fig from the anus of the same mule, on pain of death.
François Rabelais, writing in the sixteenth century, described this
extraordinary punishment in the following words:

> The inhabitants of Milan ... had rebell'd against him ... and
> turn'd the Empress out of the City, mounting her a Horse-back
> on a Mule called Thacor, with her breech foremost towards the
> old Jaded Mule's Head, and her face turn'd towards the
> Crupper. Now Frederick being return'd ... found and got the
> famous mule Thacor. Then the Hang-man, by his Order, clap'd
> a Fig into the mule's Jim-crack, in the Presence of the enslaved
> Citts that were brought into the middle of the great Market-
> place, and proclaim'd, in the Emperor's Name, with Trumpets,
> that whosoever of them would save his own Life. should

publickly pull the Fig out with his teeth, and after that put it in
again in the very individual cranny whence he had draw'd it,
without using his hands; and that whosoever refus'd to do this,
should presently swing for 't, and die in his Shoes. Some ...
chose Honourably to be hang'd ... and others ... resolved to
have at the Fig, and a Fig for't, rather than ... die in the air ...
Accordingly when they had neatly pick'd out the Fig with their
Teeth from old Thacor's Snatch-blatch, they plainly shew'd it
the Heads-man, saying *Ecco lo Fico*! (Behold the Fig!) ...

From this moment on, it was said, the phrase *far la fica* became a
common mode of derision, and the fig gesture was used to conjure
up the degradation of the Milanese captives. The symbolism here
is clear enough — the thumb protruding from the bent fingers of
the closed fist representing the fig protruding from the anus of the
mule. Although this cannot, of course, explain the origin of the
gesture, it may well have been the moment when it acquired its
insulting role. As a sexual comment, or as a protective gesture, the
fig had been in use for centuries beforehand, but we have no proof
that in Classical times it was ever employed as a gross insult, as it so
often is today. Perhaps in this capacity, at least, it is traceable to the
Barbarossa humiliation, and this strange historical incident gave it
not merely a supportive explanation, but an added message and a
new role.

DISTRIBUTION

The most common usage for the fig-sign today in Europe is as a
crude sexual comment. Of our informants, 234 gave this interpretation and told us that it can be used either as a bawdy sexual
invitation by a man to a woman, or as a comment by one man to
another about a woman's sexual qualities or availability. We found
this usage scattered over a very wide range, but it was most common
in northern Europe, especially Denmark, Holland, Belgium and
Germany. In the south it was really popular only in Tunisia.

The gesture was almost as frequent in its role as a sexual insult. Of
our informants 206 saw it as belonging to this category. For them it
was the equivalent of a forearm jerk, carrying messages such as 'get
lost', 'take this', 'up yours' and 'get stuffed'. The main centre for this
usage was not, as might have been expected, northern Italy (where
the great Barbarossa insult began), but further east in Greece and

Turkey. For some reason, the northern Sardinians and northern (Flemish) Belgians also had moderately high scores, but the strangest feature of this particular interpretation occurred in France, where there was a massive contrast between the population in central France and elsewhere. The figures for France are worth quoting:

French region	Fig as sexual insult
North	2 *out of* 30
West	0 *out of* 30
Central	27 *out of* 30
South	3 *out of* 30

This difference cannot be explained by competition with other meanings for the gesture, because France was generally rather uninterested in the fig-sign. Nearly half our French informants said that the gesture had no meaning for them whatsoever. Yet, in this one region, nearly everyone knew the fig as a gross insult. The reason behind the regional tradition is not clear, but it would be most interesting to discover how far it spreads across France and whether there are any sharp boundaries within the French-speaking zone of Europe.

In its protective role, the fig is used as an alternative to the horizontal horns, and carries much the same message: 'protection against witches', 'against spells', 'to remedy misfortune', 'to bring good luck', 'to ward off the evil eye', and so on. One or other of these protective messages was given to us by 81 informants, with the main centres being in Portugal and Sicily. Surprisingly, mainland Italy was weak in this interpretation, although traditionally and historically it is always thought to be the main centre of the protective fig. It remains today the centre for the manufacture of lucky-charm fig-amulets, but, despite this, no more than 9 per cent of our mainland Italian informants gave this particular interpretation for the gesture. Like the horn-signs, the fig seems to be an ancient gesture that is on the wane, but unlike the horn-signs, it is even losing its grip in the very territories which were its original strongholds.

The steal-your-nose joke was almost as popular as the ancient protective interpretation. Of our informants, 75 gave us this meaning, with one locality, the island of Malta, giving it as the dominant

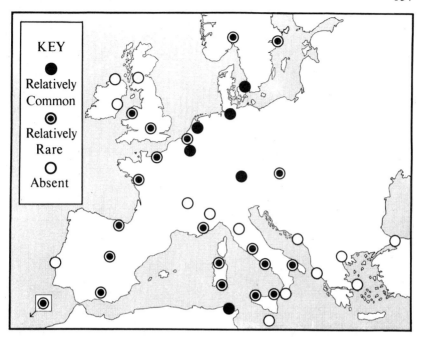

THE FIG   Meaning: sexual comment

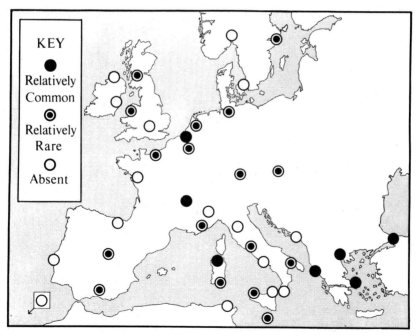

THE FIG   Meaning: sexual insult

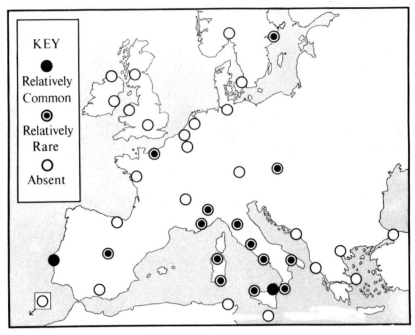

THE FIG   Meaning: protection

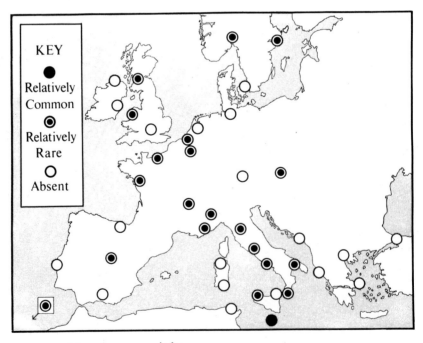

THE FIG   Meaning: nose joke

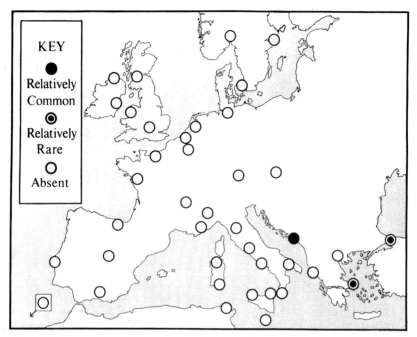

THE FIG Meaning: nothing

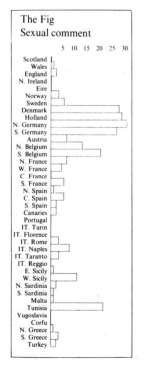

The Fig
Sexual comment

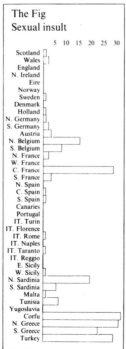

The Fig
Sexual insult

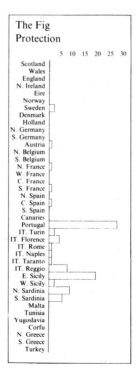

The Fig
Protection

interpretation (80 per cent). The nose-joke scatter was very wide, covering most of Europe except the south-east, where in Greece and Turkey the insulting role of the fig is so strong. In Spain there is a local variant of the joke interpretation. Instead of saying 'I've stolen your nose', the message becomes 'I've cut off your penis'. This was most common in northern Spain.

The 'I'll give you nothing' interpretation, recorded from only 32 informants, was confined almost entirely to Yugoslavia, where it was known by everyone. The message was nearly always the same: 'I'll give you nothing', 'This is all I'll give you', 'I'll give you not a fig', 'You'll get nothing'. How this separate meaning for the fig has arisen in this one locality we do not know at present.

13 The Head Toss

THE HEAD TOSS
MEANINGS:

1	Negative	302
2	Beckon	108
3	Antagonism	55
4	Superiority	50
5	Query	33
6	Salutation	24
7	Rejection	24
8	Directional	20
9	others	30
10	not used	554

(Based on 1,200 informants
at 40 locations)

DESCRIPTION

The head is tossed smartly upwards and backwards in a short jerk. The upward movement is more forceful than the downward return to the neutral position. Usually, at the same time that the head jerks back, the eyebrows are momentarily raised. There may be a soft *tschk* sound produced by the tongue as the head is tossed back, or the gesture may be completely silent. The lips may or may not be pursed. The eyes may be open or closed, or, more commonly, they are rolled upwards. In districts where the gesture is common, the basic head-toss element itself may actually be omitted, the gesturer merely pursing his lips, flicking up his eyebrows, and rolling his eyes sharply upwards — all three actions performed simultaneously — while keeping his head still. This version is only used at low intensities and at close proximity.

ORIGINS

Most people, when offering a silent 'No', shake the head from side to side, but in some regions this same message is transmitted by the head-toss gesture. Charles Darwin, in his book *The Expression of the Emotions in Man and Animals*, written in 1872, dwelt at length on the question of the derivation and distribution of these human signals of negation. He saw them originating in the infant's primary act of food rejection. By observing his own children, he found that when they were about to accept food, either from the nipple or from the spoon, they moved their heads forwards and downwards, but when they were refusing food, they turned their heads either sideways or upwards. From these observations he concluded that the adult *head nod* for *yes*, and the adult *head shake* and *head toss* for *no*, had their beginnings in these very early actions.

It is perhaps not necessary to be quite so specific in deriving the head toss from pre-adult movements. The human animal is always at pains to protect the vital facial region and any sudden surprise or frontal threat may give rise to a rapid intention movement of head-withdrawal. One form this withdrawal takes is a backward and upward tilting of the head. The head toss can therefore be derived from any small, incipient movement of head 'retreat'. This is close, of course, to the Darwinian example. In his case, the child is tilting the head away in an avoidance movement, while in the 'surprise' action the head-retreat is anticipating the need for avoidance. The added eye-closing/rolling operates both as a protection response and as a form of 'cut-off' in which the in-coming visual signals are eliminated. To put it another way, it is a conspicuous act of gaze-aversion, as well as being one of physical self-defence. Finally, there is the element of body-heightening (the anti-bow element) which accompanies the head toss, giving an assertive, non-compliant quality.

It is easy to see how these qualities can contribute to the birth of a widely accepted negation signal. What is more difficult to understand is why the head toss signal for *no* is more restricted than the alternative action of the head shake. The head shake possesses both protective and cut-off elements, but it lacks the haughty, body-heightening element of the head toss, which would seem to render the toss more suitable as a negative statement.

The explanation for the greater popularity of the head shake, cross-culturally, seems to be its distinctiveness. It lacks ambiguity. There are no other head gestures similar to it with which it could be confused. This is not the case with the head toss. As is already clear from the list of meanings we found for this gesture when making our field study, many informants gave alternative interpretations. Only 302 saw it as the *no* signal, while a total of 314 saw it as carrying one of seven other meanings. Had we investigated the head shake in the same way, it is doubtful whether any such confusion would have

The Neapolitan head toss as a negation signal.

existed. It is almost certainly this ambiguity in the case of the head toss that has helped to limit its range.

DISTRIBUTION

The head toss as a negation signal shows perhaps the most interesting of all the geographical distributions of the twenty gestures studied. It is totally absent from the whole of northern Europe, from the Iberian peninsula and from Tunisia. It is also extremely rare in northern Italy and Sardinia. But in the southern Italian region, from Naples to Sicily, in Malta, and in the Greek and Turkish region, it is recognized by almost everyone. The contrast is dramatic. In the zone where it is common there are ten sites, involving 300 informants. Of these, 288 (96 per cent) identified the gesture as meaning *no*. In the other zones there are 30 sites, involving 900 informants. Of these, only 14 informants (1.5 per cent) interpreted it in this way.

Not only is this a massive regional division, but its Italian boundary falls in the middle of a linguistic area. Somewhere between

Naples and Rome, Italians stop tossing their heads backwards for *no*, and start to display only the head shake when signalling a negative. Historically, it would appear that the change-over has something to do with the ancient Greek settlement of what is now southern Italy. The Greeks brought their culture as far north as Naples, but did not penetrate much beyond that city. It might seem far-fetched to suggest that an ancient influence of this type, dating back more than 2,000 years, could still be affecting the behaviour of modern Italians, who now experience nation-wide television programmes and who have undergone major north-south population movements. But there seems to be no other possible explanation. If it is true, then it demonstrates the remarkable tenacity and conservatism of this particular gestural difference.

We were sufficiently impressed by this to undertake a much more detailed examination of the region between Naples and Rome — the gestural 'frontier' region for the head toss. We travelled around the many small towns and villages in the district, trying to ascertain whether there was a gradual decline as one moved from north to south, or whether there was a sudden, sharp drop. The results of this enquiry have been made the subject of a special chapter later in the book (Gesture Boundaries, p. 247).

It is worth looking in some detail here at the seven other interpretations we were given for the head toss gesture, by people who were not familiar with its major role as a negative. In each case, they were confusing it with a similar, but distinct movement of the head, and the results can be tabulated as follows:

Meaning	No. of informants	Typical head movement
Negative	302	Head toss
Beckon	108	Head beckon
Antagonism	55	Head tilt
Superiority	50	Head raise
Query	33	Head cock
Salutation	24	Head jerk
Rejection	24	Head thrust
Directional	20	Head point

The *head beckon* usually involves a slight twisting of the head as it moves upwards and backwards. This difference would be quite sufficient, for someone who knows and uses the head toss proper, to

The Head Toss
Negative

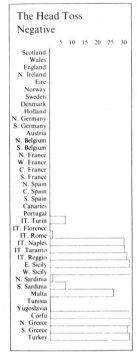

The Head Toss
Beckon

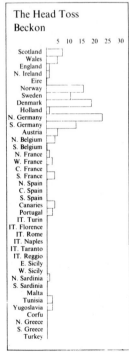

avoid any errors. But if the negative head toss is not used in a particular region, then an informant trying to identify the action could easily mistake it for someone saying 'come here'.

The *head tilt* of a man saying 'you idiot', or 'I am fed up with this', or 'how stupid', looks remarkably like a simple version of the head toss. The same *tschk* noise can be heard, and the same rolling of the eyes up to heaven, as if the gesturer, in disgust or despair, is appealing for God's help. But the head tilt is a shorter movement than the head toss, especially at high intensities.

The *head raise* of the disdainful man, signalling haughtiness, scorn, pride, or snobbery, is more of a posture than a movement. The head is held in the raised position for longer and there is no quick upward movement and return. This is the 'nose-in-the-air' posture — an anti-bowing response.

The *head cock* is quite distinct from the head toss, and it is surprising to find as many as 33 informants confusing them. When the head makes this movement, which acts as a silent question-mark, it is twisted markedly to one side, as the query, whatever it may be, is posed to the watching companion.

The *head jerk* is a backward tipping of the head that is seen as a greeting signal all over the world. The actual head movement is almost indistinguishable from that of the head toss, but confusion should not normally arise because the greeting head jerk is nearly always accompanied by a broadly smiling face. Needless to say, the negative head toss is seldom accompanied by such an expression. People living in a 'head toss zone' use the same greeting head jerk as

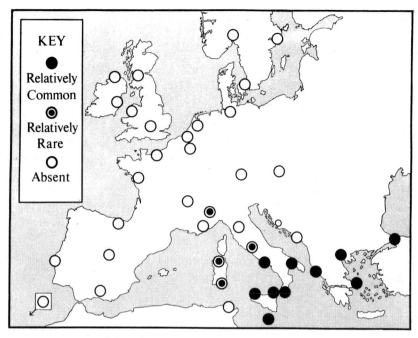

Meaning: negative

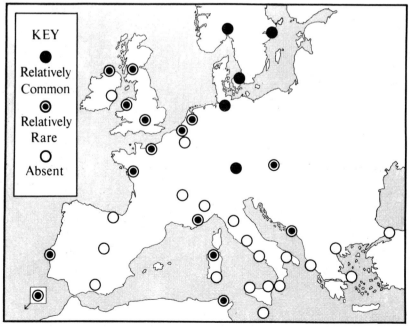

Meaning: beckon

other individuals from outside the zone, and although there is a slight risk of error, it seldom seems to occur.

The *head thrust* of the man who is saying 'clear off' or 'go away' involves a forward, jutting element that makes it comparatively easy to distinguish, especially as it is usually accompanied by a forward movement of the upper body at the same time.

The *head point* of the man saying 'over there' also involves a strong chin-jutting element, and it is hard to see how this action could be confused with the head toss, yet 20 informants interpreted our gesture in this way.

These various confusions illustrate clearly the way in which, if a particular symbolic gesture is absent from a region, the local inhabitants will re-interpret it if it is brought in by an outsider. Rather than ignore it, or admit that they really do not know what it might mean, they translate it into something familiar to them. The urge to do this seems to be so strong that they will blind themselves to small, but distinctive differences between the original gesture and the local one. How many times this happens in the ordinary course of events, as people travel more and more to faraway places, it is hard to say, but in our field studies the phenomenon was certainly a common one, as the results for this particular gesture reveal.

14 The Chin Flick

**THE CHIN FLICK
MEANINGS:**

1	Disinterest	301
2	Negative	244
3	Disbelief	20
4	others	25
5	not used	610

(Based on 1,200 informants
at 40 locations)

DESCRIPTION

The backs of the fingers of one hand are flicked forwards in an arc, brushing against the underside of the chin. This is either a single action or is repeated several times in quick succession. The head is usually tilted back as this is done, and the eyes are often directed at the companion. Sometimes the gesture is reduced in intensity, so that only a single flick is made, or the multiple flicks are performed in an abbreviated way, hardly touching the chin at all. In some regions, the flick may be performed with the front of the thumb instead of the fingers.

ORIGINS

There appear to be two separate derivations for this gesture, resulting in a double meaning. The major use of the chin flick is as a disinterest signal, and the French name for it — *la barbe* (the beard) — gives the clue as to its origin in this capacity. It is a symbolic beard-flick, the gesturer flipping his real or imaginary beard upwards and forwards at his companion. As a simple insult, this means 'I point my masculinity at you', and is associated with verbal messages such as: buzz off, shut up, get lost, don't bother me, or I have had enough of you. But it is also frequently used as a special kind of insult implying boredom: you bore me, you make me tired. In this context it may be taking its origins from the suggestion that 'you are so boring that my beard has grown long listening to you.' This may sound unlikely, and an unnecessarily complicated explanation, but there is another beard gesture, common in the Middle East, in which the hand of the gesturer indicates a long (but imaginary) beard, with the message being, 'Look how long my beard has become, listening to your boring story.' It is possible that the chin-flick gesture and the long-beard gesture have developed from a common starting point.

The boredom factor is supported by the French phrases that often accompany the chin flick: *Quelle barbe!* — what a nuisance! — and *Qu'est-ce-qu'il est barbe!* — 'He's an awful bore!'

A second meaning for the chin flick is that of a simple negative. Here it is being used as an amplification of the head toss. One of the problems with the ordinary head toss is that it communicates poorly at long distances. In a region where its use is common at close quarters, one can observe the addition of the hand element when the distance between the gesturer and his companion is increased. In

The Neapolitan chin flick gesture, from De Jorio, 1832.

these circumstances the chin-flicking movement simply underlines the fact that the head is being tossed backwards. It is as if the hand is assisting the head up and back.

A whole range of negative messages can be transmitted with this gesture. A few examples will give some idea of the way it is used. On the far side of a busy street a man whistles to a friend in charge of a news-stand. The friend performs the chin flick and the man waves and walks on. The message here was, 'No, your magazine has not arrived yet.' A motor-cruiser is being docked. The man at the bow gives a chin flick to the man at the wheel, sending the message, 'It's no good, I can't reach the mooring rope.' A car is travelling down a narrow cliff road. A driver coming in the opposite direction gives the chin flick as he squeezes past, meaning: 'Don't go on, the road is blocked.' Other negatives conveyed by the chin flick are: There is nothing doing; I haven't seen him; I can't help you; I don't want any; I don't know anything about it; or a simple no, or nothing.

DISTRIBUTION

As a sign of lack of interest, annoyance or boredom, the chin flick has a wide range across Europe, but is extremely rare or absent in the most northerly regions — the British Isles, Scandinavia and Germany. Its stronghold is in the French-speaking zones — in southern Belgium, France and in ex-colonial Tunisia. It is also common in northern Italy, Yugoslavia and southern Sardinia.

In its capacity as a simple negative, it is common only in southern Italy, Sicily, northern Sardinia, Malta and Corfu. As with the head toss, there is an interesting split between the north and south of Italy in the use of this gesture. This gives rise to a problem. What exactly are the northern Italians doing? It is clear that the French are using the gesture as an irritated beard flick, and the southern Italians are employing it as an amplified head toss, but what is it to the inhabitants of Turin, Florence and Rome? Almost all of them use the same phrase to describe the meaning of the gesture. They say, *Me ne frego, Non mi va*, or *Non mi interessa*, indicating that they couldn't care less, or that something doesn't suit them, or interest them. It is dismissive in its impact and much closer to the French meaning than the one from the south of their own country. But are they deriving it from the French beard-flipping action, or are they merely borrowing the southern negative response and loading it with a bias towards disinterest? Is it an Italian beard gesture, or a dismissive 'no'? It is

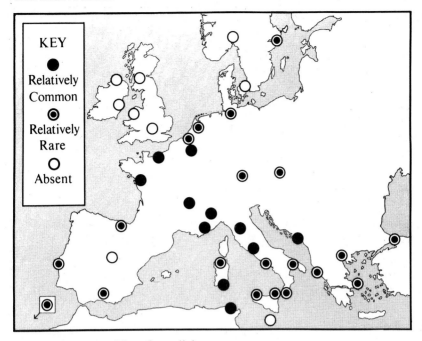

Meaning: disinterest

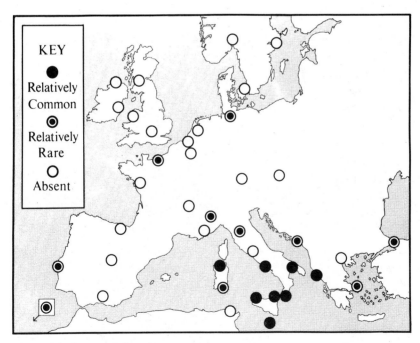

Meaning: negative

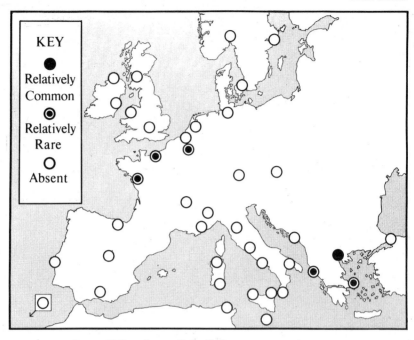

THE CHIN FLICK   Meaning: disbelief

The Italian chin flick gesture, used here as a simple negative.

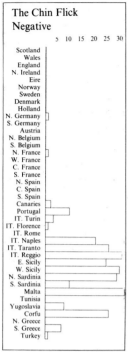

The Chin Flick
Negative

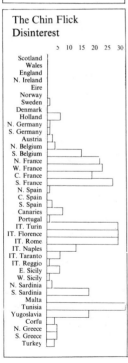

The Chin Flick
Disinterest

impossible to be certain, but it is worth pointing out that the gesture is rare or absent in mainland Greece. This seems to imply that it did not start out with the original Greek head toss and spread to the Greek colonies in south Italy. This probably indicates that the annoyance meaning for the chin flick is the ancient, basic one and that this became modified when it encountered the head toss in southern Italy. There it probably became infected by the simple, unannoyed negative meaning of the head toss, and gradually lost its irritability, becoming eventually no more than a long-distance amplification of the tossed 'no'.

It must be admitted that this is speculative, but until further field work is carried out it is the most reasonable explanation we can offer. One thing is certain, namely that a French tourist on holiday in Malta would find himself insulted by the gesture, where no insult was intended, and the context would not help him to understand. If he asked a question and was given a chin-flick 'no', he would automatically assume he was being told to 'get lost'. With tourism ever on the increase, such misunderstandings will undoubtedly multiply, and there will be a greater need for gestural fluency throughout Europe.

There are two other points which require comment. On the island of Sardinia there is a curious reversal of meaning for the chin flick as one moves from north to south. In the north of the island the gesture is predominantly negative (27 to 2 for negative to annoyed), while in the south the opposite is the case (9 to 16 for negative to annoyed). The same reversal occurs in the Greek-speaking region. Corfu is predominantly negative (24 to 3), while mainland Greece shows little response either way (0 to 4 in the north, 6 to 4 in the south). We have no explanations for these differences, and they require further investigation.

There is one minor meaning — disbelief — that is worth mapping, despite its small numbers, because it does show two regions of concentration — France and Greece. The total of 20 informants involved gave meanings for the chin flick such as 'I don't believe you', 'lies', and 'there's no truth in it'. This is a special form of the annoyed chin flick, and it would not be justified to treat this as a separate category were it not for the fact that, in his *International Dictionary of Sign Language*, Theodore Brun gives the chin flick as 'I can't believe you' in Spain. Not one of our 120 Spanish informants gave this meaning for the gesture and we are therefore inclined to view this as an error, or at least as an exaggeration. As a matter of fact, the gesture was rare in Spain in any capacity and 86 per cent of our informants there reported that they had never seen it.

15 The Cheek Stroke

THE CHEEK STROKE
MEANINGS:

1	Thin and ill	248
2	Attractive	104
3	Thinking	55
4	Success	25
5	Sad	14
6	Threat	11
7	Crafty	11
8	Effeminate	8
9	others	70
10	not used	654

(Based on 1,200 informants
at 40 locations)

DESCRIPTION

The thumb and forefinger are placed one on each cheek-bone and
then gently stroked down each cheek. The movement is soft and
caressing. There are two variants of this action: the down-stroke
may be greatly reduced, or it may be increased until the thumb and
forefinger meet at the chin.

ORIGINS

We have been able to find very few references to this gesture. The
earliest is in Andrea de Jorio's work on Neapolitan gestures, published in 1832. He explains that the significance of the cheek stroke
comes from the fact that the Greek ideal of a beautiful face was one
that was like the shape of an egg, with the contours gently diminish-
ing as one approached the chin. By stroking downwards, the thumb
and forefinger come closer and closer, as they move over the surface
of the cheeks, thus emphasizing this ideal shape. He goes on to say
that there is no way in which this derivation can be used to explain
the origin of the gesture in countries outside Greek influence, and
that some other solution must be found there. But the fact is that it is
a rare gesture in the north and west of Europe, and nearly all the

examples found today come into, or near, the Greek zone. So the explanation he offers may well be the correct one. As an alternative, however, he points out that the sight of a beautiful face makes one want to caress it, and the gesture may be no more than a simple mime, saying 'the way I am caressing *my* face, is the way I would like to caress yours'.

De Jorio makes a special point about the danger of confusing the beauty gesture with the one for thin or ill. In the latter, the thumb and forefinger are not brought gently down the cheeks, but with some force, squeezing or pinching the cheeks as they perform the down-stroke, to make the face look sunken and drawn. Despite his warning and despite the fact that the two actions are extremely easy to distinguish from one another, we found that many of our informants made this error. In fact, as the figures show, it was interpreted as the thin-and-ill gesture more than twice as often as the beauty gesture. We were always careful when miming the cheek stroke ourselves to make the down-stroke extra-gentle, but over and over

The gentle cheek stroke gesture, used as a signal for beauty. From De Jorio, 1832.

again we were given the same interpretation for the gesture: he is haggard, he is very sick, he is poorly, he is emaciated. The answer here seems to be that the beauty signal is a fading one and has been overtaken by the thin-and-ill one to such an extent that many people simply do not know the original Greek meaning. Rather than give no answer, they offer the wrong interpretation, and would presumably make this same mistake if they encountered the beauty gesture naturally, in their ordinary daily lives. Since the meanings 'beautiful' and 'ill' are so different, and would cause serious misunderstandings, it is probable that the beauty signal will go on fading and will eventually disappear altogether. The reason for the sick signal winning this struggle is probably that there is no other obvious way of saying that someone is ill with a simple gesture, whereas there are many other ways of saying someone is beautiful.

In addition to these two main meanings, we also found a rather high proportion of guesses, in areas where the cheek stroke lacked a major symbolic role. Of our informants, 55 said that the gesture meant: thinking, pondering, thoughtfulness, contemplation, or

The strong version of the cheek stroke, indicating that someone is thin or ill.

puzzling. This confuses it with the well-known chin stroke which, for some unexplained reason, has strong links with moments when people are being thoughtful. Where men have beards, it develops into repeated beard-stroking. This misinterpretation occurred despite the fact that the cheek stroke movement begins much higher up on the cheek bones than the typical chin stroke.

An unexpected interpretation was 'success', which was given to us by 25 informants. They explained that the gesture meant 'I have a full hand of beard', or that 'there is cream in my beard'.

The 14 informants who gave 'sad' as the meaning are easy to understand. They themselves gave the answer, by saying, 'he is sad, he has a long face, like this.'

Other minor meanings included threat, where the gesturers were apparently angrily stroking their beards, as if to say: 'see my beard, I am a man, not a child, and you cannot trifle with me.' Also there was 'crafty' where the statement became 'he is stroking his beard and plotting against you', the implication being that his stroking actions indicated that he was thinking hard and his thoughts were hostile. Finally, there was 'effeminate', where the cheek stroke was saying, 'he has soft, smooth cheeks, like a girl'. None of these minor meanings occurred with sufficient frequency to justify mapping them.

DISTRIBUTION

As a signal of physical attractiveness, the cheek stroke has its main centre today in Greece, especially in the north. This tallies well with Andrea de Jorio's explanation of the origin of the gesture. The curious feature of the present-day distribution outside Greece is that the main secondary centre is not, as one might expect, in southern Italy, where the Greek colonists left so many cultural legacies, but further north, in Rome. Only 3 of our 30 informants in Naples said that the gesture meant beautiful, but the figure rose to 11 in the capital city. We have no explanation for this.

The thin-and/or-ill interpretation has a very wide scatter, with no major geographical focus. It was fairly common in Germany and Holland and northern France, and again, further south, in southern Italy, northern Sardinia, Malta and Corfu.

Some of the minor meanings did, however, show remarkable localization. Of the 25 informants who identified the cheek stroke as meaning 'success', 21 of them came from our Yugoslav sample. The phrases they used included such comments as: 'I am successful', 'I

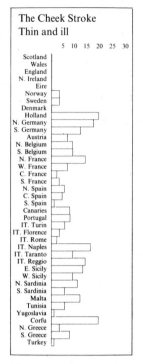

The Cheek Stroke
Thin and ill

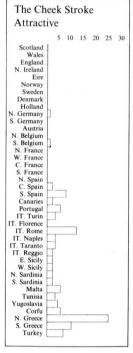

The Cheek Stroke
Attractive

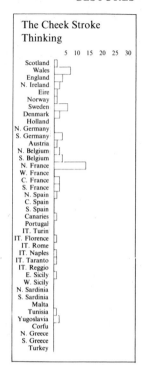

The Cheek Stroke
Thinking

have got more than I expected', 'I backed a good horse', 'I have made a good business deal', 'I have got lots of money'. It is beginning to look as though this region has a rather independent set of gestural traditions, and it would be intriguing to see if, by extending gesture map surveys further into the eastern zones of Europe, the same traditions would be found, indicating that Yugoslavia is the western edge, so to speak, of a major eastern gestural zone.

The threat signal interpretation was confined entirely to one site — Tunisia. There 11 of our informants said that the cheek stroke meant: 'I'll go to the police about you', 'I will get you for this', 'next time you will be in trouble', and 'watch out, I'll fight you'. They made the gesture in a slightly different way, pulling the thumb and forefinger down to a point below the chin, and

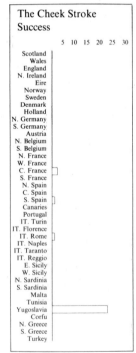

The Cheek Stroke
Success

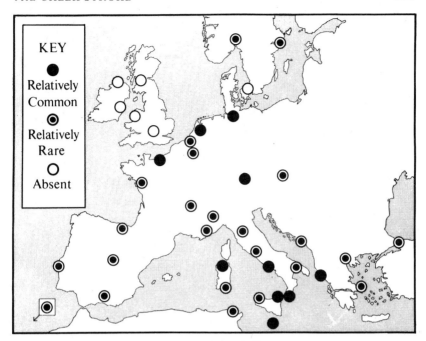

THE CHEEK STROKE   Meaning: thin and ill

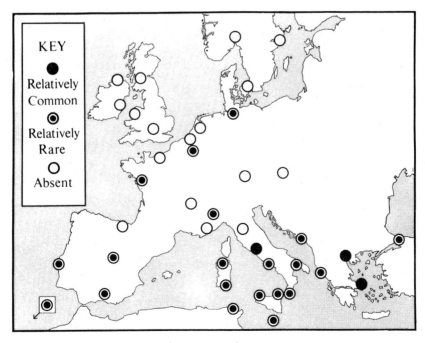

THE CHEEK STROKE   Meaning: attractive

were clearly confusing a local beard-threat gesture with the normal cheek stroke.

The use of the cheek stroke to say that a man is effeminate or homosexual was confined entirely to Turkey, where 8 informants all gave this interpretation. They gave such answers as 'he's a queer', or 'he's a pretty boy', meaning it in an insulting way. This is obviously a special usage of the basic Greek signal of 'beauty', re-applied to males, in a disparaging way.

16 The Thumb Up

**THE THUMB UP
MEANINGS:**

1	O.K.	738
2	One	40
3	Sexual insult	36
4	Hitch-hike	30
5	Directional	14
6	others	24
7	not used	318

(Based on 1,200 informants
at 40 locations)

DESCRIPTION

The clenched hand is extended, with the thumb vertically erect. In English it is better known by the popular name 'thumbs up', despite the fact that the action is commonly performed with only one hand.

ORIGINS

Few gestures can have a stranger history than the familiar 'thumbs up'. There is no doubt in the popular mind as to its origin. Everyone agrees that it hails from the days of gladiatorial combat in ancient Rome, when a decision had to be made concerning the fate of a beaten warrior. Peter Quennell, in his book on *The Colosseum*, describes what has now become the generally accepted scenario:

> In the sovereign's presence, the crowd advised their ruler. Waving cloths and displaying up-turned thumbs, they shouted 'Mitte!' (Let him go free); or, by turning down their thumbs, they vociferated 'Iugula!' — recommending that the fallen man should pay the penalty. When the emperor happened to share their feelings, he confirmed the crowd's verdict ... and ... with *pollice verso*, downturned thumb, ordered his immediate execution.

So, if the defeated gladiator had fought well, he could be spared by a
thumbs up gesture. If he had fought badly, he could be slain by a
thumbs down. From this specific use of the two thumb signals, it is
argued, came our modern usage, with the thumbs up meaning 'all's
well — O.K.' and the thumbs down meaning 'no good — failure'.
This has become the dominant interpretation of the two gestures
throughout Europe, and much of the rest of the world.

What could be simpler? The answer is that it would indeed be a
simple derivational explanation, if only it happened to be true. But it
is not. The ancient Romans did not behave in the manner ascribed to
them, and the whole story of the thumbs up 'approval' sign is based
on misunderstanding and mistranslation. It is a complete distortion
of the facts, and the true basis for our modern usage comes from a
different source altogether. What has happened is that, having
acquired our modern thumbs up and down meanings from elsewhere, we have then blatantly re-written Roman history to fit in.

There are, in reality, no ancient references to the thumbs going
either up *or* down in the Colosseum, at the vital moment of decision.
Later authors who have claimed so have simply not understood the
Latin phrases. *Pollice verso* does not mean a down-turned thumb —
it simply means a turned thumb — one that is moved in some
unspecified way. No particular direction can be assumed. The posture of the thumbs of those wishing to spare the gladiator was *pollice
compresso* — compressed thumbs. In other words, not thumbs up,
but thumbs covered up — thumbs folded away out of sight. What
the spectators did, in fact, was to extend their thumbs for a kill and
hide their thumbs for an acquittal. The reason for this is not hard to
find. If they wanted the victorious man to plunge in his sword, they
mimed the act with their hands, their extended thumbs stabbing the
air in encouragement. If they wanted to spare the defeated fighter
because he proved himself valiant in battle, they did the opposite of
sticking out their thumbs — they hid them away. This made sense in
an arena as vast as the Colosseum, where the kill/no-kill signals
would have to be strongly contrasting to be visible at all.

If this was the true situation, then how has it come to be distorted
by later writers? It is not even the case that the truth was completely
forgotten. It is recorded both in the *Oxford English Dictionary* and
in Brewer's *Dictionary of Phrase and Fable*. Sir James Murray
compiled the volume of the *O.E.D.* dealing with the letter 'T' between 1909 and 1915. Under the entry for phrases connected with
the word 'thumb', he includes the following quotation:

1880. Lewis and Short. s.v. *Pollex*: To close down the thumb
(*premere*) was a sign of approbation; to extend it (*vertere,
convertere, pollex infestus*) a sign of disapprobation.

The word *premere* refers to the pressing of the thumb, and the words
vertere, convertere, pollex infestus refer to the turning and turning
around of the 'hostile thumb'. Different words this time, but still the
same meanings and still no mention whatever of thumbs going up or
down.

Brewer's dictionary was first published in 1870 and has been
reprinted many times since then. His entry is just as clear:

In the ancient Roman combats, when a gladiator was
vanquished it rested with the spectators to decide whether he
should be slain or not. If they wished him to live, they shut up
their thumbs in their fists (*pollice compresso favor judicabatur*); if
to be slain, they turned out their thumbs ... Our popular saying,
Thumbs up! expressive of pleasure or approval is probably a
perversion of this custom.

Brewer does not hazard a guess as to why anyone should want to
pervert so simple a truth. In a moment we shall do so, but first we
want to consider some other distortions that occurred. The modern
equations: thumbs up = O.K., thumbs down = not O.K., is not the
only error that was made. Earlier authors usually made the opposite
mistake. This is hard to believe today, but the following quotations
should be convincing enough:

R. Garnett, 1887: 'They had unanimously turned their thumbs
up. "Sartor", the publisher acquainted him, "excites universal
disapprobation".'
J. Dixon, 1896: 'To turn the thumbs up. — To decide against.
The Romans in the amphitheatre turned their thumbs up when
a combatant was not to be spared.'
R. Y. Tyrrell, 1907: '"Thumbs down" means "spare him ...":
the signal for death was "thumbs up".'

What seems to have happened here is that the extended thumb has
automatically been thought of as going up, and the hidden thumb as
being kept down (rather than pointed down). But as the idea has
been passed from author to author, the distortion has hardened.
Sadly, it appears that translations from the Latin are often less than
scholarly. In one case, we can actually watch the bias change as the

years pass. There is a passage in Juvenal's third *Satire*, written at about the beginning of the second century A.D., which, in the original, refers to thumbs being either *verso* or *converso* (according to two different sources). Either way, it means that the thumbs were being turned, but makes no suggestion as to the direction. Juvenal has been translated many times, but if we select just three examples, we can see how the interpretation varies with the period.

Montaigne, in his *Essayes* of 1603 (Second Book, 26th Chapter) translates the Juvenal passage as: 'When people turn their thumbs away, they popularly any slay.' This is very restrained and correct, but he makes it the basis of a comment of his own to the effect that a thumb-sign 'of disfavour or disgrace' is 'to lift them up, and turn them outwards'. Read properly, he is still not badly distorting the original, but the phrase 'lift them up' can easily be taken to mean 'point them up', and this is undoubtedly the way many subsequent authors interpreted him.

Dryden, in his translation of Juvenal in 1693, gives the same passage as: 'Where ... with thumbs bent back, they popularly kill.' Turning away has now become bending back, and again this was taken to mean an erect thumb, even though Dryden was not specific about it.

Coming up to date, in Peter Green's 1967 translation, the passage becomes: '... and at the mob's thumbs-down, will butcher a loser for popularity's sake.' Now the meaning has gone the other way, to fit in with modern popular usage.

So, from an ambiguous beginning the distortion has taken off, first in one direction, and then in another. The question we now have to answer is what is it that controls these directions? Are they mere whims, or are there certain pressures being exerted to pull them one way or the other? First, we must consider pressures favouring the idea that thumbs up mean something unpleasant and thumbs down something pleasant. Whatever the pressure is, it has not been a particularly strong or successful one, and has lost out to its rival in modern times. A glance at the list of meanings for the thumbs up gesture, which we obtained from our informants in our present gesture-maps field study, reveals that 738 of them gave the 'O.K.' pleasant meaning, while only 36 gave an unpleasant meaning, namely that of a phallic insult. In the latter case the erect thumb is jerked in the air as a symbolic phallus, and the message is 'sit on this', or 'up yours'. This appears to be an old usage that has lost ground in the face of the increasingly popular O.K. meaning. If it was once

The O.K. version of the thumb up gesture.

better known than it is today, it could easily have led to the idea that, if an unpleasant thumb gesture was used in the Colosseum, it must have been this one.

Another clue comes from the first century A.D. writings of Pliny. In his great work, *The Historie of the World*, translated into English in 1601 by Philemon Holland, there is a passage in the second chapter of the 28th book, which reads: 'to bend or bow down the thumbs when we give assent unto a thing, or do favour any person, is so usuall, that it is growne into a proverbial speech, to bid a man put down his thumb in token of approbation.' There is no doubt here about the way Pliny viewed the gesture: thumbs down meant O.K. But he was not talking about what happened in the Colosseum. He was referring to ordinary, everyday life, and it is important to make that distinction.

If we now put together these two observations: thumbs up meaning an unpleasant insult, and thumbs down meaning a pleasant form of approval, it is possible to see how these usages, if known about by earlier authors, could have been grafted on, as it were, to the ambiguous statements about what the spectators' thumbs were doing at the gladiatorial combats. This can explain how one kind of distortion developed, but what of the other — the one leading in the opposite direction, to the popular usage of modern times?

To understand this other distortion we have to consider the basic nature of 'up' gestures and 'down' gestures. If we are feeling 'up in the air' we are feeling good, and if we are feeling 'down in the dumps' we are feeling bad. There is something inherently optimistic, positive and dominant about upward movements, and something essentially pessimistic, negative and subordinate about downward movements. This dichotomy pervades the whole of our language and our thinking, and it is obviously going to have an impact on our gestural repertoire as well. So, whatever other, more specific, influences may be at work, there is also going to be a generalized pressure tending to favour a thumbs up gesture as meaning something pleasant and a thumbs down gesture as something unpleasant. We feel that it is this basic influence that has finally favoured the modern interpretation of the thumbs up and down gestures.

There is some evidence that this is not exclusively modern. John Bulwer, in his *Chirologia* of 1644, has this to say about ordinary thumb postures: 'To hold up the thumbe, is the gesture ... of one shewing his assent or approbation. To hold up both thumbs, is an expression importing a transcendency of praise.' He quotes classical authors to support him in this view, which contradicts the statements made by Pliny. There is no way we can see to reconcile these two views and it looks as though there must have been an early conflict of thumb signals which was eventually resolved by the rise to dominance of the 'up = good' version.

The O.K. thumb up employed as a good luck patch for attachment to denim clothing.

Two other derivational clues exist to help to explain the 'thumbs up = good' equation. There is an old English saying 'Here's my thumb on it!' which was used to seal a bargain. The two people involved each wetted a thumb and then extended it, held upwards, until the two raised thumbs came into contact with one another. It is easy to see how this custom could lead to, or support the idea of holding out a raised thumb as a sign of friendly agreement or approval. Another supportive clue comes from Gérard Brault's study of *French Gestures*, where he says that admiration is expressed when 'the thumb of the right hand is held erect and pushed forward, as if pushing in a thumbtack ... The thumbs up gesture here signifies "first class", for the French indicate number one with the thumb.'

Summing up, it would be an understatement to say that the

origins of the thumbs up gesture are not as simple as most people seem to believe. The whole 'Roman arena' explanation that is so often given, appears to be largely irrelevant. The evidence as to exactly what was happening in ordinary, daily life in ancient times is still not clear and the information is contradictory. But the present-day situation is obvious enough. Everywhere the O.K. message of the thumbs up gesture has come to dominate the scene, as the gesture map on p. 194 reveals.

DISTRIBUTION

If Rome really was the ancestral home of this gesture, we would expect to find the Italian region particularly strongly represented on our gesture map. The opposite is the case, with the Italian-speaking zone, in fact, being the weakest of all, closely followed by Greece. This confirms our suspicions that the fate of gladiators played no part in the history of this gesture. It also seems to indicate that perhaps the existence of the ancient thumbs up obscenity in the Italian and Greek zones has been the main factor working against the domination of the O.K. message there. The second gesture map, dealing with the gesture as a phallic insult clearly shows that this sexual interpretation (apart from solitary informants in Belgium and Malta) is entirely limited to the Greco-Italian world. In Italy, its strongholds are in the more remote, less cosmopolitan regions, where older customs tend to die hard.

It would seem that the O.K. gesture is likely to have enjoyed its major growth in the north of Europe and then to have rapidly invaded the south. Many Italians were surprised to learn that northerners thought of the gesture as having sprung originally from Rome. To them it was a 'new thing' imported by the American G.I.s during the war. At every location we visited on mainland Italy, at least one person identified it as 'The American O.K.', helping to drive yet another nail into the 'Roman Arena' explanation.

Finally, it is perhaps worth recording in this case the wide variety of 'O.K.' messages we were given by informants. They reveal the generic nature of the gesture, encompassing many subtly differing specific signals. Answers given included the following:

All right. A.O.K., *iarriba!* (Spain), bang on, *champion* (France), everything's fine, everything's fixed, excellent, first class, *fixe* (Portugal), good luck, great, great stuff, I agree, I made it, it's a winner, it's in the bag, *kalo* (Greece), O.K., ready to go, really good, right on,

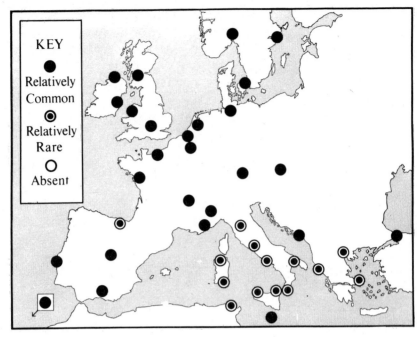

THE THUMB UP   Meaning: O.K.

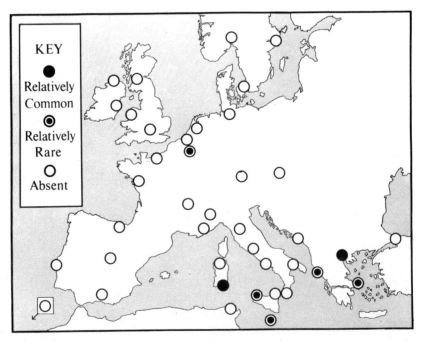

THE THUMB UP   Meaning: sexual insult

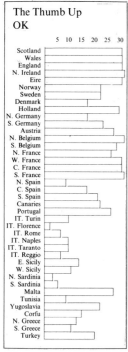

The Thumb Up
OK

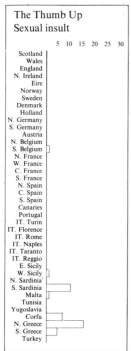

The Thumb Up
Sexual insult

solid, *Spitze* (Austria), spot on, success, superb, tops, *va bene* (Italy), very good, victory, you are right, you've done well.

This is almost exactly the same range of meanings as we found with the O.K. ring gesture, and the two can be used almost interchangeably. They are also of about equal popularity (700 for the O.K. ring and 738 for the O.K. thumbs up) and have the same widely scattered range. The major difference between them is that the O.K. ring is the more popular in Italy, and the O.K. thumbs up the more popular in France.

The distribution of the minor meanings of the thumbs up are of little interest. They are so scattered that few zonal concentrations show up, and we have not felt it worthwhile to map them. The 40 informants who interpreted the gesture as meaning 'one', ranged from Holland to Turkey. Only in Tunisia was this meaning at all popular (14 out of 30 informants). The 30 informants who saw it as a hitch-hiking signal (often called by the name 'auto-stop') were scattered right across the map, but there were never more than 4 at any one site. The 14 who interpreted it as a directional sign — a thumb point — were confined to southern regions, where this kind of guide-sign is slightly less surly in its ordinary use.

It is not safe to use the 'thumbing-a-lift' gesture in either Sardinia or Greece. The message transmitted to the passing drivers by the hopeful figures at the roadside is not 'please help us', but 'get stuffed', and does not encourage drivers to stop, except to pick a fight. Our figures show that, although both the insult meaning and the O.K. meaning are present in these countries,

in southern Sardinia and northern Greece the obscene insult is
dominant. Furthermore, with the addition of the upward jerking
movement, shared by both the insult and the true hitch-hiking
gestures, but absent from the O.K. version, far more people in those
countries would see the action in its obscene role, and the hitch-
hiking tourist would do well to imitate the local hitch-hikers, and
adopt the loosely waved, flat hand gesture we observed at Sardinian
and Greek roadsides.

The obscene version of the thumb
up gesture, used here in southern
Sardinia.

17 The Teeth Flick

THE TEETH FLICK

MEANINGS:

1	Nothing	207
2	Anger	127
3	Praise	24
4	others	65
5	not used	777

(Based on 1,200 informants
at 40 locations)

DESCRIPTION

The thumb-nail is placed behind the lower edge of the upper incisors
and then forcibly jerked forwards, making a clicking sound. At low
intensity the gesture may be made quickly, without actual contact
being made between nail and tooth.

ORIGINS

Like the fig and the horn-sign, the teeth flick appears to be a gesture
which is on the decline, with a shrinking geographical range. In our
survey we found it missing entirely in the north of Europe — in the
British Isles and Scandinavia — and yet the historical evidence
suggests that it was once common in the north.

In its earliest form it was apparently always a threat or a sign of
anger, and in England was referred to as 'biting the thumb' at
someone. The oldest reference we have been able to find dates from
1573, when a satirical poem included the phrase 'The Clerk was like
to byte his thowmis'. But perhaps the most famous early quotation is
the one from Shakespeare's *Romeo and Juliet*, where Sampson says:
'I will bite my thumb at them; which is a disgrace to them, if they
bear it.' He is trying to pick a quarrel and the victim of his insult
replies: 'Do you bite your thumb at us sir?' His reply to this is

deliberately ambiguous: 'I do bite my thumb, sir' — avoiding any reference to the direction of the insult. His victim is forced to re-state his question: 'Do you bite your thumb at us sir?' At this point Sampson asks his friend Gregory: 'Is the law on our side if I say ay?' Gregory replies 'No', so Sampson answers: 'No sir, I do not bite my thumb at you sir; but I bite my thumb, sir.' The way in which Shakespeare plays with this phrase suggests that it would have been well known to his audience and that they would have understood the seriousness of the insult, had it been specifically directed *at* someone. But there is no clue here as to why such an apparently harmless action should be so intensely provocative. A clue does come, however, in a work published four years after *Romeo and Juliet*. In *Wits Miserie*, by Thomas Lodge, which appeared in 1596, there is the phrase: 'Giving me the Fico with his thumb in his mouth', which is generally assumed to be the same gesture. It has been interpreted as a variant form of fig-sign, with the thumb going to the mouth instead of between the fingers of the closed hand. When we discussed the more typical fig-sign earlier, we mentioned the story of the humiliation of the Milanese by the Emperor Frederick Barbarossa in 1162, when he forced his captives to pluck a fig from the anus of a mule with their teeth. It is this origin which is seen by some as the explanation of the teeth flick gesture. The gesturer, by plucking his thumb (the symbolic fig) from his mouth, and aiming it directly at his victim, implies that the latter was a 'fig-plucker', in other words, a man who was prepared to humiliate himself to save his life. The phrase 'a fig for you' is sometimes used in connection with the gesture, and this would seem to confirm that the anger aroused by the teeth flick results from its message: 'you are a degraded, humiliated coward.'

It has been argued that perhaps the 'biting a thumb' gesture was a completely different action from the teeth flick, but there is an instruction in a seventeenth-century etiquette book, *The Rules of Civility*, which suggests that they are, in fact, one and the same. It reads: ''Tis no less disrespectful to bite the nail of your thumb, by way of scorn and disdain.' From this it would appear simply that 'to bite the thumb' is no more than a popular contraction of 'to bite the nail of your thumb', a fact often overlooked by Shakespearean actors, who tend to bite the whole of the thumb, rather than just flick the nail from behind the upper teeth.

The gesture remained popular in northern Europe throughout the seventeenth century, and there are many references to it in the writings of the day. It was also so well known in France, that it had acquired a special name: *La Nique*. Cotgrave's French and English dictionary of 1611 gives this definition: 'NIQUE, faire la: ... to threaten or defie, by putting the thumb naile into the mouth, and with a jerke (from th'upper teeth) make it to knacke.'

In England, it seems to have waned in importance during the eighteenth century so that, by the nineteenth, it is already being discussed in the past tense. In Chambers's *Book of Days*, published in 1863, there is the comment that: 'It is very probable that ... the act of biting the thumb was not so much a gesture of insulting contempt as a threat.' In southern Europe this decline did not occur, and we found the gesture much in evidence there during our present field research. Its threatening message was no longer dominant, however. Its most common meaning now had become one of negation.

An Italian example of the teeth flick gesture.

As a negative, the message of the teeth flick is essentially: 'I have nothing', or 'I will give you nothing'. This appears to have grown out of the original threat and, in many places, to have supplanted it. The history of this change appears to be as follows. The original message, 'a fig for you' implies base cowardice, but the offered fig also has the special quality of a worthless object. So the gesture can also be seen as the giving of something of no value. Taken one step further, it easily becomes 'I give you nothing'. This remains insulting, but by a further weakening of the hostility of the comment, it can then become 'I have nothing to give', or, as was often quoted to us by informants 'I have no money'.

In some regions the ancient savagery of the gesture has been retained and it remains a gross slur, but in others it has been softened to a simple, unloaded statement of fact — I have nothing — with no offence intended and none taken. In many regions we found that both the old and the new meaning existed alongside one another and were distinguished, presumably, by the context of the encounter in which the gesture was made. In earlier days it is unlikely that the context would have registered — merely to make the gesture, in any situation, would have been taken instantly as gross affront.

So context-dependent has this gesture become, it seems, that it has even been able to acquire a third, minor meaning, as a compliment. This is confined, as far as we can tell, to a feeding context, where the teeth flick indicates that the meal, or a particular item of food, is particularly good or tasty. This may well have arisen as a confusion with the fingertips gesture of praise, the teeth flick being co-opted, as it were, as a thumb-kissing variant.

The changes that have occurred in the meaning of the gesture over the centuries reflect the fact that the gesturers have largely forgotten its true origins. When asked today to explain the action, the man who uses it as an 'I will give you nothing' signal, has to invent an answer. He is likely to say that it means 'I will not even give you the dirt from under my finger-nail', or 'I don't even have a tooth for you', or 'I will give you only spittle, because that is all I have to spare'. These have now become supportive explanations, helping to transmit the gesture from generation to generation in its modified role. It might, of course, be argued that they represent a completely separate development, independent of the ancient threat, but sharing precisely the same action. We cannot rule this out, but considering the rather specialized nature of the movement of the thumb nail against the teeth, this seems unlikely. If we were dealing with a simple baton, such as the hand purse, or the hand ring, independent developments might be expected, but here the chances are remote.

Supporting this line of argument is the observation we made in our field study concerning the range of messages the gesture can carry today. These do not fall neatly into separate categories (except for the cases of food-praise) but blend into one another. At one end of the scale are the out-and-out threats: 'I will kill you!' The more violent words used were: rage, anger, hatred, spite and revenge. Then there are the expressions of exasperation: 'If only I could catch

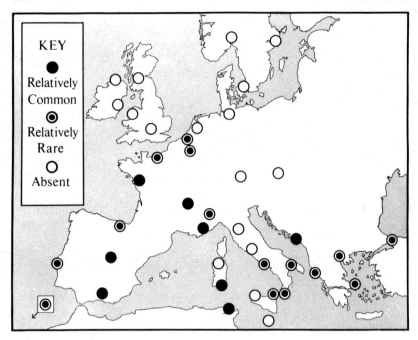

THE TEETH FLICK   Meaning: nothing

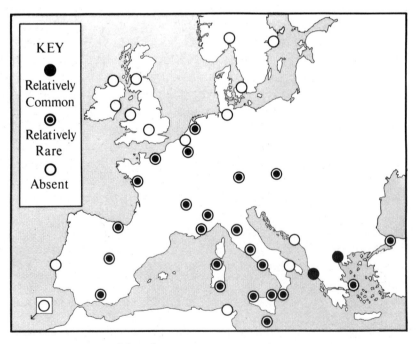

THE TEETH FLICK   Meaning: anger

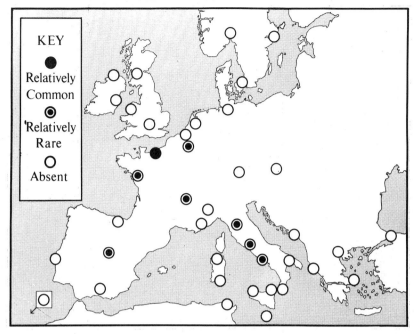

THE TEETH FLICK   Meaning: praise

you!' 'I'll get you next time!' — often tinged with regret, the gesture representing a missed opportunity for venting anger, or a bitter disappointment. Moving along the scale we come to the scornful or hostile negatives: 'You will get nothing out of me!' 'You'll get only that!' Although we have shifted now into the 'negative category' from the 'anger category', the mood is still unpleasant, and the gesture is still a deliberately unfriendly one. Finally we come to the simple, unbiased negatives, such as 'I have nothing to give you' and 'I have no money'. These are almost apologetic and far removed from the rage and hatred at the other end of the scale.

Because there exists this spectrum of meanings today, we feel that what we are seeing is one gesture in the process of evolution, rather than two independent gestures existing side-by-side, with separate origins, but we have to admit that this is mere speculation on our part, and there is no proof one way or the other.

DISTRIBUTION

The present-day distribution of the gesture in its two major meanings seems to support our interpretation of its origin. If we were

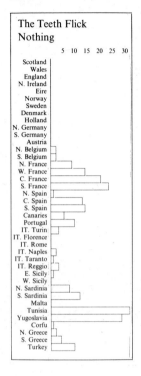
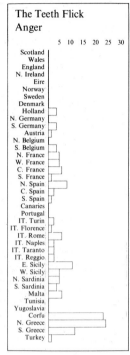
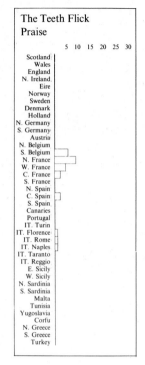

dealing with two independent gestures, we might expect to find them surviving in two distinct zones, but this is not the case. The anger meaning is still spread right across the whole of Europe (except in the north, where the gesture has vanished completely) but generally at a very low level everywhere. Only in parts of the Greek-speaking world does it survive as a commonly understood insult. As a negative it is also widely spread, again at a rather low level, but with moderate peaks of popularity in France, Spain, Tunisia, Sardinia and Yugoslavia. This combination of a very wide range with a low level of usage is typical of what one would expect for a gesture on the wane. Its once-great popularity spread it far and wide, and its decline since has left it everywhere as a remnant. Only in Tunisia does it survive as a 'saturation gesture' known to every one of our 30 informants, and with precisely the same meaning — even the same verbal accompaniment (*neegree-neegree*) — 'No money, no money'.

In its contrasting, minor meaning, as praise for food, the gesture was rare everywhere, its highest peak of occurrence being 8 out of 30 informants in northern France. Other isolated cases of praise were found in Belgium, central France and Spain, and northern Italy.

18 The Ear Touch

THE EAR TOUCH MEANINGS:

1	Effeminate	197
2	Warning	101
3	Good	32
4	Sponger	18
5	Protection	15
6	Informer	10
7	Disbelief	9
8	others	103
9	not used	715

(Based on 1,200 informants at 40 locations)

DESCRIPTION

The ear is deliberately touched with the fingers of one hand, the ear and the hand being on the same side of the body. At high intensities, both hands make contact with both ears, but this is rare. There are two major forms of this gesture, which we can call the ear-pull and the ear-flick. In the first, the ear-lobe is taken between the thumb and forefinger and tugged several times. In the second, the fingers approach the ear from behind and flick it forwards several times. Some informants said that pulling and flicking were simple alternatives, but others insisted that only pulling, or only flicking, could be used.

ORIGINS

The ear touch is one of those gestures, like the hand purse and the hand ring, which is so simple that it is capable of developing into several quite distinct symbolic gestures in different places. It has the characteristic of being widely distributed, not as a single dominant message, diffusing over a broad territory, but as a series of separate and rather rigidly localized meanings. In our field research we discovered seven such meanings and, in discussing their derivation, it is best to take them one by one, since they all appear to have different roots.

1   The ear touch as a sign of effeminacy

This is the major meaning and the symbolism involved originates from the fact that women wear ear-rings and men do not. The touching of the ear-lobe, when directed at a man says, in effect: 'You are so effeminate you ought to be wearing ear-rings, like a girl'. This is usually intended as a gross insult, and a slur on the man's masculinity. It is often specifically taken as an accusation of male homosexuality, and many of our informants told us that the message was 'you are a queer', or 'you are a pederast'. It is taken as such a serious insult in the areas where it is used that it is frequently done *about* a man, but without his knowledge. The gesturer points him out and then performs the ear touch for the benefit of his companion, saying '*he* is a queer'.

One informant gave a slightly different explanation, saying that the gesture has an early origin, dating back to the time when ship's cabin-boys were awarded a golden ear-ring at the end of a long voyage, as a reward for their sexual services to crew-members. Whether or not this second explanation has played a part in the history of the gesture, it is true to say that, at the present time, the simpler explanation of *female* ear-rings is the significance accepted by most users of the gesture today.

2   The ear touch as a warning to children

The second most common usage of the gesture was as a mimed act of tweaking a child's ear as a punishment. The adult, threatening the child, tugs at his own ear, saying in effect: 'This is what I will do to you, if you don't behave yourself.'

3   The ear touch as a gesture of praise

For one group of informants, the ear touch means: anything delicious or superlative. Most men said it applied equally to females or to food, and they used the expression 'behind the ear', pointing out that the action was always performed gently, the ear-lobe being lightly held between finger and thumb and then waggled. The derivation here is not clear, except that one informant said it came from 'kissing behind the ear'.

4   The ear touch as a protection against the Evil Eye

Here the action is essentially a tapping of the ear, and the informants who used it in this way said it was similar to touching wood, or touching metal for good luck. Although touching wood is the com-

a

b

mon superstition in the English-speaking world, in the Mediterranean region there is an even longer tradition of touching metal to ward off bad luck. This dates back to the time when metals were precious and it was the act of making contact with something of great value that was thought to have the strongest protective significance. We can only suppose that ears were touched because of the valuable metal ear-rings that were so often worn there. If metal had to be touched, then the ear-lobe was the most convenient and likely site, and this probably accounts for the survival of the gesture today.

5   The ear touch as a sign for a sponger
A man who takes advantage of another, or sponges on him for a drink, or for money, is an object of scorn. The gesturer who uses this version of the ear touch can do so either as a comment ('He is a sponger') about a third party when talking to a friend, or as a direct insult ('You are a sponger'). The origin of this usage was explained to us by one informant who said that he made the gesture about a man who came into a bar, ordered drinks, and then left without paying the bill. 'He left me hanging with the bill; he left me hanging — like an ear-lobe.'

6   The ear touch as a sign of an informer
Here the derivation is simple — it means that someone is all ears. The gesture is used to warn a friend to keep his mouth shut, because the man that is approaching will be listening to what is said and then using the information to his advantage. It means 'He is a spy', or 'He is a tell-tale who carries stories to the boss.'

7   The ear touch as a sign of disbelief
Here, again, the derivation is obvious. It means 'I can't believe my ears', or 'Do you think I am daft? Try pulling the other ear!' — the latter a variant of the more familiar 'you're pulling my leg'.

In all these cases the contact is made with the ear in a deliberate manner, and is quite distinct from the unconscious ear-fumbling or stroking that can sometimes be seen during moments of stress, or when people are deep in thought.

The Italian ear touch gesture, performed here as an ear flick with the finger approaching the ear from behind (a) and flicking it forward (b). As used by this Neapolitan, it implies that a particular man is effeminate.

DISTRIBUTION

As already mentioned, the regional distribution of this gesture shows a series of remarkably limited zones of concentration. Several of the meanings appeared only at one major site. Again, the best way to illustrate the situation will be by taking each of the seven meanings in turn:

1 Effeminacy

This is predominantly a southern Italian phenomenon, but is found throughout the Italian-speaking region, and also in Yugoslavia and Greece. It reaches its peak on the heel of Italy, where it was known to every one of our 30 informants.

2 Warning to children

This was concentrated in the Greco-Turkish region, but also had a low-level scatter in many other places, from Malta to Norway.

3 Praise

This showed a massive response (30 out of 30) in Portugal, but was totally absent in neighbouring Spain. Outside Portugal we only found two isolated cases of it, one in central France and one in northern Germany.

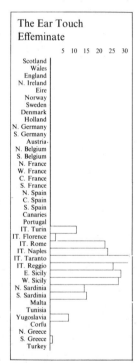

The Ear Touch
Effeminate

4 Protection against the Evil Eye

This was a Turkish meaning. Outside Turkey we found only a few cases, all in southern Italy, and although it was common in Turkey, it was totally absent from neighbouring Greece.

5 Sponger

This was restricted entirely to southern Spain and the Canary Islands, where it was moderately common in both cases.

6 Informer

This meaning was limited completely to the small island of Malta and appears to be unique to this population.

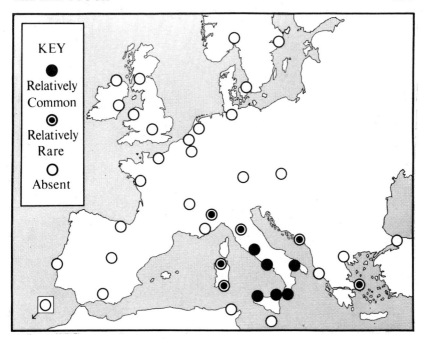

THE EAR TOUCH   Meaning: effeminate

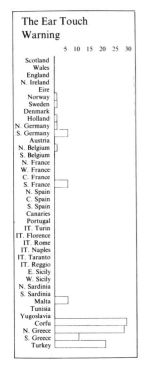

The Ear Touch
Warning

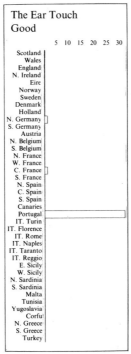

The Ear Touch
Good

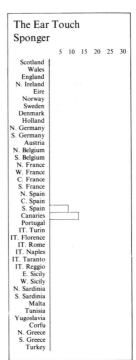

The Ear Touch
Sponger

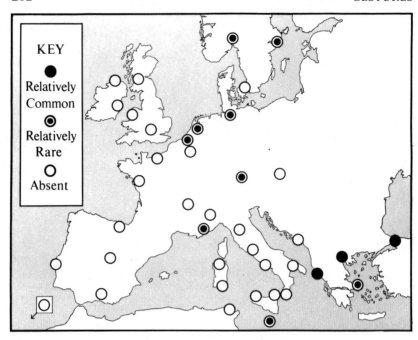

THE EAR TOUCH   Meaning: warning

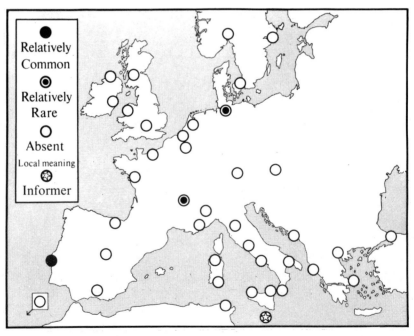

THE EAR TOUCH   Meaning: good

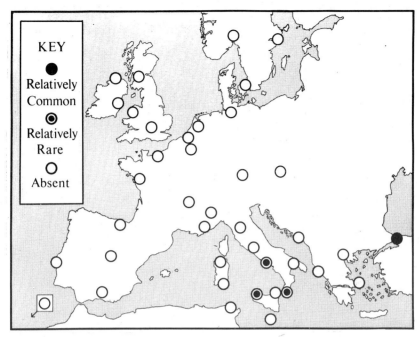

THE EAR TOUCH   Meaning: protection

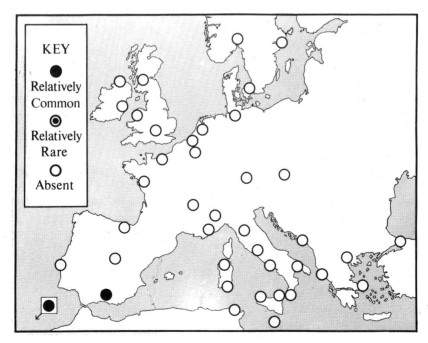

THE EAR TOUCH   Meaning: sponger

7   Disbelief
The rarest of the meanings, known only to 9 of our informants, this
was a more northerly interpretation, with its peak, if we can call it
that with such low figures, in Scotland. Five of the 9 disbelievers
were Scottish, and the others were isolated examples from Eire,
northern Belgium and northern France.

On the basis of what we have discovered in the European zone, we
would predict that, world-wide, this gesture would probably prove
to have many more local meanings, each one using the ear as the
simple starting point and then extending it symbolically in one
direction or another. Certainly, no other gesture we studied proved
to have so many highly localized meanings.

The British nose tap gesture, implying secrecy or confidentiality.

19 The Nose Tap

THE NOSE TAP
MEANINGS:

1 Complicity	110
2 Be alert	82
3 You are nosey	39
4 I am alert	31
5 He is clever	24
6 Threat	17
7 others	60
8 not used	837

(Based on 1,200 informants
at 40 locations)

DESCRIPTION

The forefinger is placed vertically alongside the nose and then gently taps it several times. Two minor variants are: the side of the nose is tapped with the tip of the forefinger; or the forefinger placed against the side of the nose is not tapped but merely held there.

ORIGINS

The gesture appears to have originated as a 'sniffing out' signal. By tapping the nose we remind our companions that we can smell out the trouble, or that someone can sniff us out. From this simple starting point, the gesture has taken off in six slightly different directions in different regions.

1   The nose tap as a sign of complicity
The message here is 'It's a secret', or 'Keep it secret', or 'Keep quiet about it'. This can be interpreted either as 'We two together have sniffed something out and we must not let anyone else in on the secret', or 'To keep our secret we must beware of nosey people trying to sniff it out'. The word 'nose' in English was slang for a police informer and was current throughout the eighteenth and nineteenth centuries. A passage from the *Cornhill Magazine* of 1862 gives a

The Sardinian nose tap, with the finger touching the tip of the nose, rather than its side. As in Britain, the dominant meaning for the gesture here is complicity or secrecy.

clear definition: 'There are a few men and women among thieves called nosers. They are so-called because they are in the secret pay of the police, giving information when the information will not lead to the crimination of themselves.' For one criminal to tap his nose to another, meant 'keep it quiet', 'there's a noser about'. From its use in the underworld, the gesture then seems to have spread to the community in general.

2   The nose tap as a friendly warning: be alert!
This message is closely related to the last one. It says 'Take care, there is danger about', and relates once more to the presence of a 'nosey' person who is trying to sniff something out. The only difference is that it does not imply any complicity or shared secret between the gesturer and the friend he is warning.

3   The nose tap as an accusation of interference
Here the nosey person is the direct recipient of the gesture, and the message becomes: 'Mind your own business', or 'Keep your nose out of my affairs', or simply 'Don't be nosey!' In this version it is often the tip of the nose that is tapped, rather than the side. Strictly speaking, this is a distinct and separate gesture, and we have handled it in the following way. If an informant, when asked the meaning of tapping the side of the nose, replies that it means 'Don't be nosey',

but then adds 'But here we usually tap the tip of the nose', we have scored this as a positive answer. If, on the other hand, he replies that tapping the side of the nose has no local meaning, but that they do have a nose-tip touch which means 'Don't be nosey', then we have scored it as a negative answer. The point is that we are investigating the recognition of the nose-side tap, and clearly, in the first instance, it would be recognized as having some meaning, and in the second instance it would not.

4   The nose tap as a sign that the gesturer is alert
For some people, the message is 'I know what's going on!', indicating that it is they themselves who are able to sniff out the truth.

5   The nose tap as a way of praising cleverness
In this case the message becomes 'He is very bright', meaning that he is good at sniffing out the truth. The difference here is that the 'sniffing' is no longer hostile or potentially dangerous. It is a comment on someone's alertness but without any element of warning, or any suggestion of a need for secrecy.

The British nose tap gesture, implying secrecy or confidentiality.

The Italian nose tap gesture acting as a friendly warning.

6   *The nose tap as a threat*

This is a special way of saying 'I am alert'. The message becomes 'I know what you are up to and if you don't stop it I will attack you.'

Clearly, all six of these meanings are very closely related to one another, and it is tempting to lump them together under the general heading of 'alertness'. But if they are separated in the way we have suggested, then gesture-mapping of the different versions reveals local biases. This then serves to illustrate the way in which a simple, basic action, such as touching the nose, can begin to lead off into a slightly different symbolic role in each region. This divergence could easily, over a long period of time, result in widely differing meanings. If these differences hardened and became more exaggerated, a situation could eventually be reached where it would be difficult to relate the various gesture meanings, one to another. With the nose tap, we seem to be at an early stage of divergence, where the relationships are still obvious.

DISTRIBUTION

Viewed as a whole, the nose tap response is confined to the British Isles, the Franco-Belgian region, the Italian-speaking region, and the island of Malta. It appears to be completely unknown in the Scandinavian countries, in Portugal and in Turkey, and is almost unknown in Holland, Germany, Austria, Spain, Tunisia, Yugoslavia and Greece. If, for the moment, we combine all six sub-meanings under the general heading of 'alertness', then we can draw up the following simple table:

Region	English-speaking zone	Franco-Belgian zone	Italian-speaking zone	Malta	Other regions
Percentage of population to which nose tap is known as some kind of 'alert' signal	61	22	51	30	10 or less

It always comes as a surprise to find a gesture that is better known in a northern region than in the gesture-rich south of Europe, but the nose tap appears to be one of these, with its strongest representation coming from the British Isles. If we now break down the general category of alertness, into its six sub-categories, it will emerge that it is in only two of its six categories that the English-speaking regions score heavily.

1   Complicity
The use of the nose tap to indicate a shared secret is confined largely to English-speaking and Italian-speaking areas, with the two peaks occurring in Scotland and Sardinia. Overall, this was the most popular sub-meaning for the gesture, accounting for 110 informants.

2   Be alert!
Almost as popular, with a total of 82 informants, was the friendly warning. This was almost non-existent in the north, but was strongly favoured on the Italian mainland, with the peak at Rome and Naples.

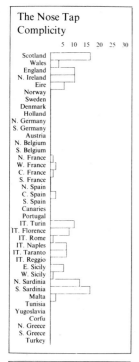

The Nose Tap
Complicity

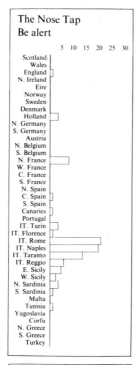

The Nose Tap
Be alert

The Nose Tap
You are nosey

The Nose Tap
I am alert

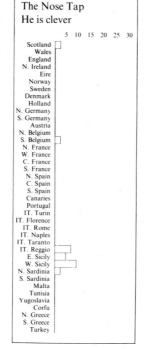

The Nose Tap
He is clever

The Nose Tap
Threat

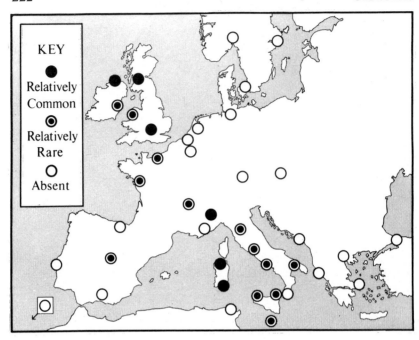

THE NOSE TAP   Meaning: complicity

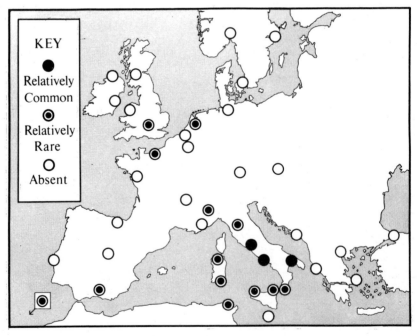

THE NOSE TAP   Meaning: be alert!

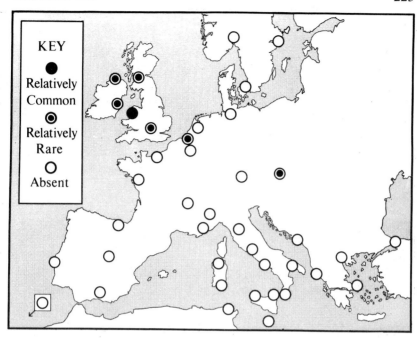

THE NOSE TAP   Meaning: you are nosey

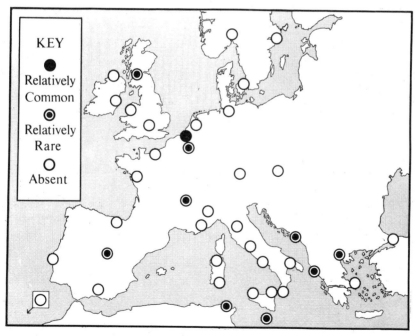

THE NOSE TAP   Meaning: I am alert

3   *You are nosey!*

As an accusation of interference, the gesture was almost entirely confined to the English-speaking region, with only two isolated cases elsewhere. Its peak came in Wales, where 50 per cent of the sample gave this interpretation.

4   *I am alert!*

This version had a wide scatter but at a very low level everywhere except in the Flemish-speaking zone of northern Belgium, where it reached the 40 per cent level.

5   *He is clever*

This interpretation has not been mapped because it showed no real peak anywhere. It was confined mostly to the southern Italian-speaking region, especially Sicily.

6   *Threat*

Again, a low-level, wide scatter, with no strong peaks, the highest level being 13 per cent in northern Sardinia and Malta.

20 The Palm-back V-Sign

**THE PALM-BACK
V-SIGN MEANING:**

1	Victory	390
2	Two	213
3	Sexual insult	156
4	Horns	11
5	others	43
6	not used	387

(Based on 1,200 informants
at 40 locations)

DESCRIPTION

The hand is raised in front of the body, with the palm towards the
gesturer's face and the forefinger and middle finger extended to form
a V shape. The other two fingers are fully bent. The hand is jerked
upwards in the air one or more times.

ORIGINS

Although the dominant meaning for this gesture is 'victory', we
want to consider first its role as an obscene insult. This is the older
meaning and its true origin has been the subject of much debate.
Even today, its primary derivation is still in doubt, and the best we
can do is to present the ten rival explanations that have been put
forward. The reason why there are so many is because of the strong
taboo associated with the gesture (its public use has often been
heavily penalized). As a result, there is a tendency to shy away from
discussing it in detail. It is 'known to be dirty' and is passed on from
generation to generation by people who simply accept it as a recognized obscenity without bothering to analyse it. When asked to
do so, they do not like to admit that they really cannot explain its
precise form. Were it a simple phallic insult, like the forearm jerk,
there would be no problem — it would represent an upthrusting

penis. But a V-shaped penis creates something of a quandary. True, the kangaroo possesses a forked penis, but to suggest that that animal had anything to do with the symbolic origins of the obscene V-sign is too far-fetched. Hence the dilemma. Here, now, are the ten ways in which people have sought to solve this dilemma:

1   The obscene V-sign as a corrupted form of the Victory sign

This is one explanation we can dispose of with ease, but it has been seriously suggested and must therefore be examined. The idea is that the Churchillian Victory sign, introduced during the Second World War, was deliberately reversed as an insult. The Churchillian version is performed with the palm facing *outward*, away from the face of the gesturer. By rotating the hand through 180 degrees, it has been suggested that it was possible to create an insulting distortion of the original message. In other words, the reversal of the hand posture reversed the meaning of the sign — from victory to defeat. Instead of saying 'I wish you victory', the gesture now said 'I wish you defeat', rather in the way in which K.O. is the opposite, both in form and meaning, of O.K.

The historical facts are against this explanation. In the case of the V-for-Victory sign we know, for once, the exact date on which the gesture was invented and the name of its inventor. It was not Churchill himself, although it was he who made it famous. It was a Belgian lawyer named Victor De Lavelaye (inspired perhaps by his own forename?) and the date was January 14th, 1941. De Lavelaye was unhappy about the use of the letters R.A.F. as a resistance graffito. The letters were being scrawled on walls in Belgium by the underground, as a method of insulting the Nazis, but in a foreign language they lacked clarity and he was looking for something simpler and more universally understood. He hit on the idea of V for Victory because it fitted not only the English word, but also the Flemish *vrijheid* and the French *victoire*. After his initial broadcast, proposing the V, the B.B.C. mounted a highly successful propaganda campaign employing the morse code symbol for V (dot-dot-dot-dash) and the opening bars of Beethoven's Fifth Symphony. It was after this that Churchill took up the sign and used it publicly at every opportunity. Nazi propagandists became so alarmed at the success of the symbol, that they started their own counter-project, V for *Viktoria*, but it was too late. The Allied V-sign had swept occupied Europe, and was already indelibly associated with the anti-Nazi movement.

We have gone into the history of the Victory-V in some detail because, by establishing beyond doubt its late date of arrival on the scene, we can eliminate it completely from the list of possible candidates to explain the origin of the insult-V. The latter has been known for centuries and nothing as modern as the Victory sign can possibly have played a part in its development. The earliest record of the insult-V we have been able to find comes from the sixteenth-century writings of François Rabelais, in the following passage: Panurge is carrying on a gestural 'duel'. He makes an explicit copulation sign and then ... 'stretched he out the forefinger, and middle finger or medical of his right hand, holding them asunder as much as he could, and thrusting them towards Thaumast.' He then makes another rude sign, and his enemy 'began to waxe somewhat pale, and to tremble ...'

That was written in 1532, and in the next century, in 1611, George Chapman, in his comedy *May Day*, has the following line: 'As often as he turns his back to me, I shall be here V with him.' This passage is quoted in late Victorian times to illustrate that 'to make V', as it was called, was a 'derisive' gesture.

Coming nearer the present day, the earliest photograph of an insult-V we have been able to find is one taken at a football match in the year 1913, where one of the watching crowd is unmistakably making the gesture as a rude sign. We also went to the length of

The earliest known photograph of the insulting British version of the palm-back V-sign gesture. This picture was taken at a football match in 1913.

Conservative leader Mrs Thatcher making a palm-back V-sign at a
moment of triumph, following an election gain. She appears to be using
the insulting version of the gesture, under the impression that it is the
Victory-V sign (Associated Press Photo).

broadcasting an appeal for information of any pre-war use of the
insult-V and were rewarded with letters from men who had both
seen and used it long before the war. Taken together, this evidence
makes the insulting version the original one and the Victory version
a very late arrival. There is some evidence, in fact, that Churchill,
unaware of the existence of the rude, palm-back form, originally
used this in error on certain occasions. There is early film of him
unwittingly making the rude V-sign at his troops and thereby in-
advertently telling them to 'get stuffed', instead of wishing them
victory in battle. Since all later film records show him performing the
gesture palm-out, it seems certain that someone must have taken
him on one side and gently explained the problem, so that the final
and surviving form of the Victory sign became fixed and distinct
from its unsavoury predecessor. (Even today, however, not all poli-
ticians have learnt this lesson, as our photograph of Mrs Thatcher
reveals.)

*"I understand you've
sacked your gardener."*

The palm-back V-sign is so well
known in Britain, as an insult,
that it has become the subject of
a *Punch* cartoon by Albert.
(Reproduced by permission of *Punch.*)

2   The obscene V-sign as a modified cuckold horn-sign

Farmer and Henley in their vast *Slang Dictionary*, published at the
turn of the century, consider the V-sign insult to be a form of
cuckold sign, with the forked fingers representing the cuckold's
horns. They say:

'V = a symbol of cuckoldry, the letter being occasionally printed
in that connection. Hence to make V = to make horns: the first and
second fingers are derisively forked out.' It is always possible that,
when the English imported the continental cuckold sign they distorted it and, instead of employing the first and fourth fingers to make
the pair of horns, used the first and second instead. If this is the case,
then this would probably be the originating source for the modern
insult-V, but the cuckold sign died out long ago in the British Isles,
and it seems more likely that some other symbolism was involved.

3   The obscene V-sign as an enlarged phallus

In Roman times, the obscene, phallic finger-jerk was the middle-
finger jerk, done with that digit alone erect. The only difference
between this ancient insult and the modern insult-V is that the latter
employs an extra finger, and it has been suggested that this is no
more than a symbolic amplification — a doubled, or enlarged phallus. Certainly many men today think of the gesture as essentially
phallic and the gesture is sometimes done with the two fingers
parallel instead of spread wide apart. By both doubling *and* spreading the phallic element, it creates an enlarged diameter and thereby
increases its insulting power. Against this argument must be set the
fact that, if one wishes to amplify the phallic symbol, then the use of
the whole fist and forearm, as in the forearm jerk, is surely the most
effective and dramatic way of doing so.

4   *The obscene V-sign as a double penis*

A slight variant on the last interpretation is one that sees the two forked fingers as representing, not one enlarged penis, but two separate penises. One informant explained to us that he uses the gesture to mean 'one penis for her vagina and one for her anus'.

5   *The obscene V-sign as symbolically inserted fingers*

A more popular explanation is that, instead of being symbolically phallic, the forked fingers represent merely themselves, inserted into the vagina during sexual foreplay. The spreading of the forefinger and middle finger into the V shape then represents an attempt to provide maximum vaginal stimulation by stretching the passage as widely as possible.

The insulting V-sign gesture seen in a British restaurant.

6   The obscene V-sign as spread female legs
Another popular interpretation switches the symbolism from the
male to the female. Here, the sign is read as meaning 'her legs are
wide apart, like this, ready for copulation'. There is some evidence to
support this, from the Arab world. There, there is an obscene gesture
in which the forked fingers are jerked upwards several times, under
the gesturer's nose, so that the tip of his nose protrudes through the
V shape, as if it were a penis being pushed through the legs. By
performing a low-intensity version of this gesture, with the jerked
hand approaching, but not actually touching the nose, an action is
made which looks exactly like the typical insult-V.

7   The obscene V-sign as open female genitals
Here the spread fingers represent the spread labia of the female
genitals, and the argument is the same as for the last interpretation.
Some people see the Arab nose-jerk gesture in this way. Others see
the sign simply as a gesture saying 'you have an open orifice'.

8   The obscene V-sign as the female pubic triangle
The dark pubic patch of the human female forms a natural V-shape
which has been used by artists as a female symbol since prehistoric
times. It has been suggested that the insult-V sign is no more than a
digital representation of this triangle.

9   The obscene V-sign as an eye-poking gesture
One suggestion that sees the insult-V as a hybrid gesture, envisages it
as a combination of the ancient middle-finger jerk with the two-
fingered eye-poking gesture. The latter is normally performed palm-
down, with the stiff first and second fingers aimed directly and
horizontally towards the enemy's eyes, but in the hybrid form, this
hand posture is seen as twisted round to add to it the quality of the
upward, middle-finger jerk. The idea is that this gives two hostile
elements at the same time: I will poke your eyes out + up yours.

10   The obscene V-sign as a covert middle-finger jerk
This final explanation also takes the ancient middle-finger gesture as
its starting point, but sees it modified in a different way. G. Legman,
the expert on erotic folklore, tells us that, during the 1960s, when
American hippies took over the Victory-V sign as a more generalized peace sign, they would deliberately reverse it into the palm-
back, obscene form, as a way of insulting the police. In the United

States, the obscene V-sign is not normally used as an overt insult. In its place there is the classic middle-finger gesture. This is such a strongly offensive American gesture that to direct it towards the police would produce immediate retaliation of a more-than-gestural kind. In order to insult the police in a way which was sufficiently ambiguous to prevent them from taking any action, the hippies rotated their peace-signs, still shouting 'peace', but giving what, to their friends, was clearly a veiled form of the phallic finger. Legman says, 'the gesture so made is a covert form of the usual single-finger *digitus impudicus*.'

This last explanation reveals the way in which the insult-V can develop independently as an obscene gesture — re-evolving in another country and at another time. Clearly this particular development was parasitic on the already existing Victory-V or peace-V sign, and could not have occurred at any time before the Second World War. Since we have demonstrated that the obscene V-sign did exist before that period, it follows that the gesture must have originated at least twice, and the chances are that it may even have had several separate beginnings. There is no way of proving this, however, and there is no way, either, of choosing between the great variety of suggested sources for this gesture. Some, we suspect, are mere inventions; others have no doubt played an important supportive role, providing a back-up for the use of the gesture once they have been concocted. But which of the many was the primary, originating symbolism, when the gesture first began, we cannot say. Perhaps it began as a variant of the old horn-sign and then, when the cuckold insult faded away in the British Isles, it lingered on, without any supporting explanation until, after many years had passed, more specifically sexual interpretations began to be placed on the way the forked fingers were held. Unfortunately, early records of such items of human behaviour are so scarce that we may never know the answer.

The fact that the origins of the insult-V are so confused and contradictory does not, however, seem to have reduced its popularity. According to Iona and Peter Opie in their study of *The Lore and Language of Schoolchildren*, it is now the most favoured of all offensive gestures made by British children, having supplanted that long-time winner, the cock-a-snook. The Opies wrote their book in 1959, and since then a famous event has occurred which has not only increased the popularity of the gesture even more, but has also

'Please accept this poster as a recognition by Barker & Dobson of your invaluable services over the years in selling Victory V. The poster commemorates the famous incident at Hickstead on Sunday August 15th when Harvey Smith raised his fingers in a Victory V salute. Some people still insist on mistaking this Churchillian gesture for something improper. But we have always assumed it was an endorsement by Harvey of a brand he has known and loved since he was knee-high to a hurdle. You can judge for yourself when Harvey repeats the performance in the new Victory V television commercial which will be entertaining millions of viewers beginning mid-November.

Right Show-jumper Harvey Smith making his V-sign gesture at the Hickstead meeting, as seen on British television. He is clearly using the palm-back version of the gesture. *Above* Harvey Smith recently used the sign to advertise Victory-V lozenges, but now the hand position has been reversed.

provided it with a name: The Harvey Smith.

The incident occurred at the British Jumping Derby at Hickstead on August 15th, 1971. Harvey Smith, a brilliant and colourful show-jumping personality, was competing on a horse called Mattie Brown, with which he had won the title the previous year. Before the contest he had an argument with the owner of the Hickstead course who, in the presence of press reporters had said that he thought Harvey Smith had 'no chance' of winning again. This made Harvey Smith even more determined to succeed, and succeed he did. In his autobiography he describes what then followed:

> I felt overwhelmed by a mixture of pleasure, relief, relaxation of tension, and as I circled my little horse before pulling him up I had no thought in my mind of gesturing in any way. Then, absolutely on the spur of the moment, I raised two fingers on my right hand in the direction of that balcony overlooking the Devil's Dyke (the judges' balcony). It was a V for Victory; it was meant to show how delighted I was that Mattie Brown had become the only horse ever to win the British Jumping Derby in successive years. If it was also interpreted as an 'up you' to those on that balcony who had made it plain that they wanted Mattie Brown to lose, then all well and good ... But above all, the gesture was meant to be light-hearted and the crowd received it as such.

Fortunately for the history of the gesture, but unfortunately for Harvey Smith, the Hickstead judges did not react in a light-hearted way. Five hours after the event was over, they sent the rider a telegram which read: 'Because of your disgusting behaviour at the end of your jump-off in the Derby the directors and I have disqualified you and all prize-money [£2,000] is forfeited. You will also be reported to the stewards of the B.S.J.A. [The British Show Jumping Association].' It was signed by the owner of the Hickstead course.

Harvey Smith fought this decision and, after an enquiry at which a television recording of the incident was screened, it was decided that the gesture had, after all, been light-heartedly made. He won the day and his victory in the jumping event was reinstated. But to his annoyance he was never allowed to forget that gesture. It rapidly became part of British folklore and his name became synonymous with it. It was no longer the 'two fingers' gesture, or the 'up yours' — it was now simply 'The Harvey Smith' and it has remained so in the eight years since he made it. A sympathizer, writing to Harvey

Smith shortly after the incident, pointed out to him the unusual nature of his achievement: 'Dear Mr Smith, It is given to very few of us to achieve the distinction of being responsible for introducing a new phrase into the English language. "To be or not to be", "England expects", "You never had it so good" have stood the test of time. Now it seems we are to have a new one. Many a lady will, in future, be relieved of the necessity of making a certain unladylike gesture by simply saying instead: "A Harvey Smith to you".'

In 1977 the title became even more entrenched when the landlord of an inn at Petteridge, in Kent, re-named his establishment 'The Harvey Smith' and hung outside it a newly painted inn-sign displaying a picture of the show-jumper in the act of making the famous gesture. Local civic officials called it 'distasteful' and there was a new controversy, but the landlord reported that his trade had immediately doubled.

We have told this story in some detail because it is precisely this kind of detail we are lacking with so many of the other gestures. Some such tale could perhaps have been told about a medieval jester who became famous for 'cocking-a-snook', which would help us to understand that gesture's early history, but such records do not seem to exist. In the case of The Harvey Smith we are lucky enough to have been able to watch a title for a gesture enter the language and, in so doing, to strengthen its hold on the popular imagination.

DISTRIBUTION

The obscene interpretation of the palm-back V-sign is confined almost entirely to the British Isles, where it is known to virtually the entire population. Of our English-speaking informants, 95 per cent viewed it in this way. Apart from four isolated cases, it was absent from the whole of the rest of our study region, with one exception. Significantly, that exception was the island of Malta, where 30 per cent interpreted it in the British way. This is not surprising when one remembers that nearly all Maltese speak English, read English publications and see English films and TV programmes. The British colonial influence on the island is still enormous, with regard to customs and culture, even though there has been complete political independence for a number of years.

So we are faced with the rare occurrence of a gesture unique to British culture. Why it should have failed to travel and spread its range is not entirely clear, but we can offer a partial explanation.

Outside the English-speaking region, the role of the insult-V is taken over by the forearm jerk. The same verbal accompaniments are employed: 'up yours', 'get stuffed', 'piss off', 'get lost', and so on. In the British Isles, this usage of the forearm jerk is not common. Instead, it is used as a vulgar sexual compliment. In other words, the rest of Europe has a perfectly good obscene jerk of its own — the gestural niche is filled — and they do not need ours to add to their repertoire. We, having our own two-fingered version, do not need theirs and so, when we borrow it we convert it into a new message — a lewdly admiring comment, rather than a straight insult.

We cannot be certain about the relative antiquity of these two alternative gestures, but we do know that the middle-finger jerk is more ancient than either, with 2,000 years of history behind it. Could it perhaps be that that is the ancestral gesture, from which both the others have stemmed, by a process of amplification? At the present time it seems a reasonable guess.

Leaving the insulting version of the palm-back gesture, we must briefly consider its other usages. Since it is not known as an obscenity outside the British Isles, it is available for other interpretations. Almost everywhere it is commonly mistaken for the Churchillian victory sign. Non-English speaking communities make no distinction between the palm-front and the palm-back forms of the gesture. They see both versions as meaning the same thing: victory or peace. In Austria and Yugoslavia almost everyone interprets the gesture this way, but elsewhere the average response is nearer to 50 per cent. In Greece and Turkey the figures are lower, and there is a special reason for this, which can be understood by looking at the third gesture map.

This last map shows the distribution for the third major meaning of the palm-back V-sign. Here it means simply 'two'. The gesturer is seen as holding up his hand to signal two of something — two drinks, please, or two chairs needed. This was an interpretation given by a small number of people almost everywhere, but in Greece and Turkey the numbers are much higher (an average of 69 per cent for the whole region). This explains why the local scores for the 'victory' interpretations were much lower than average (only 22 per cent), but it leaves the question of why Greeks and Turks should be so keen to use this particular form of hand posture for signalling two of something. As far as the Greeks are concerned, the answer lies in the presence of a savagely insulting local gesture, the *moutza*. We have mentioned this briefly before. It is the Byzantine gesture symbolizing

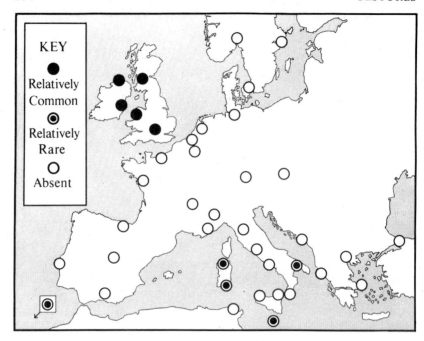

THE PALM-BACK V-SIGN   Meaning: sexual insult

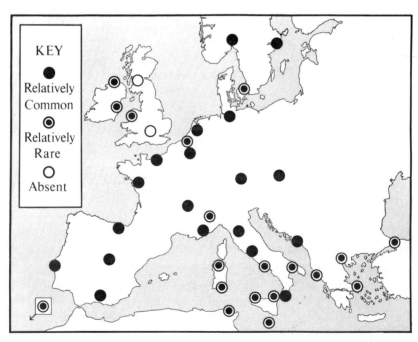

THE PALM-BACK V-SIGN   Meaning: victory

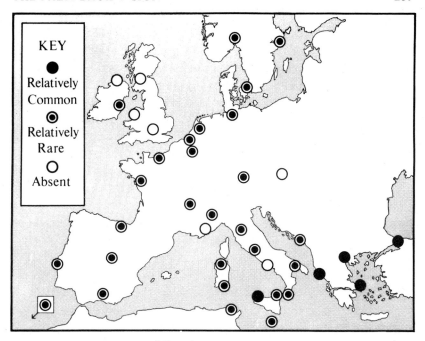

THE PALM-BACK V-SIGN Meaning: two

The Palm-back V-Sign
Sexual insult

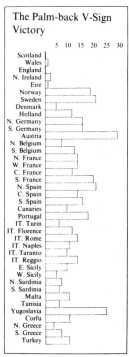

The Palm-back V-Sign
Victory

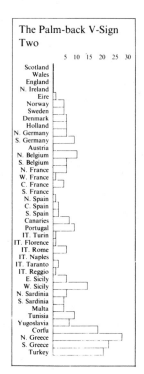

The Palm-back V-Sign
Two

the thrusting of a handful of filth into the face of a paraded prisoner. In it, the flat hand pushes forward towards the insulted man's face, as if miming the act. Any gestures remotely resembling this action are tabooed for fear of being mistaken for the gross insult. There is a particular form of the *moutza*, known as the half-*moutza*, in which only the first two fingers are erect, the third and fourth being fully bent. This is a slightly milder insult — only 'half a handful' is being thrust forward — but it is still a strong enough insult to be taken seriously. Anything similar to it must be avoided, and this includes, of course, ordering two drinks with two raised fingers and the palm facing the companion. Anyone ordering two drinks is therefore extremely careful — in Greece — to do so with the palm held back. This idea is so strongly ingrained, that when shown the palm-back V-sign, many Greeks think immediately of their special form of signalling 'two, please'. Hence the high scores in their region for this particular interpretation, and the low scores for the rival meaning.

This explanation is less satisfactory for the Turks, because we were unable to find any evidence of the existence of the *moutza* gesture in modern Istanbul. We can only suppose that, in Byzantine days, it was present but has since disappeared, leaving behind the special 'two' sign as a last vestige of its earlier influence.

There is one final interpretation of a minor kind that deserves a brief comment. Eleven of our informants (out of the total of 1,200) saw the palm-back V-sign as meaning 'horns' or 'cuckold'. They were scattered across various sites in France, Spain, Portugal and Italy. They were giving us, in effect, an ancient interpretation of the gesture, the one that we said earlier might well have played a part in its ancient development. They slightly strengthen our suspicions, but we remain unconvinced. Several of the rival claims are equally appealing. The truth is that we will probably never know, because the detailed study of the origins of symbolic gestures has never been taken seriously until now, and the literature on the subject is somewhat sparse. We can only hope that when new gestures arise in the future, they will not suffer the same fate.

Beckoning and Waving

In addition to questioning our informants about the 20 key symbolic gestures, we also asked them to demonstrate the way in which they beckon someone to come towards them and the manner in which they wave goodbye to someone who is leaving. The form of the movement used in each case was recorded, noting the position of the hand and the movements made. This was done because preliminary observations indicated that there were regional differences in these signals and we wanted to find out whether there were characteristic zonal distributions of the various forms.

It soon emerged that for beckoning there were two dominant hand postures: *palm-up* and *palm-down*. Other differences, such as the number of fingers used, varied erratically and were of less importance. There were also a number of minor methods employed, such as beckoning with the head, or making a sideways sweep of the arm, but these too showed little in the way of characteristic geographical distribution and we have ignored them when producing gesture maps. In making these maps we have simply combined all cases where the beckoning hand was held palm uppermost, regardless of how many fingers were employed in making the movement (for the first map) and all cases where it was held with the palm facing downwards, again regardless of other details (for the second map).

With waving there was a similar situation, only here the two dominant postures were *palm-show* and *palm-hide*. If the palm of the waver was visible to the person at whom the action was directed, then, regardless of whether the hand was waved laterally, vertically, or was held more or less still, we classified the gesture as palm-show. If the palm was not visible — that is, if it was held towards the gesturer himself — we called the gesture a palm-hide wave. When this distinction was made and two further gesture maps were prepared, it became clear that, as with beckoning, there was a characteristic distribution for each of these major types.

When these four responses — palm-up beckon/palm-down beckon/palm-show wave/palm-hide wave — are examined as a group, it emerges that each country in our study zone can be classified as belonging to one of five categories, depending on their particular beckon/wave combination. The categories are as follows:

	Palm-up beckon	Palm-down beckon	Palm-show wave	Palm-hide wave
A	COMMON	*rare*	COMMON	*rare*
B	*rare*	COMMON	COMMON	*rare*
C	*rare*	COMMON	*rare*	COMMON
D	*moderate*	*moderate*	COMMON	*rare*
E	*rare*	COMMON	*moderate*	*moderate*

TABLE I

Category A   The combination of palm-up beckon and palm-show wave was found throughout northern and central Europe, covering the following regions: British Isles, Scandinavia, Holland, Germany, Austria, Belgium and France. It also occurred in Yugoslavia.

Category B   The combination of palm-down beckon and palm-show wave was found in Spain, Malta, Tunisia, S. Greece and Turkey. In other words, this was confined to countries bordering the Mediterranean, but excluding Italy, Corfu and N. Greece.

Category C   The combination of palm-down beckon and palm-hide wave was confined to the Italian-speaking region, including not only the mainland, but also the islands of Sicily and Sardinia.

Category D   In this special category there was no dominance of one type of beckon over the other, but there was a strong preference for the palm-show wave. This arrangement was encountered in Portugal and N. Greece.

Category E   Here there was a strong preference for the palm-down beckon, but no dominance of one type of wave over the other. This arrangement was found only on the island of Corfu.

The significant feature of this summary is that there is only one clear-cut combination missing, namely the palm-up beckon with the

Palm-up Beckon

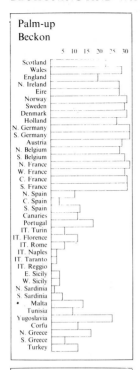

Palm-down Beckon

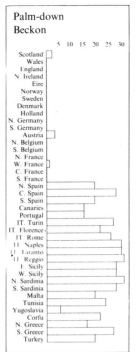

Palm-show Wave

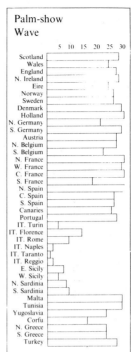

Palm-hide Wave

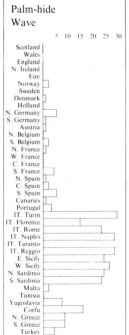

Italian beckon.

Italian wave.

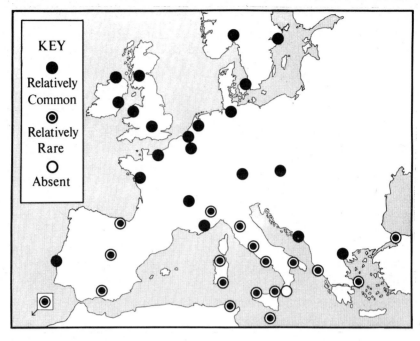

PALM-UP BECKON

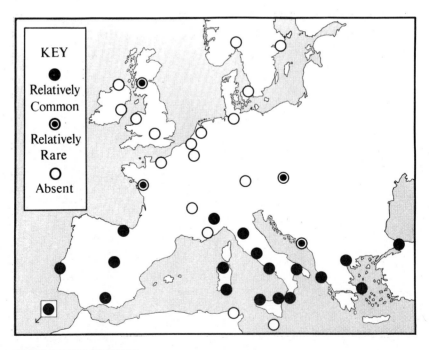

PALM-DOWN BECKON

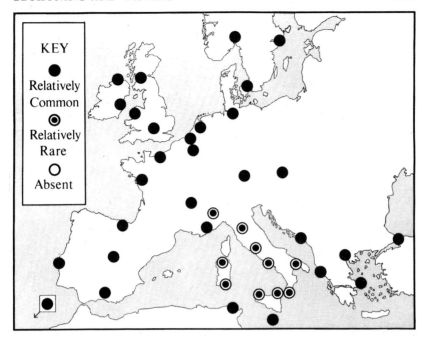

PALM-SHOW WAVE

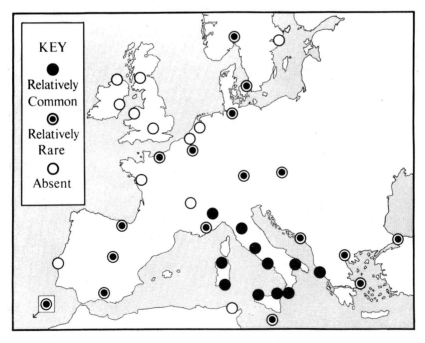

PALM-HIDE WAVE

palm-hide wave. The reason for this is simple enough: the two actions look almost identical and can easily be confused. The palm-hide wave is typically Italian and to a northern European it appears as if the waver is beckoning. Conversely, the northern, palm-up beckon looks like a wave to an Italian. Even in the two minor categories, D and E, where the distinctions are less sharp, one of the two confusable gestures is rare in each case, thus reducing ambiguity.

This is an elegant example of the way in which local gesture systems develop in such a way that signal-clarity is achieved.

Gesture Boundaries

There are cases where a gesture is known and used in one city but not the next, and instances where a gesture is used to convey quite distinct and different messages in two adjacent sites. Most cases of gesture disappearance and meaning-change can be shown to correspond with national or linguistic boundaries. This is hardly surprising considering the cohesive effects of national identity and the use of a common language. What is surprising, however, is to find that some gestures occur in one part of a linguistically homogeneous country but not another, or to discover that they change their meaning within a nationally and linguistically defined region. Gesture boundaries which do not correspond to a customs or language barrier present a special and tantalizing problem for the simple reason that they need to be explained in terms other than nationality and language. There are several instances of intra-national and intra-linguistic boundaries that invite study. Both the ring gesture in France, which switches from *O.K.* in the north, to *zero* in the south, and the chin flick in Italy, which moves from a dismissive gesture in the north to a simple negative in the south, are interesting examples of meaning change, while the head toss, which is virtually absent in northern Italy and common in the south, offers a clear case of gestural disappearance within the same country.

The gesture that we chose to study in this connection was the head toss. On our initial gesture-mapping trip through Italy we had discovered a boundary for the head toss between Rome and Naples. While almost every one of our Roman informants had reported that the gesture was absent in the capital, nearly every one of their Neapolitan counterparts said that it was used locally. The question now arose as to the exact nature and location of the head toss boundary. Was the boundary defined by a steep and dramatic disappearance of the gesture or was there a gradual decline as one proceeded north? Similarly, was Naples no more than an isolated outpost, surrounded by a sea of headshakers, or was there a gestural connection between it and those sites that we had sampled to the south? These questions and the prospect of being able to map the occurrence of a gesture across a wide expanse of territory prompted us to embark on a detailed study of the exact location of the head toss in the region.

The method that we selected for this operation differed in several respects from the one we had employed in our '20 gestures' study. Instead of requiring informants to report on current practice in that area we asked them to describe what they did personally. Adults of both sexes and all ages were interviewed and our question, very simply, was 'How do you indicate "no" with your head?' This question was followed by another, which consisted in asking the respondent to identify the message that was conveyed by the chin flick. We had decided to examine the geographical distribution of this second gesture because we had already discovered that the disappearance of the head toss was associated with the transition of the chin flick from a straightforward negative to a gesture of disinterest. Responses to the first question were assigned to one of five categories, so that a respondent was regarded as (1) only using a head toss (2) using the head toss more frequently than the head shake (3) using both with roughly equal frequency (4) using the head shake more frequently than the head toss or (5) only using the head shake. This provided us with a five-point scale on which to place each informant. Responses to the second question were recorded verbatim and later subjected to the type of analysis we had used for our 20 key gestures.

When we began the study we were in command of two facts, namely that all Italians use the head shake and that Neapolitans use the head toss while Romans do not, and the task that confronted us was to locate not only the point or area at which the gesture disappeared between these two sites, but also the extension of this boundary across the full extent of Italy. It goes without saying that this type of operation, far from being organized along established principles, involves a high degree of surmise and guess-work. It also inevitably requires that one retrace one's steps in order to obtain information between the areas of extreme response. In order to complete the study it was necessary to sample a variety of sites from Rome to Naples and beyond, and from the Tyrrhenian coast to towns on the Adriatic. By the end of the head toss survey we had visited at least 75 cities, towns and villages and interviewed more than 750 people. The information we had assembled allowed us to plot the frequency of the head toss from one side of Italy to the other. This information is depicted in Map A on pp. 254–5. Here each circle represents ten respondents. A solid circle indicates that at least 80 per cent of the respondents reported using the head toss and at least half the sample used the gesture at least half the time. An open circle indicates that at least 80 per cent of the sample denied using the head toss, and a grey circle represents a sample of intermediate character. As a shorthand, solid circles can be taken to indicate a dominant head toss area, grey circles to indicate an infrequent use of this gesture, and open circles to indicate the presence of an exclusive head shake area. This three-fold classification allows us to identify two separate isokines for the head toss. The first, which encompasses and contains all the solid circles, begins from just north of Naples. It starts by encircling the city and then extends south, hugging the coastline until it goes off the map and re-emerges again on the Adriatic where once again a preponderance of head tosses are found beside the coast. Our second isokine separates the grey circles from the open circles. Here we find the line begins just north of Naples, moves north-east across the calf of Italy until it reaches the main autostrada coming down the east coast, at which point it dips south, and then rises again to include the Gargano peninsula.

In order to make sense of our informants' responses it has been necessary to construct these two separate isokines. Not only does this give some coherence to the pattern that we observe, but it also enables us to identify the 'steepness' of the transition from the dominant head-toss and the dominant head-shake region. Steepness can, of course, be seen as the closeness of the two isokines, and it is clear that the most dramatic case of steep transition occurs just north of Naples where the dominant head-toss region and the dominant head-shake region come to within 10 kilometres of each other. We are accustomed to the fact that gestures differ between countries, and even that they change within the same country, but to discover a gesture boundary with such a narrow band of transition was, by any standards, quite unexpected.

We decided, therefore, to pursue this issue with a fine-grained analysis of the area just north of Naples. In our original '20 gestures' study we had already plotted the distribution of the head toss in ten separate Italian sites, and then gone on to a detailed analysis of its use within the Italian Meridian. The third phase of this study involved a more powerful microscope, as it were, where each point represented the response of a single individual rather than a summary index of the responses of 30 or 10 informants. In practical terms our procedure involved an extension of the method used in the second phase of the study. Map B, on page 255, shows the area that was sampled, roughly the region extending north of Naples between the main autostrada and the coastline. It shows quite clearly that exclusive and dominant head-tossers are to be found in Naples and the area extending northwards towards the Volturno river. It also shows that the gesture has almost completely disappeared by the time one reaches the Garigliano river and the Aurunci mountains. Diagram I, on page 251, has been constructed by dividing the area between Naples and the Aurunci into eight discrete zones. It gives the numbers of people who reported personally using the head toss in each zone and provides a graph of the transformed percentage data. The graph shows that there are three significant drops in the use of the head toss as one moves north; the first occurs between the Volturno and the flat area to the north of the river, the second between this plain and the southern slopes of the Massico range, and the third between the northern slopes of the Massico and the southern banks of the Garigliano. If we combine the first two steps we see that a short and simple journey from the Volturno to the ridge of the Massico will take one from an area in which almost every individual uses the gesture to an area where only one in every three people uses the gesture (a distance of about 16 kilometres), and that an extension of this journey would bring one to a region where virtually nobody uses the gesture (a total distance of about 21 kilometres).

We are now in a position to answer our initial question about the nature and location of the head-toss boundary in Italy. Map A showed that there are two distinct isokines for the gesture. Map B and Diagram 1, which provide a more detailed examination of the area north of Naples, show how the movement of the head toss has been constrained by the geography of the region.

The clue to the pattern of the head-toss boundary in southern Italy consists in the fact that the head toss is also the most dominant gesture of negation in Greece. Southern Italy was well known to the Greeks at the time of the Odyssey. Odysseus, having escaped the amorous overtures of Circe, had visited the land of the Cimmerians in the area, and in the 11th book we also find mention of the region between present-day Naples and the Phlegrean Fields, reputedly the entrance to the Underworld. Aside from their epic encounters, the Greeks also engaged in trading in this area — from about 1400 to 1200 B.C. — but it was not until the foundation of a small settlement on the island of Ischia in about 690 B.C. by a group of Euboeans that we see the beginnings of *Magna Graecia*. This island settlement enjoyed only a brief existence and a more permanent post was later established at Cumae, which is just north of Pozzuoli and about 20

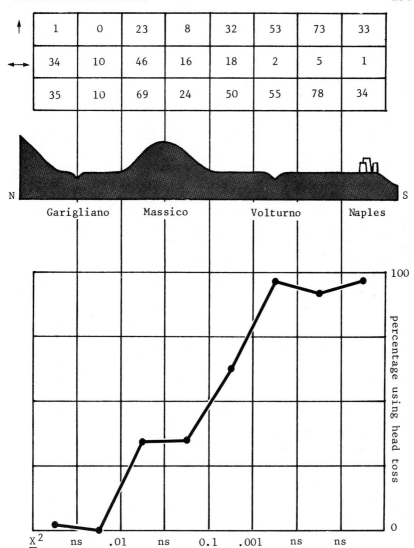

1	0	23	8	32	53	73	33
34	10	46	16	18	2	5	1
35	10	69	24	50	55	78	34

Garigliano Massico Volturno Naples

$\underline{X}^2$ ns .01 ns 0.1 .001 ns ns

DIAGRAM 1 Numbers of respondents in the eight zones between
Naples and the Aurunci mountains who reported using the head toss (↟),
and the numbers who reported using the head shake only (↔).

kilometres from Naples. In time, other outposts appeared at Naxos,
Catane, Rhegium, Syracuse, Metapontum, Tarentum, and so on, and
by the time Cumae had begun to decline Neapolis had begun to
increase in influence over the immediate area. The name Neapolis,
new city, was probably given to the area by a group of new Greek

colonists. Hitherto it had been called Partenope, after the Siren who had flung herself into the sea for the love of Odysseus. Up until the fourth century B.C. Naples was a great metropolis, centre of the Greek trading posts in the North Tyrrhenian Sea. In 326 B.C. all this changed. After a two-year siege she fell to the Romans, and soon afterwards other Greek settlements capitulated. Nevertheless, *Magna Graecia*, and the whole ethos of Greek life, continued to exert a long and lasting influence on the Romans and the indigenous population.

We know that Cumae gave its alphabet to the Etruscans and the Romans, and a casual stroll through any local museum will be sufficient to remind the visitor of the Greek presence in southern Italy. But the fact that goes unnoticed, and which this study serves to disclose, is that the Greeks also left an indelible mark on the everyday actions of the local inhabitants in the form of the head toss. Pompey, Virgil, Cicero and Ovid, not to mention Nero, were all ardent Grecophils, and Roman contact with what had once been *Magna Graecia* only served to reinforce their respect for things Greek. They adopted many of their habits and much of the Greek point of view, but for all this emulation it was never a wholesale borrowing. One aspect of Greek colonial life that the Romans did not borrow was the head toss, but here it is important to note that although they did not take on every aspect of Greek behaviour, equally they did nothing to suppress or discourage its continued use by others.

If we compare the information in Map A with any map depicting Greek settlements on the Tyrrhenian coast we find a surprising fit — a fit not only in terms of the areas in which the Greeks settled, but one in terms of names of towns in the area. We find places like Cumae, Naples and, further to the south, Paestum and Agropoli. As we know, the Greeks established coastal outposts, and it is here that we found a pronounced use of the head toss. The Greek settlement argument does not, however, explain the presence of the dominant head-toss zone on the Adriatic coast, because they never established permanent trading posts on this particular section of the eastern border of Italy. Nevertheless, Greek influence in this region was by no means absent. We know that there had been repeated contacts between mainland Greeks and the indigenous Italics in Apulia, and that during the expansion of *Magna Graecia* the Iapygi had entered and settled in the area. The Iapygi emigrated from what is now Albania and South Dalmatia. We know that they had dealings with the Greeks both before and after they settled in Apulia and that by 300 B.C. the area was heavily hellenized. It seems likely that this particular form of Greek influence led to the introduction of the head toss into this area. Alternatively, the Iapygi, about whose gestural habits history has left no record, may have used the head toss themselves and introduced the action into the region without the assistance of the Greeks. Either way it is noteworthy that while Naples and the Greek settlements of the west were being exposed to the pressure of Italics moving south, Apulia remained almost totally unaffected by these population movements and their attendant cultural influences. Furthermore, we know that the south of Italy remained continually attached to the Byzantine Empire until the Middle Ages. After Justinian had recaptured peninsular Italy in the mid-sixth century there were two subsequent invaders from the north. In the seventh century the Lombards gained control of north and central Italy, with the exception of such areas as Venetia, Rimini, Ancona and Rome, and did penetrate into the south, establishing a principate at Benevento. But they never managed to take Naples or the whole of Calabria and Bruttium. In the next invasion, that of the Carolingians, the progress to the south was further curtailed, with the result that Italy tended to be cut into two, with its northern part attached to the Holy Roman Empire, and its southern part to the Mediterranean. In the third quarter of the ninth century Basil II of Byzantium began the reconquest of this southern area. Bari fell in 875 and all of Calabria and Apulia came firmly under Byzantine control. The hellenization which ensued was apparently much more clear-cut in Calabria, which, we are told, positively teemed with Greek monks, but the two areas did not lose their Byzantine status until the Normans expelled the Greeks from mainland Italy during the eleventh century. This later contact with the Byzantine Empire could itself explain the presence of the head toss on the eastern coast, or it could have served to support a gestural system which had been introduced into Apulia much earlier.

We find therefore that there are two separate head-toss zones in southern Italy, and that these require quite separate historical explanation. With the passage of time, and quite independently of any reason for the introduction of this gesture, there has been some seepage of the head toss into the hinterland, but it is by no means pre-eminent in these areas.

Map B shows how the presence of the head toss corresponds with the Massico range, and here again it looks as though this range of

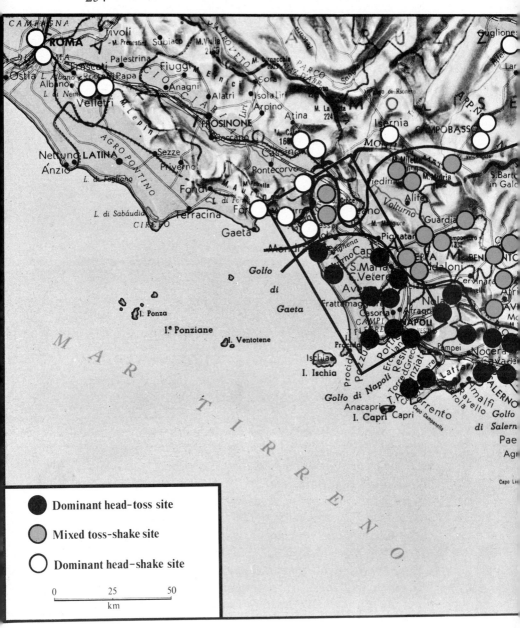

Dominant head-toss site

Mixed toss-shake site

Dominant head-shake site

0   25   50
km

MAP A   MAP B

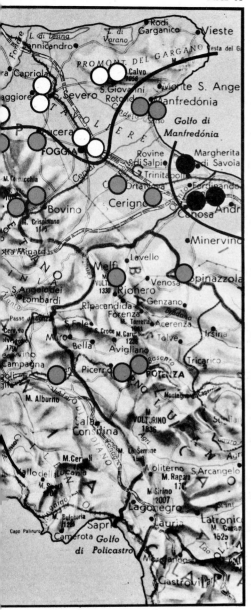

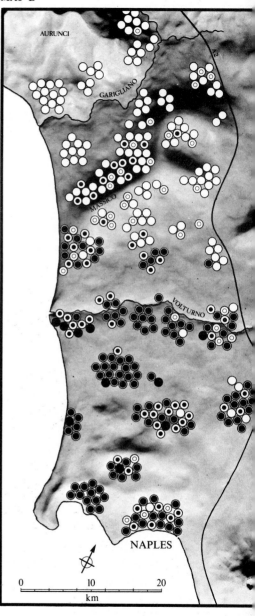

MAP A (the black rectangle on this map shows the area depicted in detail in MAP B, *right*).

● Exclusive head-tosser
◉ Dominant head-tosser
⊙ Uses toss and shake equally
◎ Dominant head-shaker
○ Exclusive head-shaker

hills is responsible for impeding the movement of the people who originally introduced the gesture or those who later adopted it as their own. However, more careful examination of the region shows that the Volturno valley was, until recently, a swamp region, and it therefore seems unlikely that the Massico hills would not have had the opportunity of presenting a barrier to the head toss. What seems more likely is that the Volturno basin presented an obstacle to the original Greek settlers and later inhabitants of the area. These swamps were drained only in the 1930s and it is probable that with subsequent shifts of the local population the head toss moved north to its present position. The highly fertile plain which extends from Naples and Vesuvius to Capua on the Volturno is known as the *Terra Di Lavoro*. This is the most fertile part of Campania, due to the mixture of alluvial deposits and volcanic ash. As one approaches the sea and the river mouths, fertility decreases as the result of the water-logging of these alluvial deposits. The *Terra Di Lavoro* was certainly cultivated as far back as the Greeks, and Livy mentions a *Fossa Greca*, which suggests that primitive irrigation has been conducted here from the earliest times. On the other hand the areas around the river mouths have always been marshy and malaria-ridden. It was only in this century when intensive land reclamation was organized under the Mussolini regime that the area around the mouth of the Volturno became agriculturally productive and habitable.

One possible objection that can be levelled at the interpretation we have offered is that there are places elsewhere in the Mediterranean where the Greeks established permanent trading centres, but which now show no signs of a negative head toss. For example, they had an important settlement at Massalia (Marseilles) and yet the head toss appears to be completely absent from the south of France. While the Greeks undoubtedly introduced the head toss to their settlements in France, Spain, Africa and elsewhere it is likely that the later abandonment of these centres also marked the disappearance of the head toss from these areas. It seems as though there are at least three requirements that have to be satisfied before a colonial habit is incorporated and sustained within an indigenous set of practices. The first is that the colonization be extensive, the second that the local population be receptive and favourably inclined towards the settlers, and the third is that subsequent historical events be conducive to its continued existence. The Greek settlements in *Magna Graecia* satisfied all of these conditions, while those in other sectors of the Mediterranean did not. The establishment of posts throughout *Magna Graecia* was extensive and the attitude of the local population appears to have been highly favourable, and long after the collapse of the Greek Empire there were several regions in southern Italy which continued to enjoy a relationship with Greece. Therefore it is not surprising to discover that isolated Greek outposts elsewhere in the Mediterranean failed to leave the kinds of gestural marks on the local inhabitants that we find so clearly imprinted in southern Italy today.

One final issue needs to be discussed in connection with this study of gesture boundaries. Alongside our detailed study of the head toss we also investigated the geographical distribution of the various messages conveyed by the chin flick in the area. An examination of the responses obtained to our second question revealed that as the head toss disappears, so too the chin flick changes from a simple negative to a sign of dismissiveness. What is interesting here is that the chin flick does not appear to have been introduced by the Greeks for the simple reason that it is not used in Greece today. As we saw earlier the chin flick has two major zones of meaning. In the first, which extends through France into northern Italy, the gesture expresses a form of annoyance or dismissiveness, while in the second, which extends south of the Massico range, it is employed as a simple negative. Considered together, these facts suggest that the chin flick was originally used as a dismissive gesture, but that with the introduction of the head toss into the south it became seconded into a negative role by the head toss. Now, instead of indicating disinterest, it served the function of amplifying the head toss. It became, as it were, a way of tossing the head with the assistance of the hand. If this is correct, then it demonstrates very neatly how the introduction of a new gesture into an established repertoire can have repercussions for the semantic role of items already in the system.

Gesture boundaries are only one of a number of interesting issues that emerge from the serious study of gesture. This particular investigation has shown how it is possible to proceed from a gross level of analysis, where countries or cities are compared with each other, to an extremely detailed level at which gestures are mapped from village to village. The virtue of this type of approach is that it eliminates speculation about the location of gesture boundaries and provides the foundation on which explanations for these boundaries can be built.

DATA USED TO CONSTRUCT MAPS A AND B

In the detailed study of the head toss in central Italy all respondents were assigned to one of five categories, ranging from those who reported using only the head shake (1) through to those who reported using only the head toss (5). The data that were collected in this study and which were subsequently used to construct Maps A and B are given below. In each case the name of the site is followed by the number of respondents that fell into each of the five negative head-movement categories:

Exclusive head shake	1
Dominant head shake	2
Shake and toss equal	3
Dominant head toss	4
Exclusive head toss	5

DATA USED TO CONSTRUCT MAP A
(Sites given in rough west-to-east sequence)

	1	2	3	4	5		1	2	3	4	5
Roma	22	0	0	0	0	Vietri	1	3	5	5	8
Velletri	20	2	0	0	0	Mercato	4	3	10	3	0
Cassino	17	4	0	0	0	Avellino	5	3	6	2	0
Formia	10	0	0	0	0	Altavilla	2	0	0	0	0
S. Apollinare						Benevento	7	8	4	0	0
– S. Andrea						Guglienesi	13	0	0	0	0
– S. Ambrogio	14	1	0	0	0	Agropoli	0	3	7	2	0
Minturno	13	0	0	0	0	Casalnuovo					
Cellole	10	0	0	0	0	Monterotara	10	0	0	0	0
Roccamonfine	7	2	1	0	0	Motta	7	3	0	0	0
Sessa Aurunca	11	2	3	0	0	Greci	8	2	0	0	0
Mondragone	2	3	6	9	0	Eboli	3	12	4	1	0
Castel Volturno	0	0	6	1	4	Osara di Puglia	8	2	0	0	0
Teano	10	1	0	0	0	Lucera	5	5	0	0	0
Capua	1	4	3	7	1	S. Severo	20	0	0	0	0
Trentola-Aversa	1	0	11	9	1	Buccino	2	5	2	1	0
Marcianise	2	0	3	10	0	Foggia	18	2	0	0	0
Pozzuoli	0	0	0	12	0	Melfi	6	3	1	0	0
Napoli	1	3	6	12	0	S. Giovanni					
Caserta	9	6	1	6	0	Rotóndo	17	1	2	0	0
Calazzo	9	7	0	5	0	Orta Nova	5	3	3	2	0
Piedimonte Matese	9	8	1	3	0	Potenza	11	3	3	3	0
Isernia	10	0	0	0	0	Albano di Lucania	2	4	2	2	0
Boiano	6	6	1	0	0	Cerignola	3	4	3	0	0
Guardia	3	3	4	0	0	Manfredonia	15	5	0	0	0
Campobasso	24	1	0	0	0	Trinitapoli	2	3	2	3	0
Nola	2	5	8	3	0	Canosa di Puglia	4	8	4	10	0
Palma Campania	0	0	5	1	3	Spinazzola	4	5	1	0	0
Sarno	2	0	0	6	2	Matera	4	8	5	3	0
Sorrento	0	2	4	12	2	Bari	1	8	3	8	0

DATA USED TO CONSTRUCT MAP B
(Sites in the eight zones, from north to south)

	1	2	3	4	5		1	2	3	4	5
S. Apollinare	7	1	0	0	0	Montanaro	0	1	0	0	0
S. Ambrogio	2	0	0	0	0	Carinola	5	1	0	0	0
S. Andrea	5	0	0	0	0	Sparanise	6	0	0	1	0
Castelforte	4	0	0	0	0	Francolise	2	1	0	0	0
Santi Cosma						Nocellero	3	0	2	0	0
e Damiano	3	0	0	0	0	Pizzone	0	0	3	4	0
Minturno	13	0	0	0	0	Mondragone	2	3	6	9	0
Cellole	10	0	0	0	0	Capua	1	4	3	7	1
						Brezza	0	0	0	1	0
Cave	7	3	0	0	0	S. Maria la					
Spicciano	4	0	0	0	0	Fossa	1	1	0	8	0
Marzano Appio	2	0	0	0	0	Grazzanise	0	0	0	8	0
S. Carlo	5	0	0	0	0	Cancello	0	0	2	2	0
Vigne	1	1	0	0	0	Arnone	0	0	1	4	0
Roccamonfine	7	2	1	0	0	Castel Volturno	0	0	6	1	4
Ponte	1	0	0	0	0						
Sessa Aurunca	11	2	3	0	0	Marcianise	4	0	3	12	0
Sorbello	2	1	3	0	0	Villa Literno	0	0	1	17	1
Carano	2	2	1	0	0	Casal di Principe	0	0	0	1	1
Piedimonte						Trentola-Aversa	1	0	11	9	1
Massicano	5	0	3	0	0	Marina di Lago					
						di Patria	0	0	0	5	1
Teano	10	1	0	0	0	Marano di Napoli	0	1	2	6	1
Casale	4	1	0	0	0						
Casanova Carani	1	2	0	0	0	Pozzuoli	0	0	0	12	0
Falciano del						Napoli	1	3	6	12	0
Massico	1	3	1	0	0						

Gestural Distance

The 40 sites that we investigated in our '20 gestures' study ranged across the full extent of western Europe — from Stockholm in the north to Tunisia in the south, and from the Canaries in the west to Istanbul in the east. The actual physical distances between these sites are often tabulated in a good atlas. If not they can readily be calculated. But their gestural counterparts are nowhere to be found. This section, therefore, is concerned with distances between sites expressed in gestural terms.

It is sometimes said that the gestures used in one country are either similar to or different from those employed in another. Scandinavians, for example, are said to be similar to each other by virtue of the paucity of their manual vocabulary, and the French, for instance, are often held up as a nation with a unique gestural profile. In the sections which have dealt with the 20 key gestures we have tried to identify the precise manner in which countries differ from or are similar to each other in relation to particular gestures and messages. We have also gone some way towards indicating where certain gestural stereotypes are either correct or unfounded. It now remains to see just how similar these sites are in relation to the full range of gestures — in short, to calculate the gestural distances between the 40 sites.

A distance score was computed between every pair of sites. This was done by summing the number of significant differences across all the gesture-meaning categories shown in the tabulated results section. Significant differences were calculated using a Chi-squared test. If, for example, the number of informants who reported the local use of the fingertips kiss gesture for praise in one site was ·significantly greater or less than the corresponding number of people reporting its use in another, then these two sites would be regarded as different in relation to the 'fingertips kiss — praise' category. By performing the same calculation across all the gesture-meaning categories and then summing the number of significant differences it was possible to derive a numerical index of the gestural distance between two sites, and by performing the same analysis on all pairs of sites it was possible to produce a similarity matrix showing the derived gestural distances between all pairs of sites. These gestural distance scores ranged between 0 and 27. Because the pattern of similarity and differences between the sites does not readily emerge when one is required to scrutinize such a large matrix of numbers we have simplified the picture by converting the gestural distance score between each pair of sites to one of four symbols. The scheme is as follows:

0 – 6	significant differences	=	white
7 – 13	significant differences	=	light grey
14 – 20	significant differences	=	dark grey
21 – 27	significant differences	=	black

Diagram 2 presents a similarity matrix of all 40 sites. Note that the darker the shading the more different the sites, and that bold lines have been used to separate the countries. Looking at the matrix several interesting points emerge:

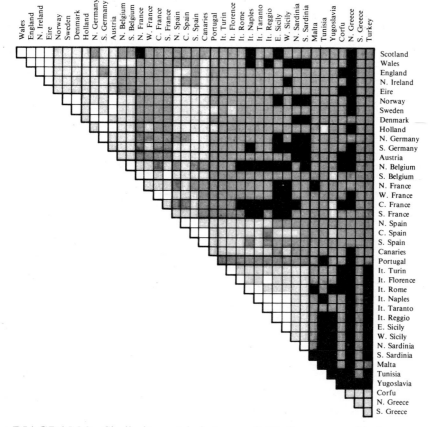

DIAGRAM 2   Similarity matrix between all 40 sites expressed in terms of gestural distances.

1   The most striking feature of the table is that the distances between sites are smaller within countries than they are between countries. Within-country comparisons are to be found in the triangular sections along the diagonal, and between-country comparisons in the remainder of the matrix. Within the British Isles, for example, the distances between Scotland, Wales, England, Northern Ireland and Eire are at a minimum. The same occurs in the case of Germany, France, Spain, Italy and Greece, and interestingly enough within the Scandinavian complex. In fact, Norway, Sweden and Denmark are no more different from each other than the separate sites that constitute the British Isles' sample. This can probably be explained in terms of the relatively low level of response in Scandinavia rather than in terms of any substantive similarity between sites that have gesturally rich vocabularies.

2   Several countries show a greater resemblance to one country rather than another. For instance, the Scandinavian trio appear to be more similar to the British Isles, Holland, Germany and, surprisingly, Spain than they are to France, Italy, Malta, Tunisia, Yugoslavia, Greece and Turkey. Likewise, Italy is shown to be more similar to Spain than it is to any other country. Another marked similarity is that between Greece and Turkey.

3   Several countries show a noticeable dissimilarity to certain countries rather than to others. The most dramatic case of this appears to be the large gestural distances between Malta, Tunisia and Yugoslavia, and between these and all the other countries.

4   There is no obvious relationship between map distance and gestural distance. We see that certain countries which are situated close together, and which have enjoyed a long history of contact, have small gestural distances. While others which have even fewer miles between them might as well be at opposite ends of the Mediterranean. Malta and Tunisia, separated by a relatively short stretch of sea, show a pronounced difference, and much the same holds for Yugoslavia and Greece.

It is clear from the diagram that, as we might expect, gestural distances within countries are shorter than those between countries. Beyond this, however, it should be remembered that there are often quite striking differences within countries where specific gestures are concerned, and that the type of analysis which we have presented here depends entirely on the 20 gestures that we studied and the various meanings that emerged in the process of our investigation.

Gesture Concepts

We set out to record the facts concerning our key gestures and their distribution across Europe, but inevitably, as our study developed, we also began to formulate a number of gestural concepts. Some of these have already been mentioned under the heading of a specific gesture, and one of them — Gesture Boundaries — has been treated separately. But to conclude the book it may be helpful if we summarize the various concepts briefly, as a kind of extended glossary.

GESTURE FLOW

When we look at a gesture map for a particular gesture, and see it ranging across a large part of Europe, there are two ways to explain its broad distribution. Either it arose in one place — the primary location — and then spread outwards from that site, or it arose independently at a number of sites. In the case of mimic gestures, such as the imitation of putting food into the mouth, as a sign of hunger, it is highly likely that there was no single place of origin. The gesture is used around the world and is quickly understood by almost anyone who sees it. But with symbolic gestures showing a restricted geographical range, the chances are that in every case there was a primary location where the gesture was first invented, and that it then diffused outwards from this location, spreading in various directions until it arrived at its present-day distribution, as shown on our maps. This process of diffusion is what we are calling Gesture Flow. In theory, there is nothing to stop a useful symbolic gesture of this kind from flowing with equal speed in all directions until it covers the whole area of human habitation around the globe. In practice, this does not occur. The flow is opposed by a variety of factors. We have been able to identify a number of these gesture flow barriers:

1 Cultural prejudice barriers
Sometimes two adjoining cultures develop a prejudice against one another's customs. If, for instance, there has been a long-standing rivalry between two neighbouring states or nations, the gestures of one may be shunned by the other. To adopt the foreign gesture would be disloyal, or would smack of affectation. Some Englishmen,

asked if they ever kiss their fingertips, might reply that 'only Continentals do that', for example. This is not a case of the Englishmen being ignorant of the gesture, but rather that they consider it unBritish and therefore to be avoided.

Such prejudices seem to be behind a number of the sharp changes in gesture-use that crop up at modern national boundaries today. It does not affect all gestures, of course, but in the instances where it occurs the difference can be dramatic. Between Spain and Portugal, for instance, there are marked contrasts in the use of the fingertips kiss, the eyelid pull, the fig, and the ear touch. Other similar changes occur between France and Italy, France and Spain, and Germany and Italy. But not all of these can automatically be ascribed to cultural prejudice. There are other factors at work, such as:

2   Linguistic barriers
If a particular gesture is closely related to a verbal phrase, this may tend to reduce its penetration rate into a culture lacking the phrase in question. A slang expression is often closely associated with a symbolic gesture and if the slang expression defies simple translation, then the gesture may become 'language-tied' to some extent.

3   Ideological and religious barriers
Any gesture that is linked to specific political or religious beliefs may find its gesture flow impeded in areas outside the zones of influence of the politics or religions involved. Tunisia and Turkey, for instance, do not use the crossed-fingers gesture as a protective sign, since it has developed from a Christian symbol, the cross, which is foreign to their religious beliefs.

4   Geographical barriers
Where there is a stretch of water or a mountain range between two populations, the gesture flow will be impeded by simple obstruction. Two sites separated by only a few miles of sea or mountain, may be gesturally as distant as two sites far apart elsewhere, but divided only by easily traversed land masses. The English Channel, separating the British region from the continent, or the North Sea separating the Scandinavian countries from the rest of Europe, are two cases in point.

5   Gesture taboos
In addition to these barriers, gesture flow may be impeded by the

existence of local taboos. Public kissing, for example, may be so
heavily suppressed in one culture that gestures such as the fingertips
kiss cannot thrive there.

6   Gesture obscurity

A piece of symbolism based on some highly localized cultural feature — a particular animal, for example, or a particular food — will
be meaningless in other places and will therefore travel badly. The
cheek screw is a good illustration of this, based as it is on the perfect
preparation of Italian pasta, which makes it just right 'on the tooth',
and provides the basis for this action of the finger against the cheek.

7   Gesture niches

If a culture already possesses a popular gesture to express a particular idea, then other foreign gestures expressing the identical idea
will find it hard to invade, because their 'niche' is already fully
occupied, and an additional gestural expression would be superfluous. This seems to have been important in limiting the spread of a
number of the gestures we studied. For instance, where the thumbs-
up gesture for O.K. is widely used, the ring gesture will find it hard to
make an impression as it spreads across from country to country.
But where there is no common O.K. sign, the invasion will be
quicker and more complete. Where cultures, such as that of the
Arabs, already have a rich collection of insulting gestures, European
insults will not fare well.

8   Gesture replacement

Gestures are rather like a kind of visual slang and, just as slang
words may sometimes go out of fashion, so may they. Repeatedly we
heard of a gesture, such as the horn-sign or the fig, as being used by
'old people', implying that it had become quaintly old-fashioned
and was no longer used by the younger 'smarter set'. Old slang
words are usually pushed out by new ones and the same is true with
gestures. The nose-thumb gesture, as we saw earlier, is losing ground
among British school-children today, and is being replaced by the
more virulent V-sign insult. In the years to come, the V-sign may
gain ground and eventually overtake the older taunt, limiting its
range and impeding its further flow. Despite this, however, it must
be admitted that many gestures have stood the test of time and have
resisted the whims of changing fashion.

GESTURE SOURCES

In tracking down the origins of the symbolic gestures, we found two main sources. The first is that of *Baton Signals*. These gesticulatory movements of the hands which serve to emphasize the spoken word, have been at the root of both the hand purse and the ring gesture, at least in some of their meanings. Other gestures, by contrast, have their beginnings in some specific historical invention, as with the nose-thumb and the horn-sign. These two sources — the baton and the historical event — differ in two characteristic ways. The baton type tend to have many meanings, derived from the original gesticulatory emphasis, but little or no written history, while the historical type tend to have a single dominant meaning, but many different derivational explanations. In the latter case, there has to be one *Initiating Explanation*, and a whole series of later, *Supporting Explanations* which, although in a sense untrue, nevertheless come to act as if they were true, and thereby help to keep the gesture alive by giving it a satisfying, if incorrect, background.

TYPES OF SYMBOLIC GESTURE

It is possible to group certain symbolic gestures under convenient headings, but it should be stressed that we are not, in so doing, attempting to provide a complete or systematic arrangement, nor are the gesture-types we list here necessarily mutually exclusive.

1   Class-restricted gestures
Some people, when asked about a particular gesture, retorted that only the inarticulate need to 'wave their hands about'. They felt it was unsophisticated to admit to gesturing themselves, although, ironically, they often gesticulated animatedly when making this point. Essentially, what they were saying is that *certain kinds* of gestures are class-restricted, and this is true enough. But to generalize, as they sometimes did, to include all gesturing, and to look upon the use of the hands as always indicative of a failure to find the right words, is a gross exaggeration. People who are inarticulate are often equally limited in their gestural expressiveness, and people who are articulate are often extremely sensitive in their use of manual signals. But when it comes to certain types of symbolic gesture, then the class distinctions do begin to emerge. This is

particularly true of insulting gestures. Joke insults are common among children, for example, and many symbolic gestures such as the popular nose-thumbing action are largely confined to the younger members of the population. More serious, obscene gestures are also class-restricted to a great extent and are rare among the more sophisticated sectors of society. By contrast, the more polite or complimentary gestures are used by almost all sectors of society, although even here, there is a tendency for men to employ them more often than women.

2   Emancipated gestures

Certain gestures are performed today without reference to their symbolic origins. In some cases, the emancipation is so complete that the symbolic origins of an action are no longer certain and have become the subject of extravagant speculations. Earlier, we referred to the way in which this situation can lead to the development of Supportive Explanations regarding the origins of gestures — explanations which, although unfounded, help to keep the gestures alive. This certainly happens, but even so, for many people a symbolic gesture is simply something to be copied without question. They see that it is used rudely or in a complimentary way and do likewise without ever asking why such an action should carry such a message. Where the matter does eventually become discussed, then the Supportive Explanations may start to play a part, but in their absence a gesture is far from dead or in danger of dying. It would be interesting to question a large number of people who use a particular gesture, to see how many of them have ever considered its origin and how many simply accept it for what it is. We suspect that the latter group would be by far the larger.

3   Hybrid gestures

Most symbolic gestures are single units and they rarely combine with one another to produce complex gestures. In a few cases, however, we did find hybrids. For example, in Tunisia, the flat hand-chop threat gesture is combined with the ring gesture to produce a ring-chop. And the forearm jerk was sometimes combined with the fig or the horn-sign to produce a double-impact insult. But these are the exceptions to the rule, and in general it can be stated that symbolic gestures, unlike words, work singly as isolated units. They may be strung together, one after the other in a torrent of abuse or a shower of praise, but they seldom appear simultaneously.

4   Conservative gestures

Some gestures are comparatively modern, but many more seem to have lasted for centuries unchanged. In general terms, it could be said that symbolic gestures tend to be highly conservative, not only in their form, but also in their meanings and even, in some instances, in their distributions. The case of the head toss analysed in detail earlier, reveals that it is possible for the distribution of a gesture to last in its original form for over 2,000 years. It remains to be investigated why some gestures are more susceptible to fashion-changes and fashion-replacement, than others. It also remains to be seen how well the present distributions we have reported in this book will stand up to future years of increased mobility and media exposure. With films and television on an increasingly international scale, we may yet see a weakening of gesture conservatism. To repeat our survey some decades in the future would give the answer.

5   Illegal gestures

Some gestural activities can still bring police prosecution in certain countries. We encountered this in Germany and in Malta. In Germany, drivers making the temple-screw gesture for 'crazy' can be and have been arrested and prosecuted. In Malta we were warned not to make the forearm jerk in the street when interviewing informants. In England, certain obscene gestures, such as the palm-back V-sign, might easily be construed as 'insulting behaviour' in the legal sense if directed offensively at police. These and other examples reflect the great power of symbolic gestures in hostile social encounters, and equate them with the worst swear words available, which can also carry similar penalties.

6   Variant gestures

Just as a word may vary in pronunciation from place to place, so too a symbolic gesture may change its form slightly in different localities, while retaining the same meaning over the whole range. In such cases we can speak of gesture dialects. This occurs where there is one key element in a particular gesture that gives the basic clue to its meaning. Providing that essential ingredient is present, other details can vary considerably. We noticed that this occurred most where the essential feature of the gesture was itself uncommon or unlikely. To give some examples: the horn-sign requires the projection of a pair of sharp points. This is not a common signal to make and is unlikely to arise accidentally or incidentally. It is therefore possible to present the 'paired projection' configuration in a number of ways (two fingers from one hand, one finger from each of two hands, etc.). The forearm jerk can also appear in a variety of ways because phallic jerking movements of the arm are not likely to be confused with other arm actions. The ear touch gesture is also variable, there being no other ear-contact signal that is in common use with which it can be confused. Future field studies of an even more detailed kind may well be able to demonstrate that these variant forms are arranged in a series across the major range of a symbolic gesture, just as a species of animal may show a series of gradually changing local forms. In other words, it may eventually be possible to demonstrate the existence of *gesture clines*.

7   Multi-message gestures

Almost all our key gestures turned out to have more than one distinct meaning. We had expected this to happen, but the phenomenon was much more common and frequent than we had anticipated. There are two main ways in which a gesture acquires multiple meanings. First, there is the generality of the original source, which enables it to become particularized in different ways in different regions. For example, a gesture that involves contact with the eye or the nose can lead to a whole range of seeing or smelling symbolisms. The gesture says no more, initially, than *eye* or *nose*, and as one moves from region to region the interpretation of this general signal can shift, 'seeing' things or 'smelling' things in different ways: I am alert/he is alert/he is dangerous/you must be alert, and so on. Each particular version of alertness gradually becomes a local tradition for the basic eye or nose message. Second, there is the possibility of a gesture becoming multi-message because it is multi-derivational. In other words, the original action has several quite distinct starting points leading to totally distinct meanings. The ring gesture, for instance, becomes an O.K. sign, a zero sign or an orifice insult, according to the way its form is symbolically interpreted.

These two processes produce different kinds of multi-message gesture — the first being less heterogeneous than the second. With the first it is always possible to see the relationships between the different local messages, but with the second there is always a striking contrast between the varying interpretations, giving rise to the possibility of major confusions in regions of gesture-meaning overlap.

Gesture Confusions

Misinterpretation of gestures stems from several factors. Apart from the overlap phenomenon, where one gesture meaning invades the area of another and comes into conflict with it, there is also the obvious case of travellers moving into a zone where their own gesture repertoire is out of tune. It is clear from our gesture maps that there is a considerable possibility of this wherever tourists, travellers and immigrants are concerned. International political and business meetings are also at risk, although the more cosmopolitan individuals involved will have become wary of misreading foreign gestures and will be alerted to the possible dangers of misconstruing the moods and intentions of their companions.

One particular phenomenon we encountered repeatedly was that of *gesture-blurring*. If asked the meaning of a gesture which was unknown to him, an informant, wishing to be helpful, would often interpret it as the local gesture nearest to it in form. A cheek screw is seen as a temple screw, simply because of the screwing action of the forefinger against part of the head. The meaning therefore becomes 'crazy', the informant assuming that the questioner himself is making an error. Or the hand purse becomes a feeding gesture, because the fingers appear to be holding imaginary food near the mouth. The fact that the informant himself would never perform the gesture in quite that way when signalling 'food', does not deter him. He would rather offer *some* interpretation than admit ignorance. Although this blurring of gestural distinctions was occurring during an interview, rather than in a more natural social situation, there is reason to believe that, where visitors and travellers are concerned, similar errors must arise in the ordinary course of events. Knowledge of the gestures of other cultures would clearly alleviate this problem, and it is to be hoped that, in future, tourist guides will include a gestural glossary alongside the usual helpful phrases for use in foreign lands.

Tabulated Data

The table on the following pages shows the number of informants out of 30 who reported that a gesture was used to convey a particular meaning in each of the 40 locations. All maps and histograms have been constructed from this data.

	PRAISE / FINGERTIPS KISS	SALUTATION / FINGERTIPS KISS	PROTECTION / FINGERS CROSS	OK – GOOD / FINGERS CROSS	FRIENDSHIP / FINGERS CROSS	BREAK FRIENDSHIP / FINGERS CROSS	COPULATION / FINGERS CROSS	SWEAR OATH / FINGERS CROSS	MOCKERY / NOSE THUMB	QUERY / HAND PURSE	GOOD / HAND PURSE	FEAR / HAND PURSE	LOTS / HAND PURSE	EMPHASIS / HAND PURSE	CRITICISM / HAND PURSE	SLOWLY / HAND PURSE	GOOD / CHEEK SCREW	CRAFTY / CHEEK SCREW	EFFEMINATE / CHEEK SCREW	CRAZY / CHEEK SCREW	I AM ALERT / EYELID PULL	BE ALERT / EYELID PULL	PRAISE / EYELID PULL	COMPLICITY / EYELID PULL	BOREDOM / EYELID PULL	SEXUAL INSULT / FOREARM JERK	SEXUAL COMMENT / FOREARM JERK	STRENGTH / FOREARM JERK	DEPARTURE DEMAND / FLAT HAND FLICK	DEPARTURE DESCRIPTION / FLAT HAND FLICK	DEPARTURE REQUEST / FLAT HAND FLICK	OK GOOD / RING	ORIFICE / RING	ZERO / RING	THREAT / RING	CUCKOLD / VERTICAL HORN	GENERAL INSULT / VERTICAL HORN	PROTECTION / VERTICAL HORN	CURSE / VERTICAL HORN	CUCKOLD / HORIZONTAL HORN	PROTECTION / HORIZONTAL HORN
SCOTLAND	9	0	16	4	5	0	0	–	28	0	–	0	0	6	0	0	0	0	0	0	4	–	0	4	0	11	19	0	0	0	25	2	–	0	0	0	0	0	0	0	0
WALES	2	8	16	1	0	0	0	0	27	0	0	0	0	2	0	0	0	0	0	0	2	15	0	0	0	6	20	0	0	0	21	2	0	0	0	0	0	0	0	0	0
ENGLAND	11	5	21	3	1	0	0	0	28	0	–	0	0	2	0	0	0	0	0	0	7	4	0	2	0	19	0	0	0	0	24	1	0	0	0	0	0	0	0	0	0
N. IRELAND	9	4	19	0	0	0	0	0	27	0	0	0	0	3	0	0	0	0	0	0	13	–	0	0	0	16	7	0	0	0	20	1	0	0	0	0	0	0	0	0	0
EIRE	2	–	16	3	–	0	0	0	21	0	0	0	0	2	0	0	0	0	0	0	9	0	0	0	0	–	20	3	0	0	24	0	0	0	0	0	0	0	0	0	0
NORWAY	5	13	19	0	0	0	0	0	23	0	2	0	0	–	0	0	0	0	0	0	10	0	0	0	0	3	3	12	0	0	29	0	–	0	0	0	0	0	0	0	0
SWEDEN	9	16	11	–	0	0	–	–	28	–	0	0	0	2	0	0	0	0	0	–	6	2	0	0	0	2	17	0	0	0	19	3	0	0	0	0	0	0	0	0	0
DENMARK	20	10	16	0	0	0	0	–	29	0	4	0	0	–	0	0	0	0	0	0	16	0	0	0	0	–	1	8	0	0	21	0	5	0	0	0	0	0	0	0	0
HOLLAND	27	0	3	4	–	0	0	0	30	2	4	0	0	9	0	0	0	0	0	0	9	14	–	0	0	4	6	0	0	0	29	0	0	0	2	0	0	0	0	0	0
N. GERMANY	20	10	7	0	0	0	–	–	28	0	7	0	0	2	0	0	0	0	0	0	12	0	21	4	0	0	0	4	0	0	21	6	0	0	0	0	0	0	0	0	0
S. GERMANY	22	8	8	0	0	0	0	0	28	0	5	0	–	1	0	0	0	0	0	0	13	19	7	0	0	0	11	5	0	–	23	6	0	0	–	0	0	0	0	0	0
AUSTRIA	11	21	9	10	0	0	0	0	30	0	–	0	0	4	0	0	0	0	0	0	7	7	2	0	0	9	3	–	0	0	27	0	0	0	2	–	0	0	0	0	0
N. BELGIUM	26	4	11	0	0	0	0	2	30	0	0	23	0	2	0	0	0	0	0	0	7	17	11	0	0	16	3	5	3	0	15	0	13	0	2	0	0	0	0	0	0
S. BELGIUM	23	8	3	–	0	0	0	0	30	0	0	19	0	0	0	0	0	0	0	0	29	–	0	0	0	23	–	4	10	7	17	0	9	5	0	0	0	0	3	0	0
N. FRANCE	22	22	8	3	–	0	0	0	28	0	–	7	12	0	–	0	0	0	0	0	28	2	0	0	0	21	5	2	18	8	0	14	0	10	0	0	0	0	0	0	0
W. FRANCE	21	21	5	2	–	0	0	0	30	0	–	1	25	0	–	0	0	0	0	0	30	0	0	0	0	30	0	0	8	19	9	0	17	0	–	0	0	0	1	0	0
C. FRANCE	23	22	10	–	0	0	0	0	25	0	3	0	18	0	–	0	0	0	0	0	30	0	0	0	0	30	0	0	13	14	0	7	0	21	0	0	0	0	9	0	0
S. FRANCE	23	–	2	0	–	0	–	8	28	–	0	8	5	4	0	0	0	0	0	0	28	0	–	0	0	28	0	–	15	14	0	9	–	16	0	6	0	0	3	13	4
N. SPAIN	16	8	–	0	2	0	0	0	27	0	–	16	0	0	0	0	0	2	0	0	6	30	23	0	0	24	3	–	7	0	0	13	–	–	0	25	0	0	0	25	0
C. SPAIN	24	2	8	–	0	0	0	0	27	0	4	0	17	0	0	0	0	–	0	0	2	2	27	0	0	22	2	0	2	7	0	27	0	0	0	27	0	0	0	27	0
S. SPAIN	23	5	5	–	0	0	0	0	28	0	5	0	8	0	0	0	0	25	0	0	5	5	25	0	0	23	–	5	6	0	0	19	0	–	0	24	0	0	–	24	0
CANARIES	22	8	12	0	–	0	0	–	24	2	9	0	6	0	0	0	0	–	5	24	0	0	0	0	0	21	2	–	0	29	0	29	0	0	0	26	0	0	0	26	0
PORTUGAL	3	27	6	0	0	0	–	23	0	10	–	4	3	0	0	0	0	0	0	0	15	13	2	0	0	30	0	2	0	18	–	3	0	26	2	0	0	21	0	0	0
IT. TURIN	9	10	8	4	–	0	0	0	28	27	0	0	0	0	0	0	15	8	0	0	3	25	0	0	26	0	4	20	0	5	0	17	–	0	29	0	0	0	17	6	0
IT. FLORENCE	11	13	9	0	2	0	0	0	28	27	0	0	–	–	0	0	25	–	0	0	0	9	7	0	0	28	0	0	21	–	0	12	–	5	0	29	0	0	19	19	9
IT. ROME	9	6	–	2	0	0	0	0	21	26	0	0	0	–	0	0	28	0	0	–	24	24	2	–	0	30	0	0	29	0	0	18	0	0	29	0	0	0	19	19	4
IT. NAPLES	10	12	5	3	3	–	0	–	23	30	0	0	0	0	0	0	29	0	0	0	3	24	–	0	0	29	0	0	29	0	0	25	0	0	2	30	0	0	23	5	0
IT. TARANTO	13	12	5	3	0	0	0	0	24	30	0	0	0	0	0	0	27	0	0	0	3	23	–	0	0	28	0	2	28	–	0	22	0	0	28	28	0	2	27	–	0
IT. REGGIO	10	15	5	–	0	0	0	0	25	29	0	0	0	0	0	0	26	3	0	0	2	21	0	–	0	28	0	–	28	2	0	20	–	0	27	27	2	0	18	0	0
E. SICILY	8	18	15	4	0	0	0	0	25	30	0	0	0	0	0	0	29	0	0	0	2	25	0	2	0	25	0	0	29	0	0	20	–	0	–	30	0	0	20	6	0
W. SICILY	8	16	6	3	0	0	0	2	28	30	0	0	0	0	0	0	26	3	0	0	3	22	0	0	0	29	0	0	28	0	0	23	0	–	0	30	0	0	26	6	0
N. SARDINIA	3	3	23	2	–	0	0	0	5	26	22	0	2	0	0	0	0	22	2	0	3	14	–	0	0	29	0	0	17	2	8	13	0	0	27	27	0	–	22	5	0
S. SARDINIA	8	16	2	–	0	0	0	2	25	26	0	0	0	–	0	0	21	–	0	0	5	15	–	0	0	28	0	–	11	5	0	11	4	0	25	27	0	0	17	3	0
MALTA	2	7	28	4	2	4	0	2	3	29	–	0	0	0	0	27	0	0	0	0	6	6	–	0	2	28	–	2	0	0	0	6	11	23	0	17	2	3	0	23	0
TUNISIA	20	20	7	0	0	4	–	0	5	0	5	0	0	0	0	20	0	0	0	0	8	8	0	0	13	0	11	–	19	18	0	0	–	12	0	13	–	0	0	0	0
YUGOSLAVIA	8	29	0	11	–	0	3	0	30	30	0	0	19	0	0	0	0	0	8	29	2	0	0	0	28	–	19	–	10	0	24	0	0	7	13	–	3	4	2	4	4
CORFU	8	22	–	–	0	17	–	7	30	–	29	0	0	0	0	0	–	0	3	6	0	2	0	0	0	11	8	0	9	0	0	0	0	0	2	4	–	0	2	4	–
N. GREECE	24	6	–	0	0	6	0	28	29	0	0	0	0	0	0	0	–	0	0	0	22	8	–	4	11	–	0	0	0	11	0	0	0	0	2	0	0	0	0	0	0
S. GREECE	20	10	0	0	0	3	0	–	27	0	29	0	0	0	0	0	0	0	0	0	14	0	–	–	0	28	7	0	–	3	2	0	0	0	0	2	0	0	0	0	0
TURKEY	26	2	0	0	0	5	0	0	21	0	29	0	0	0	0	0	0	0	0	0	30	0	0	0	0	25	2	2	2	–	2	0	0	0	6	0	0	0	0	0	0

Gesture	Meaning
HORIZONTAL HORN	INSULT
HORIZONTAL HORN	THREAT
HORIZONTAL HORN	CURSE
FIG	PROTECTION
FIG	SEXUAL COMMENT
FIG	SEXUAL INSULT
FIG	NOSE JOKE
FIG	NOTHING
HEAD TOSS	NEGATIVE
HEAD TOSS	BECKON
CHIN FLICK	NEGATIVE
CHIN FLICK	DISINTEREST
CHIN FLICK	DISBELIEF
CHIN FLICK	SUCCESS
CHEEK STROKE	THIN ILL
CHEEK STROKE	SAD
CHEEK STROKE	ATTRACTIVE
CHEEK STROKE	EFFEMINATE
CHEEK STROKE	THINKING
CHEEK STROKE	CRAFTY
CHEEK STROKE	THREAT
THUMB UP	OK
THUMB UP	SEXUAL INSULT
TEETH FLICK	NOTHING
TEETH FLICK	ANGER
TEETH FLICK	PRAISE
EAR TOUCH	EFFEMINATE
EAR TOUCH	WARNING
EAR TOUCH	GOOD
EAR TOUCH	SPONGER
EAR TOUCH	PROTECTION
EAR TOUCH	INFORMER
EAR TOUCH	DISBELIEF
NOSE TAP	COMPLICITY
NOSE TAP	BE ALERT
NOSE TAP	YOU ARE NOSEY
NOSE TAP	I AM ALERT
NOSE TAP	HE IS CLEVER
NOSE TAP	THREAT
V SIGN	INSULT
V SIGN	VICTORY
V SIGN	TWO
V SIGN	HORNS
PALM-UP BECKON	COME HERE
PALM-DOWN BECKON	COME HERE
PALM-SHOW WAVE	GOODBYE
PALM-HIDE WAVE	GOODBYE

Bibliography

In addition to the works mentioned in the text, we have attempted to provide a fairly comprehensive bibliography on the subject of gesture, as we feel there is a need for an up-to-date list of references on this subject. The last to appear was by Francis Hayes in 1957, and since that time many new works have been published.

Abercrombie, D. 1973. *Problems and Principles in Language Study*. Longman, London. (See Chapter VI for discussion of Gesture.)

Adams, F. A. 1891. *Gesture and Pantomimic Action*. Albany, New York.

Aldis, O. 1975. *Play Fighting*. Academic Press, New York.

Allport, G. W. and P. E. Vernon. 1933. *Studies in Expressive Movement*. Hafner, New York. (Reprinted 1967.)

Alsop, S. 1960. 'How to speak French without saying a word,' *Saturday Evening Post*, Dec. 24–31, pp. 26–9.

Altner, G. (editor). 1976. *The Nature of Human Behaviour*. Allen and Unwin, London.

Ambrose, J. A. 1960. 'The Smiling and Related Responses in Early Human Infancy'. Ph.D. Thesis, University of London.

Anderson, J. D. 1920. 'The language of gesture', *Folk-Lore*, 31, p. 70. (On Bengali gestures.)

Anon. 1914. 'Glossary of international gestures', *Travel*, 22 (Feb.), p. 35.

Anon. 1926. *Asia Magazine*, 26 (4), p. 320. (Tibetan upward jerk of right thumb combined with tongue protrusion as greeting to fellow-traveller.)

Anon. 1941. 'Mexico says it with gestures', *Pemex Travel Club Bulletin*, 3 (Nov.–Dec.), pp. 5–6. (For a description of 25 Mexican gestures.)

Anon. 1946. 'Speaking of pictures. French gestures', *Life Magazine*, 21· (Sept. 16), pp. 12–15.

Anon. 1961. *Asiatic Society of Bengal*, 3, p. 619. (Persian gestures.)

Anthriotis, N. P. 1947. 'Ancient and modern Greek hand and facial gestures', *Morphais* (Thessaloniki). Feb. 1947, pp. 90–2. (In Greek.)

Arditi, Marchese. 1825. *Il Fascino*. Naples.

Aresty, E. B. 1970. *The Best Behavior*. Simon and Schuster, New York.

Argyle, M. 1967. *The Psychology of Interpersonal Behaviour*. Penguin, Harmondsworth.

Argyle, M. 1969. *Social Interaction*. Methuen, London.

Argyle, M. (editor). 1973. *Social Encounters. Readings in Social Interaction*. Penguin, Harmondsworth.

Argyle, M. 1975. *Bodily Communication*. Methuen, London.

Argyle, M. and M. Cook. 1976. *Gaze and Mutual Gaze*. Cambridge University Press, Cambridge.

Aristophanes (ed. T. Bergk, Lipsiae, 1903). *Comoedias*. Pax, line 1350. (For fig sign.)

Aubert, C. 1927. *The Art of Pantomime*. Paris.

Austin, G. 1806. *Chironomia; or, a treatise on rhetorical delivery*. London.

Austin, M. 1927. 'Gesture in primitive drama', *Theatre Arts Magazine*, 11 (August), pp. 594–605.

Bacon, A. M. 1875. *A Manual of Gestures*. Griggs, Chicago.

Barakat, R. A. 1969. 'Gesture systems', *Keystone Folklore Quarterly*. Fall issue, pp. 105–21.

Barakat, R. A. 1973. 'Arabic gestures', *J. Popular Culture*, pp. 749–87.

Barakat, R. A. 1975. 'On ambiguity in the Cistercian sign language', *Sign Language Studies*, 8, pp. 275–88.

Barakat, R. A. 1975. *The Cistercian Sign Language. A study in non-verbal communication*. Cistercian Publications. Kalamazoo, Michigan.

Barber, J. 1831. *A Practical Treatise on Gesture, Chiefly Abstracted from Gilbert Austin's Chironomia*. Cambridge, U.S.A.

Barrère, A. and C. G. Leland. 1889. *A Dictionary of Slang, Jargon and Cant*. Ballantyne Press.

Barrois, J. 1850. *Dactylogie et langage primitif restitués d'après les monuments*. Firmin Dido, Paris.

Barsley, M. 1966. *The Left-handed Book*. Souvenir Press, London.

Barsley, M. 1970. *Left-handed Man in a Right-handed World*. Pitman.

Barzini, L. 1964. *The Italians*. Hamish Hamilton, London.

Basore, J. W. 1928. *Seneca: the Moral Essays*. (See Vol. 1, Book 3, *De Ira*, for gestures of anger.)

Basto, C. 1938. 'A linguagem dos gestos em Portugal', *Revista Lusitana*, 36, pp. 5–32.

Bastock, M., D. Morris and M. Moynihan. 1953. 'Some comments on conflict and thwarting in animals', *Behaviour*, 6, pp. 66–84.

Bastow, A. 1936. 'Peasant customs and superstitions in 13th century Germany', *Folk-Lore*, 47, pp. 313, 328.

Bates, J. A. V. 1975. 'The communicative hand' in *The Body as a Medium of Expression*. Allen Lane, London. pp. 175–94.

Bateson, G. and M. Mead. 1942. *Balinese Character*. New York.

Bauer, L. 1898. 'Einiges über Gesten der syrischen Araber', *Zeitschrift des Deutschen Palaestina-Vereins*. Leipzig. pp. 59–64.

Bauer, L. 1903. *Volksleben im Lande der Bibel*. Leipzig.

Bauml, B. J. and F. H. Bauml, 1975. *A Dictionary of Gestures*. Scarecrow Press, Metuchen, New Jersey.

Bayley, H. 1912. *The Lost Language of Symbolism*. Williams and Norgate, London. (Last reprinted in 1974 by Ernst Benn, London.)

Bee, J. 1823. *Sportsman's Slang*. London.

Beinhauer, W. 1930. *Spanische Umgangssprache*. Berlin. (See pp. 113, 131, 170, 191 and 202 for Spanish gestures.)

Beinhauer, W. 1934. Über Piropos. Eine Studie über spanische Liebessprache', *Volkstum und Kultur der Romanen*, 7, pp. 111–63.

Beinhauer, W. 1942. *El Carácter Español*. Madrid.

Bell, C. 1806. *Essays on the Anatomy of Expression*. Longman, Hurst, Rees and Orme, London.

Bell, C. 1824. *Essays on the Anatomy and Philosophy of Expression*. London.

Bell, C. 1872. *The Hand; its Mechanism and Vital Endowments*. (8th edition) Bell and Daldy, London.

Bell, D. C. and A. M. Bell. 1902. *Bell's Standard Elocutionist*. Hodder and Stoughton, London.

Benthall, J. and T. Polhemus. 1975. *The Body as a Medium of Expression*. Allen Lane, London.

Birdwhistell, R. L. 1952. *Introduction to Kinesics*. University of Louisville, Kentucky.

Birdwhistell, R. L. 1970. *Kinesics and Context. Essays on body motion communication*. University of Pennsylvania Press, Philadelphia.

Birdwhistell, R. L. 1975. 'Background considerations to the study of the body as a medium of "expression"', in *The Body as a Medium of Expression*. Allen Lane, London. pp. 36–58.

Birenbaum, A. and E. Sagarin (editors). 1973. *People in Places. The sociology of the familiar*. Nelson, London.

Blackmur, R. P. 1935. *Language as Gesture*. New York.

Blackmur, R. P. 1946. 'Language as gesture', in *Accent Anthology* (Ed. K. Quinn and C. Shattack). New York.

Blake, W. H. 1933. *A Preliminary Study of the Interpretation of Bodily Expression*. Columbia University, New York. (Reprinted in 1972 by AMS Press, New York.)

Boardman, J. 1964. *The Greeks Overseas*. Penguin, Harmondsworth.

Bogen, H. and O. Lipman. 1931. *Gang und Charakter*. Leipzig.

Bolinger, D. L. 1946. 'Thoughts on Yep and Nope', *American Speech*, 21, pp. 90–5.

Bonifacio, G. 1616. *L'arte dei cenni con la quale formandosi fauella visibile, si tratta della muta eloquenza, che non è altro che un facondo silentio*. Vicenza.

Boring, E. G. and E. B. Titchener. 1923. 'A model for the demonstration of facial expression', *American J. Psychol.*, 34, pp. 471–85.

Born, W. 1945. *Fetish, Amulet and Talisman*. CIBA Symposium 7 (7), Basle.

Bowers, R. H. 1948. 'Gesticulation in Elizabethan acting, *Southern Folklore Quarterly*, 12, pp. 267–77.

Boyvin de Vavrouy. 1636. *La Physionomie ou des Indices que la Nature a Mis au Corps Humain* ... Louis de Vandosme, Paris.

Bragaglia, A. G. 1930. *Evoluzione del Mimo*. Ceschina, Milan.

Brault, G. J. 1963. 'Kinesics in the classroom. Some typical French gestures', *The French Review*, 36 (Feb 4), pp. 374–82.

Bredtmann, H. 1889. *Der sprachliche Ausdruck einiger der gelaufigsten Gesten in den altfranzösischen Karlsepen*. Marburg.

Brewer, E. C. 1962. *Dictionary of Phrase and Fable*. Cassell, London. (See p. 902 for thumb-up and thumb-down interpretation.)

Brewer, W. D. 1951. 'Patterns of gesture among the Levantine Arabs', *American Anthropologist*, 53, pp. 232–7.

Broadbent, R. J. 1901. *A History of Pantomime*. Simpkins, Marshall.

Broeg, B. 1957. *Signals ... The Secret Language of Baseball*. The Gilette Co., Boston.

Brufford, R. (n.d.) *Teaching Mime*. Methuen, London. (Chapter 10: 'Other countries and other times'.)

Brun, J. 1967. *La Main*. Delpire, Paris.

Brun, T. 1969. *The International Dictionary of Sign Language*. Wolfe, London.

Bruyne, L. de. 1943. 'L'Imposition des mains dans l'art chrétien', *Riv. di arch. crist.*, 20, pp. 41–153.

Budge, E. A. W. 1930. *Amulets and Superstitions*. Oxford University Press, London. (See p. 172 for an ancient Egyptian fig-sign amulet.)

Buhler, K. 1933. *Ausdruckstheorie; das System an der Geschichte aufgezeigt*. Jena.

Bulwer, J. 1644. *Chirologia; or the Naturall Language of the Hand. Whereunto is added Chironomia: or, the Art of Manual Rhetoricke*. London.

Bulwer, J. 1648. *Philocophus; or the Deafe and Dumbe Man's Friend*. London.

Bulwer, J. 1649. *Pathomyotomia, or a Dissection of the Significative Muscles of the Affections of the Minde*. London.

Bulwer, J. 1650. *Anthropometamorphosis; Man Transform'd; or the Artificial Changeling*. London. (Re-issued in 1654 as: *A View of the People of the Whole World*.)

Burke, T. 1949. *The Streets of London*. London. (See p. 94 for London street gestures.)

Burton, R. 1800. *The Anatomy of Melancholy*. London. 2 vols.

Burton, R. F. 1862. *The City of the Saints*. London. (Chapter 2: 'The Indian Pantomime'.)

Buzby, D. E. 1924. 'Interpretation of facial expression', *Amer. J. Psychol.*, 35, pp. 602–4.

Caballero, R. 1898–1900. *Diccionario de Modismos*. Madrid.

Callisen, S. A. 'The evil eye in Italian art', *The Art Bulletin*, University of Chicago, 19, pp. 450–62.

Cannon, W. B. 1929. *Bodily Changes in Pain, Hunger, Fear and Rage*. Appleton-Century, New York.

Cardona, M. 1953–4. 'Gestos o ademanes habituales en Venezuela. Archivos venezolanos de folklore'. *Caracas, Univ. Cent. de Venezuela, ano II–III*, tomo II (3), pp. 159–66.

Carmichael, L. *et al.* 1937. 'Study of the judgment of manual expression as presented in still and motion pictures', *Journal of Social Psychology*, 8 (Feb.), pp. 115–42.

Caroso, F. 1600. *Della Nobiltà di Dame*. Venice.

Carpenter, E. and M. McLuhan. 1970. *Explorations in Communication*. Cape, London.

Carthy, J. D. and F. J. Ebling (editors). 1964. *The Natural History of Aggression*. Institute of Biology, Symp. 13. Academic Press, London. (See p. 37 for first use of term 're-motivating activities'.)

Casa, G. della. 1774. *Galateo: or, a Treatise on Politeness and Delicacy of Manners*. Dodsley, London.

Chance, M. R. A. 1962. 'An interpretation of some agonistic postures: the role of "cut-off" acts and postures'. *Symp. Zool. Soc.*, 8, pp. 71–89.

Chomentovskaja, O. 1938. 'Le comput digital, histoire d'un geste dans l'art de la Renaissance italienne', *Gazette des Beaux-Arts*, 20, pp. 157–72.

Cicero, M. T. 1468. *De Oratore*. Rome. (Fifteenth-century edition of the ancient works of Cicero. English trans., N. Guthrie, London, 1742.)

Cicourel, A. V. 1975. 'Gestural-sign language and the study of non-verbal communication', in *The Body as a Medium of Expression*. Allen Lane, London. pp. 195–232.

Clark, W. P. 1885. *Indian Sign Language*. Washington, Philadelphia.

Clodd, E. 1900. *The Story of the Alphabet*. New York.

Cocchiara, G. 1932. *Il Linguaggio del Gesto*. Bocca, Torino.

Cody, I. E. 1925. *How: Sign Talk in Pictures*. Boelter, Hollywood.

Cody, I. E. 1972. *Indian Talk*, N.E.L., London.

Coleman, C. 1832. *The Mythology of the Hindus*. London.

Cook, A. B. 1907. 'Cykoφanthc', *Classical Review*, London, 21, pp. 133–6. (For fig sign.)

Coomaraswamy, A. and G. K. Duggirala (translators), 1936. *Nandikesvara, The Mirror of Gestures*. Wehye, New York.

Cosgrove, D. 1954. *A Study of the Reliability of Judging Emotions as Expressed by the Hands*. Master's Thesis, University of Detroit.

Coss, R. 1965. *Mood-provoking Visual Stimuli*. Univ. of California Press.

Cossetta, A. 1946. *Natural Gestures and Postures in Speech*. Kansas City, Missouri. (On gestures and salesmanship.)

Cotgrave, R. 1611. *A Dictionaire of the French and English Tongues*. Adam Islip, London.

Craig, A. E. 1941. *The Speech Arts; A Textbook of Oral English*. New York. (See chapter on 'Pantomime and Gesture'.)

Cranach, M. von and I. Vine (editors). 1973. *Social Communication and Movement*. Academic Press, London.

Cresollius, L. 1620. *Vacationes Autumnales sive De perfecta Oratoris Actione et Pronunciatione*. Paris. (3 vols. Appears to be the earliest post-classical study of gestures.)

Critchley, M. 1939. *The Language of Gesture*. Arnold, London.

Critchley, M. 1975. *Silent Language*. Butterworth, London.

Croce, B. 1935. 'Il linguaggio del gesto', in *Varietà di Storia Letteraria e Civile*. Serie Prima. Bari.

Cushing, J. H. 1892. 'Manual concepts', *American Anthropologist*, 5, pp. 289–317.

Cutner, H. 1940. *A Short History of Sex-Worship*. Watts, London. (See p. 35 for fig symbolism.)

Cuyer, E. 1902. *La Mimique*. Paris. (See pp. 307–51 for a brief dictionary of gestures.)

D'Alviella, G. 1894. *The Migration of Symbols*. London.

D'Angelo, L. 1969. *How to be an Italian*. Price, Sterne, Sloane. Los Angeles.

Daremberg, C. and S. Edmond. 1877. *Dictionnaire des antiquités grecques et romaines*. Paris. 5 vols.

Darwin, C. 1872. *The Expression of the Emotions in Man and Animals*. John Murray, London.

Davidson, L. J. 1950. 'Some current folk gestures and sign language', *American Speech*, 25 (Feb.), pp. 3–9.

Davidson, L. J. 1951. *A Guide to American Folklore*. Univ. Denver Press.

Davis, F. 1971. *Inside Intuition. What we know about non-verbal communication*. McGraw-Hill, New York.

Davis, R. C. 1934. 'Specificity of facial expressions; correction of a statistical misinterpretation in Landis' experiment', *J. General Psychol.*, 10 (Jan.), pp. 42–58.

De Gubernatis, A. 1878. *La Mythologie des plantes*. Reinwald et Cie, Paris.

De Haerne, D. 1875. *The Natural Language of Signs*. American Annals of the Deaf and Dumb.

De Jorio, A. 1832. *La Mimica degli Antichi Investigata nel Gestire Napoletano*. Naples.

Devereaux, G. 1949. 'Some Mohave gestures', *American Anthropologist*, 51, pp. 325–6.

Drechsler, P. 1906. *Sitte, Brauch, und Volksglaube in Schlesien*. Leipzig. vols. (For Silesian gestures.)

Dumas, G. and A. Ombredane. 1930. *Nouveau Traité de psychologie*. Paris. 5 vols.

Dyer, T. T. F. 1883. *Folk Lore of Shakespeare*. Griffith and Farran, London.

Efron, D. 1972. *Gesture, Race and Culture*. Mouton, The Hague. (First published in 1941 as: *Gesture and Environment*. King's Crown Press, New York.)

Efron, D. and J. P. Foley, Jr. 1937. 'Gestural behavior and social setting', *Zeit. f. Sozialforsch.*, 6, pp. 152–61.

Eibl-Eibesfeldt, I. 1970. *Ethology. The Biology of Behavior*. Holt, Rinehart and Winston, New York.

Eibl-Eibesfeldt, I. 1971. 'Zur Ethologie menschlichen Grufsverhaltens II', *Zeit. f. Tierpsych.*, 29, pp. 196–213.

Eibl-Eibesfeldt, I. 1972. *Love and Hate. The Natural History of Behavior Patterns*. Holt, Rinehart and Winston, New York.

Eibl-Eibesfeldt, I. 1973. 'The expressive behaviour of the deaf-and-blind born', in *Social Communication and Movement*. Academic Press, London. pp. 163–94.

Eisenberg, P. 1940. 'Motivation of expressive movement', *J. Gen. Psychol.*, 23 (July), pp. 89–101.

Ekman, P. 1969. 'The repertoire of nonverbal behavior', *Semiotica*, 1 (1), pp. 49–98.

Ekman, P. 1970. 'Universal facial expressions of emotion', *Californian Mental Health Research Digest*, 8 (4), pp. 151–8.

Ekman, P. 1971. 'Universal and cultural differences in facial expressions of emotion', *Nebraska Symp. on Motivation*.

Ekman, P. (editor). 1973. *Darwin and Facial Expression*. Academic Press, New York.

Ekman, P. 1976. 'Movements with precise meanings', *J. Communication*, 26 (3), pp. 14–26.

Ekman, P. and W. V. Friesen. 1968. 'Nonverbal behavior in psychotherapy research', *Research in Psychotherapy*, 3, pp. 179–216.

Ekman, P. and W. V. Friesen. 1969. 'The repertoire of nonverbal behavior: categories, origins, usage and coding', *Semiotica*, 1 (1), pp. 49–98.

Ekman, P. and W. V. Friesen. 1969. 'Nonverbal leakage and clues to deception', *Psychiatry*, 31 (1), pp. 88–106.

Ekman, P. and W. V. Friesen. (1971) 'Constants across cultures in the face and emotion', *J. Personality and Soc. Psych.*, 17 (2), pp. 124–9.

Ekman, P. and W. V. Friesen. 1972. 'Hand movements', *J. Communication*, 22, pp. 353–74.

Ekman, P. and W. V. Friesen. 1974. 'Detecting deception from the body or face', *J. Personality and Soc. Psych.*, 29 (3), pp. 288–98.

Ekman, P. and W. V. Friesen. 1974. 'Nonverbal behavior and psychopathology', in *The Psychology of Depression: Contemporary Theory and Research*. Winston and Sons, Washington, D.C. pp. 203–32.

Ekman, P. and W. V. Friesen. 1975. *Unmasking the Face*. Prentice-Hall, New Jersey.

Ekman, P. and W. V. Friesen. 1976. 'Measuring facial movement', *Envir. Psychol. and Nonverbal Behav.*, 1 (1), pp. 56–75.

Ekman, P., W. V. Friesen and P. Ellsworth. 1972. *Emotion in the Human Face*. Pergamon Press, New York.

Ekman, P., W. V. Friesen and K. R. Scherer. 1976. 'Body movement and voice pitch in deceptive interaction', *Semiotica*, 16:1, pp. 23–7.

Ekman, P., W. V. Friesen and S. S. Tomkins. 1971. 'Facial affect scoring technique: a first validity study', *Semiotica*, 3 (1), pp. 37–58.

Ekman, P., E. R. Sorensen and W. V. Friesen. 1969. 'Pan-cultural elements in facial displays of emotion', *Science*, 164, pp. 86–8.

Elworthy, F. 1895. *The Evil Eye*. John Murray, London.

Elworthy, F. 1900. *Horns of Honour*. John Murray, London.

Engel, J. J. 1785–6. *Ideen zu einer Mimik*. Berlin. 2 vols. (repub. 1804, 1810). In French: *Idées sur le geste et l'action théâtrale*. Paris, 1788–9. 2 vols.

Farmer, J. S. and W. E. Henley. 1909. *Slang and its Analogues*. Privately printed. (See entries for 'Horn', 'Fig', 'V', 'Sight', 'Fork', and 'Coffee-milling', which relate to gestures.)

Fast, J. 1970. *Body Language*. Evans, New York.

Feldman, S. 1959. *Mannerisms of Speech and Gesture*. New York.

Fenichel, O. 1928. 'Die "lange Nase"', *Zeit. f. Anwendung der Psychoanalyse auf die Natur- und Geisteswissen*, 14, pp. 502–4. (On thumbing a nose.)

Fernberger, S. W. 1928. 'False suggestion and the Piderit model', *Amer. J. Psychol.*, 40 (Oct.), pp. 562–8.

Fernberger, S. W. 1930. 'Can emotion be accurately judged by its facial expression alone?', *J. Criminal Law and Criminology*, 20 (Feb.), pp. 554–64.

Field, C. 1918. 'Salutes and Saluting, Naval and Military', *J. Roy. United Service Inst.*, 63, pp. 42–9.

Fields, S. J. 1953. 'Discrimination of facial expression and its relation to personal adjustment', *J. Soc. Psychol.*, 38, pp. 63–71.

Firth, R. 1973. *Symbols, Public and Private*. Allen and Unwin, London.

Fischer, H. E. 1955. 'My case as a prisoner was different', *Life Magazine*, 38 (26) (June 27), p. 157. (American prisoners photographed making gestures in a Chinese prison.)

Fisher, S. and S. E. Cleveland. 1968. *Body Image and Personality*. Dover, New York.

Flachskampf, L. 1938. *Spanische Gebärdensprache*. Erlangen. (Reprinted from *Romanische Forschungen*, 52, pp. 205–58.) (For Spanish gestures.)

Frijda, N. H. 1953. 'The understanding of facial expression of emotion', *Acta Psychologica*, 9, pp. 294–362.

Frobenius, L. 1909. *The Childhood of Man*. Seeley, London. (See Chapter 6: 'Sign and gesture language'.)

Gambers, H. S. 1937. *Curiosa Sexualis*. Brijmohan, Amritsar. (See p. 143 for fig-sign.)

Garry, R. 1888. *Elocution, Voice and Gesture*. Bemrose, London.

Geiger, P. and R. Weiss. 1951. *Atlas de Folklore Suisse*. Basle. (For distribution of greetings.)

George, S. S. 1916. 'Gesture of affirmation among the Arabs', *Amer. J. Psychol.*, 27 (July), pp. 320–3.

Gifford, E. S. 1958. *The Evil Eye: Studies in the Folklore of Vision*. Macmillan, New York.

Giles, P. 1913–14. 'A far-travelled story', *Aberdeen University Review*, 1, pp. 259–64. (On the Zeichendisput: man holds up fingers, opponent misinterprets meaning.)

Giraudet, A. 1895. *Mimique, physiognomie et gestes*. Paris.

Godefroy, 1884. *Dictionnaire de l'ancienne langue française. IXième–XVième Siècle*. Paris.

Goffman, E. 1961. *Encounters*. Bobbs-Merrill Co., Indianapolis.

Goffman, E. 1963. *Behavior in Public Places*. Free Press, New York.

Goffman, E. 1967. *Interaction Ritual*, The Penguin Press, London.

Goffman, E. 1969. *The Presentation of Self in Everyday Life*. The Penguin Press, London.

Goffman, E. 1970. *Strategic Interaction*. Blackwell, Oxford.

Goffman, E. 1971. *Relations in Public*. The Penguin Press, London.

Goffman, E. 1974. *Frame Analysis*. The Penguin Press, London.

Goldberg, B. Z. 1931. *The Sacred Fire*. Jarrold, London. (See p. 106 for fig-sign.)

Goldberg, I. 1938. *The Wonder of Words*. New York. (See pp. 53–7.)

Goldsmith, E. 1924. *Life Symbols as Related to Sex Symbolism*. New York.

Goldziher, I. 1886. 'Über Gebärden und Zeichensprache bei den Arabern', *Zeit. f. Völkerpsychol. und Sprach.*, 16 (4), Berling, pp. 369–86.

Goldziher, I. 1906. 'Zauberelemente im Islamischen Gebet', *Orientalische Studien. Theodor Noldeke zum 70. Geburtstag I*. Giessen. pp. 303–29.

Gombrich, E. H. 1966. 'Ritualized gesture and expression in art', *Phil. Trans. Roy. Soc.*, London B. 251 (772), pp. 393–401.

Goodland, R. 1931. *A Bibliography of Sex Rites and Customs*. London. (For sexual gestures.)

Grant, E. C. 1968. 'An ethological description of non-verbal behaviour during interviews', *Brit. J. med. Psychol.*, 41, pp. 177–84.

Gratiolet, P. 1865. *De la Physionomie et des mouvements d'expression*. Paris.

Gray, G. W. 1934. 'Problems in the teaching of gesture', *Quart. J. Speech Education*, 10, p. 238–52.

Green, J. R. 1968. *Gesture Inventory for the Teaching of Spanish*. Chilton Books, Philadelphia.

Green, L. 1929. *Einführung in das Wesen unserer Gesten und Bewegungen*. Berlin.

Grimas, A. J. (editor.) 1967. 'Pratiques et langages gestuels', *Langages*, 10.

Gubbins, J. K. 1946. 'Some observations on the evil eye in Greece', *Folk-Lore* (London) 62 (Dec.), pp. 195–8.

Gubernatis, A de. 1872. *Zoological Mythology*. Trubner, London. (See Vol. 2, pp. 232–4, for cuckold.)

Guenther, J. 1930–1. 'Kultur der Geste – Geste des Kulturs', *Gestalt*, 3, pp. 41–8.

Guildford, J. P. and M. Wilkie. 1930. 'New model for the demonstration of facial expressions', *Amer. J. Psychol.*, 42, pp. 436–9.

Guthrie, R. D. 1976. *Body Hot Spots. The anatomy of human social organs and behavior*. Van Nostrand Reinhold, New York.

Hacks, C. 1887. *Le Geste*. Paris.

Haddon, A. C. 1907. 'The gesture language of the Eastern Islanders of Torres Straits', *Camb. Anthrop. Exped. to Torres Straits, Reports*, 3, pp. 261–2.

Hadley, L. F. 1887. *A List of the Primary Gestures in Indian Sign-talk*. Anadarko, Indian Territory.

Hadley, L. F. 1890. *A Lesson in Sign Talk*. Fort Smith, Arkansas.

Hadley, L. F. 1893. *Indian Sign Talk*. Chicago.

Haiding, K. 1955. 'Von der Gebärdensprache der Märchenerzähler', *Folklore Fellowship Communications Helsinki, Academia Scientiarum Fennica*, No. 155, pp. 1–16. (On Austrian gestures.)

Haigh, A. E. 1907. *The Attic Theatre*. Oxford.

Hall, E. T. 1959. *The Silent Language*. Doubleday, New York.

Hall, E. T. 1966. *The Hidden Dimension*. Bodley Head, London.

Hall, G. S. 1921. 'Gesture, mimesis, types of temperament and movie pedagogy', *Pedagogical Seminary*, 28, pp. 171–201.

Halliwell, J. O. 1881. *A Dictionary of Archaic and Provincial Words*. John Russell Smith, London.

Hamalian, L. 1965. 'Communication by gesture in the Middle East', *Etc; A Review of General Semantics*, 22, p. 43.

Hapgood, R. 1966. 'Speak hands for me: gesture as language in *Julius Caesar*', *Drama Survey*, 53, pp. 162–70.

Hass, H. 1970. *The Human Animal*. Putnam, New York.

Hayes, F. C. 1940. 'Should we have a dictionary of gestures?' *S. Folk-lore Quarterly*, 4, pp. 239–45.

Hayes, F. C. 1941. 'Beckoning', *American Notes and Queries*, 1, p. 142.

Hayes, F. C. 1941. 'Gesture', in *Encyclopedia Americana*. New York.

Hayes, F. C. 1942. 'Just a gesture', *Collier's Magazine*, 109 (Jan. 31), pp. 14–15.

Hayes, F. C. 1951. 'Gestos o ademanes folklóricos', *Folklore Americas*, 11, pp. 15–21.

Hayes, F. C. 1957. 'Gestures: a working bibliography', *S. Folk-lore Quarterly*, 21, pp. 218–317.

Hayner, P. C. 1956. 'Expressive meaning', *J. Philosophy*, 53, pp. 149–57.

Henderson, A. V. 1971. 'Hand Sign Language', *The Rome Weekly*, April 25 – May 1, p. 16.

Henley, N. M. 1977. *Body Politics; Power, Sex and Nonverbal Communication*. Prentice-Hall, New Jersey.

Hess, E. 1975. *The Tell-tale Eye*. New York.

Hewes, G. W. 1955. 'World distribution of certain postural habits', *American Anthropologist*, 57, (2) (Part 1, April), pp. 231–44.

Hewes, G. W. 1957. 'The anthropology of posture', *Sci. Amer.*, 196 (Feb.), pp. 123–32.

Higgins, D. D. 1942. *How to Talk to the Deaf*. Chicago.

Hildburgh, W. L. 1946. 'Apotropaism in Greek vase-painting', *Folk-Lore* (London) 62 (Dec.), pp. 154–78.

Hildburgh, W. L. 1951. 'Psychology underlying the employment of amulets in Europe', *Folk-Lore*, 62, p. 242.

Hindmarch, I. 1973. 'Eyes, eye-spots and pupil dilation in non-verbal communication', in *Social Communication and Movement*. Academic Press, London. pp. 299–321.

Hocart, A. M. 1939. 'The mechanism of the evil eye', *Folk-Lore* (London) 49, pp. 156–7.

Hoffman, W. J. 1895. *The Beginnings of Writing*. New York. (See Chapter 6: 'Gesture signs and attitudes'.)

Hoffmann-Krayer, E. and H. Bachtold-Staubli. 1927. *Handwörterbuch des deutschen Aberglaubens*. Berlin.

Hoppe, R. 1937. *Die romanische Geste im Rolandslied*. Koenigsberg.

Howes, M. 1975. *Amulets*. Hale, London.

Huber, E. 1931. *Evolution of Facial Musculature and Facial Expression*. Johns Hopkins Press, Baltimore.

Hughes, H. 1900. *Die Mimick des Menschen auf Grund voluntarischer Psychologie*. Frankfurt.

Hulin, W. S. and Katz, D. 1935. 'Frois-Wittmann pictures of facial expressions', *J. Exp. Psychol.*, 18 (Aug.), pp. 482–98.

Irwin, F. W. 1932. 'Thresholds for the perception of difference in facial expression and its elements', *Amer. J. Psychol.*, 44 (Jan.), pp. 1–17.

Izard, C. E. 1971. *The Face of Emotion*. Meredith, New York.

Jakobson, R. 1972. 'Motor signs for "Yes" and "No"', *Lang. in Soc.*, 1, pp. 91–6.

James, W. T. 1932. 'A study of the expression of bodily posture', *J. Genetic Psychol.*, 7, pp. 405–37.

Jarden, E. and W. Fernberger. 1926. 'Effect of suggestion on judgment of facial expression of emotion', *Amer. J. Psychol.*, 37 (Oct.), pp. 565–70.

Jenness, A. 1932. 'Effects of coaching subjects in the recognition of facial expressions', *J. General Psychol.*, 7, pp. 163–78.

Jennings, A. 1932. 'Differences in the recognition of facial expression of emotion', *J. General Psychol.*, 7, pp. 192–6.

Johannesson, A. 1949. *Origin of Language*. Reykjavik.

Johannesson, A. 1952. *Gestural Origin of Language*. Reykjavik and Oxford.

Johnson, H. G., P. Ekman and W. V. Friesen. 1975. Communicative body movements: American emblems', *Semiotica*, 15 (4), pp. 335–53.

Jones, H. 1968. *Sign Language*. E.U.P., London.

Jones, H. P. 1918. *Dictionary of Foreign Phrases and Classical Quotations*. Grant, Edinburgh. (See p. 93 for thumb-down gesture.)

Jousse, M. 1923. 'Études de psychologie linguistique; le style oral, ryth-mique et mnemotechnique chez les verbo-moteurs', *Arch. de Philo-sophie*. 2 (4), pp. 236–40.

Jousse, M. 1929. *Études sur la psychologie du geste. Les Rabbis d'Israel. Les Récitatifs rythmiques parallèles*. Paris.

Jousse, M. 1931. 'Méthodologie de la psychologie du geste', *Revue des Cours et Conférences*, pp. 201–18.

Jousse, M. 1936. 'Le mimisme humain et l'anthropologie du langage', *Revue Anthropologique*, 7–9, pp. 201–15.

Kakumasu, J. 1968. 'Urubu sign language', *Int. J. of Amer. Ling.*, 34, pp. 275–81.

Kany, C. E. 1960. *American-Spanish Euphemisms*. Berkeley and Los Angeles.

Kapsalis, P. T. 1946. 'Gestures in Greek Art and Literature'. Ph. D. Thesis, Johns Hopkins University.

Kaulfers, W. V. 1931. 'Curiosities of colloquial gestures', *Hispania*, 14, pp. 249–64.

Kaulfers, W. V. 1932. 'Handful of Spanish', *Education*, 52 (March), pp. 423–8.

Kendon, A. 1972. 'Some relationships between body motion and speech', in *Studies in Dyadic Communication* (ed. A. Siegman and B. Pope). Pergamon Press, Oxford.

Kendon, A. 1973. 'The role of visible behaviour in the organization of social interaction', in *Social Communication and Movement*. Academic Press, London. pp. 29–74.

Kendon, A. 1977. *Studies in the Behavior of Social Interaction*. Indiana University, Bloomington.

Kendon, A. and A. Ferber. 1973. 'A description of some human greetings', in *Comparative Ecology and Behaviour of Primates* (ed. R. P. Michael and J. Crook). Academic Press, London.

Key, M. R. 1975. *Male/Female Language*. Scarecrow Press, Metuchen, New Jersey.

Key, M. R. 1975. *Paralinguistics and Kinesics. Nonverbal Communication*. Scarecrow Press, Metuchen, New Jersey.

King, W. S. 1949. 'Hand gestures', *Western Folklore*, 8, pp. 263–4.

Kleen, T. 1924. 'Hand-poses of the priests of Bali', *Asia*, 24 (Feb.), pp. 129–31.

Kleen, T. 1924. *Mudras. The Ritual Hand-poses of the Buddha Priests and the Shiva Priests of Bali*. Kegan Paul & Co., London.

Kleinpaul, R. 1888. *Die lebende Sprache und ihre Weltstellung*, Leipzig.

Kleiser, G. 1915. *Kleiser's Complete Guide to Public Speaking*. Funk and Wagnall, New York. (See pp. 198–213 on gesture.)

Kline, L. W. and D. E. Johannsen. 1935. 'Comparative role of the face and of face-body-hands as aids in identifying emotions', *J. Abnormal and Soc. Psych.*, pp. 415–26.

Klitgard, C. 1934. 'Skaelsord og foragtelig gestus', *Danske Studier*. Copen-hagen. pp. 88–9. (For Danish insult gestures.)

Knight, R. P. 1892. *The Symbolic Language of Ancient Art and Mythology*. New York. (See pp. 29–30 for the fig-sign.)

Knowlson, J. R. 1965. 'Idea of gesture as a universal language in the 17th and 18th centuries', *J. Hist. Ideas,* 26, pp. 495–508.

Koenig, O. 1976. 'Behaviour study and civilization', in *The Nature of Human Behaviour*. Allen and Unwin, London. pp. 153–210.

Kohlbrugge, J. H. F. 1926. *Tier- und Menschenantlitz als Abwehrzauber*. Bonn.

Kroeber, A. L. 1958. 'Sign language inquiry', *Int. J. of Amer. Ling.*, 24, pp. 1–19.

Krout, M. H. 1931. 'Symbolic gestures in clinical study of personality', *Trans. Illinois State Acad. Sci.*, 24, pp. 519–23.

Krout, M. H. 1935. 'Autistic gestures', *Psych. Monog.*, 46 (4), pp. 1–126.

Krout, M. H. 1935. 'The social and psychological significance of gestures', *J. Genetic Psychol.*, 47, pp. 385–412.

Krout, M. H. 1937. 'Further studies in the relation of personality and gesture; a nosological analysis of autistic gestures', *J. Exp. Psychol.*, 20. pp. 167–72.

Krout, M. H. 1942. *Introduction to Social Psychology*. Harper, New York. (See Chapter 6: 'Symbolism'.)

La Barre, W. 1947. 'The cultural basis of emotions and gestures', *J. Personality*, 16, pp. 49–68.

La Barre, W. 1964. 'Paralinguistics, kinesics, and cultural anthropology', in *Approaches to Semiotics* (ed. T. A. Sebeok). Mouton. The Hague. pp. 191–220.

La Fin. 1692. *Sermo Mirabilis, or the Silent Language*. London. (An early suggestion for finger-language for the deaf-mutes, but preceded by Jerome Cardano, Pedro Pone de León and John Bulwer.)

Lake, E. F. C. 1933. 'Some notes on the evil eye round the Mediterranean basin', *Folk-Lore* (London) 44, pp. 93–8.

Lamb, W. 1965. *Posture and Gesture*. Duckworth, London.

Lamb, W. 1968. 'To make a gesture', *20th Century*, 177, pp. 30–3.

La Meri. 1941. *The Gesture Language of the Hindu Dance*. Columbia University Press, New York.

Landis, C. 1924. 'Studies in emotional reaction: II', *J. Comp. Psychol.*, 4, pp. 447–509.

Landis, C. and W. A. Hunt. 1939. *The Startle Pattern*. New York.

Langdon, S. 1919. 'Gesture in Sumerian and Babylonian prayer', *J. Roy. Asiatic Soc.*, pp. 531–56.

LaPiere, R. T. and P. R. Farnsworth. 1949. *Social Psychology*. McGraw-Hill, New York. (See Chapter 6 on gesture.)

Lavater, J. C. 1789. *Essays on Physiognomy*. John Murray, London.

Lawrence, R. M. 1898. *The Magic of the Horseshore*. Boston.

Lawson, J. 1957. *Mime*. London.

Leach, M. (editor). 1972. *Standard Dictionary of Folklore, Mythology and Legend*. N.E.L. London. (See article by C. F. Potter on 'gesture', pp. 451–3.)

Le Faucher, M. 1657. *Traité de l'action de l'orateur*. Paris.

Leite de Vasconcellos Pereira de Mello, J. 1892. *Sur les Amulettes portugaises*. Lisbon. (For the fig-sign.)

Leite de Vasconcellos Pereira de Mello, J. 1917. *A Linguagem dos Gestos.* Ethnografia Artistica III. Separata da Alma Nova, Lisboa 2.

Leite de Vasconcellos Pereira de Mello, J. 1925. *A Figa.* Porto, 1925.

Leroi-Gourhan, A. 1964. *Le Geste et la parole.* Albin Michel, Paris.

Leroy, O. 1935. *A Dictionary of French Slang.* Harrap, London.

Licht, H. 1963. *Sexual Life in Ancient Greece.* Routledge and Kegan Paul, London. (See pp. 367 and 370 for the fig-sign.)

Lieth, L. von der. 1967. *Dansk Døve-tegnsprog.* Akademisk Forlag, Copenhagen.

Liggett, J. 1974. *The Human Face.* Constable, London.

Ljung, M. 1965. 'Principles of a stratificational analysis of the Plains Indian sign language', *Int. J. of Amer. Ling.*, 31, pp. 119–27.

Loomis, G. 1956. 'Sign language of truck drivers', *Western Folklore*, 5, pp. 205–16.

Lowen, A. 1958. *Physical Dynamics of Character Structure.* Grune and Stratton, New York.

Lucas, J. 1675. *Actio Oratoris, seu de gestu et voce.* Paris.

Lutz, F. 1908. 'Inheritance of the manner of clasping hands', *Amer. Naturalist*, 42, pp. 195–6.

Lutz, F. 1927. *The Technique of Pantomime.* Berkeley, California.

Lutz, H. F. 1936. 'Speech consciousness among Egyptians and Babylonians', *Osiris*, 2, pp. 1–27.

Lyall, A. 1930. *It Isn't Done, or The Future of Taboo Among the British Islanders.* Kegan Paul, Trench, Trubner and Co., London.

Lynn, J. G. and D. R. 1943. 'Smile and hand dominance in relation to basic modes of adaptation', *J. Abnormal and Soc. Psychol.*, 38, pp. 250–76.

Lyall, A. 1956. 'Italian sign language', *20th Century*, 159, pp. 600–4.

McCord, C. 1948. 'Gestures (at the University of California, Berkeley)', *Western Folklore*, 7, pp. 290–2.

MacHovec, F. J. 1975. *Body Talk.* Peter Pauper Press, Mt Vernon, New York.

Mackay, C. 1877. *The Greek Etymology of the Languages of Western Europe.* Trubner and Co., London.

Maclay, G. and H. Knipe. 1972. *The Dominant Man.* Delacotre Press, N.Y.

Malecot, J. L. 'A note on gesture and language', *Quart. J. Speech*, 13, p. 439.

Mallery, G. 1879. 'Sign language among the North American Indians compared with that among other peoples and deafmutes', *U.S. Bureau of Ethnology*, 1, pp. 263–552.

Mallery, G. 1881. *The Gesture Speech of Man.* Salem.

Mallery, G. 1891. *Greetings by Gesture.* New York.

Mantegazza, P. 1904. *Physiognomy and Expression.* Scott, London.

Maple, E. 1972. *Superstition and the Superstitious.* Barnes, New York. (See p. 133 for finger-crossing as act of making the sign of the cross.)

Maranon, G. 1950. 'The psychology of gesture', *J. Nerv. and Ment. Diseases*, 122, pp. 469–97.

Marcadé, J. 1961. *Roma Amor.* Negel, Geneva. (See pp. 26 and 92 for fig and horn signs.)

Marsh, P. 1978. *Aggro: The Illusion of Violence.* Dent, London.

Marsh, P., E. Rosser and R. Harré. 1978. *The Rules of Disorder*. Routledge and Kegan Paul, London.

Mawer, I. 1932. *The Art of Mime*. London.

Meerloo, J. A. M. 1971. *Intuition and the Evil Eye*. Servire, Wassenaar.

Mehta, S. S. 1914. 'Modes of salutation', *J. Anthropol. Soc. Bombay*, 10, pp. 263–72.

Merryman, M. 1945. *Portuguese: A Portrait of the Language of Brazil*. Rio de Janeiro. (See chapter on: 'The eloquence of Brazilian hands'.)

Michaelis, C. F. 1818. *Die Kunst der rednerischen und theatralischen Declamation*. Leipzig. (Founded on Austin's *Chironomia*.)

Michel, C. 1776. *L'Instruction des sourds et muets, par voies des signes méthodiques*. Paris.

Michel, K. 1910. *Die Sprache des Körpers*. Leipzig.

Minervini, G. 1852. *Monumenti antichi inediti*. Naples. (For fig-sign as seen on Greek vases.)

Mitchell, M. E. 1968. *How to Read the Language of the Face*. Macmillan, New York.

Mitton, A. 1949. 'Le langage par gestes', *Nouvelle Revue des Traditions Populaires*, 1, pp. 138–51.

Montaigne, M. de. 1603. *The Essayes*. London. (Reprinted by Scolar Press, Menston, Yorkshire in 1969.) (See Book Two, Chapter 12 for comments on bowing, kissing etc.)

Morris, C. W. 1938. *Foundations of the Theory of Signs*. Chicago.

Morris, C. W. 1946. *Signs, Language and Behavior*. New York.

Morris, D. 1967. *The Naked Ape*. Jonathan Cape, London.

Morris, D. 1969. *The Human Zoo*. Jonathan Cape, London.

Morris, D. 1970. *Patterns of Reproductive Behaviour*. Cape, London.

Morris, D. 1971. *Intimate Behaviour*. Jonathan Cape, London.

Morris, D. 1977. *Manwatching. A field-guide to human behaviour*. Jonathan Cape/Elsevier, London/Oxford.

Moser, O. 1954. 'Zur Geschichte und Kenntnis der volkstümlichen Gebärden', *Sonderdruck aus Carinthia I, Mitteilungen des Geschichtsvereines für Kärnten*, 144, Heft 1–3, Klagenfurt, pp. 735–74. (For the use of the fig-sign in Carinthia between 1570 and 1670.)

Mosher, J. A. 1916. *Essentials of Effective Gestures*. New York.

Mosher, J. A. 1931. *A Complete Course in Public Speaking*. New York. (See Part II, Gesture, pp. 1–82.)

Mountford, C. P. 1938. 'Gesture language of the Ngada tribe of Warburton ranges, Western Australian', *Oceania*, 9, No. 2, pp. 152–5.

Mower, I. 1932. *The Art of Mime*. Methuen, London. (Chapters 2, 3, 4.)

Munari, B. 1963. *Supplemento al Dizionario Italiano*. Muggiani, Milan.

Napier, J. 1962. 'The evolution of the hand', *Sci. Amer.*, 207 (6), pp. 56–62.

Neckel, G. 1935. 'Über eine allgemeine Geste des Schmerzes', *Archiv für das Studium der neueren Sprachen*, 167, p. 64.

Neville, H. 1900. 'Gesture', in *Voice, Speech and Gesture*. Deacon, London.

Nierenberg, G. I. and H. Calero. 1971. *How to Read a Person Like a Book*. Hawthorn, New York.

Ohm, T. 1948. *Die Gebetsgebärden der Völker und das Christentum*. Leiden. (On prayer gestures.)

Olofson, H. 1974. 'Hausa language about gesture', *Anthropol. Ling.*, 16 (1).

Opie, I. and P. Opie. 1959. *The Lore and Language of Schoolchildren*. Clarendon Press, Oxford. (For crossed fingers.)

Orton, H. and N. Wright. 1974. *A Word Geography of England*. Seminar Press, London.

Ott, E. A. 1902. *How to Gesture*. New York.

Paget, R. A. S. 1930. *Human Speech*. New York.

Paget, R. A. S. 1935. *This English*. London.

Paget, R. A. S. 1937. 'Gesture language', *Nature*, 139, p. 138.

Paget, R. A. S. 1944. 'Origin of language, gesture theory', *Science*, 99, pp. 14–15.

Paget, R. A. S. 1946. 'Gesture as a constant factor in linguistics', *Nature*, 158, p. 29.

Papas, W. 1972. *Instant Greek*. Papas, Athens.

Parrish, W. M. 1947. *Speaking in Public*. New York.

Partridge, E. 1937. *A Dictionary of Slang and Unconventional English*. Routledge, London.

Pavitt, T. and K. Pavitt. 1914. *The Book of Talismans*. Rider and Son, London. (See pp. 93–4 for the fig-sign and the cornuta.)

Pei, M. 1950. 'Gesture language', *Life Magazine*, Jan. 9, pp. 79–81. (Illustrated article estimates 700,000 gestures around the world.)

Phillot, D. C. 1906. 'A note on the mercantile sign language of India', *J. and Proc. Roy. Asiatic Soc. Bengal*, N.S. 3, pp. 333–4.

Phillot, D. C. 1907. 'A note on the sign, code and secret language, etc., amongst the Persians', *J. and Proc. Roy. Asiatic Soc. Bengal*, N.S. 3, pp. 619–22.

Pitre, G. 1877. 'Gesti ed insegne del popolo Siciliano', *Rivista di letteratura popolare*, 1, pp. 32–43. (For Sicilian gestures.)

Pitre, G. 1889. *Usi e Costumi del Popolo Siciliano*. Palermo. (See Vol. 2, p. 349, for Sicilian gestures.)

Pliny. 1601. *The Historie of the World*.

Potter, C. F. 1972. 'Gestures', in *Funk and Wagnall's Standard Dictionary of Folklore, Mythology and Legend*. N.E.L., London. pp. 451–3.

Poyatos, F. 1975. 'Gesture Inventories: fieldwork methodology and problems', *Semiotica*, 13 (2), pp. 199–227.

Praetorius. 1677. *De Pollice*. Leipzig.

Quennell, P. 1971. *The Colosseum*. Readers Digest. London.

Quintilian, M. F. 1470. *Quintiliani Institutiones Oratoriae*. Rome. (Fifteenth-century edition of the first century A.D. writings of the Roman rhetorician Quintilian. English trans. by J. Patsall 1774.)

Rabanales, A. 1954–5. 'La Somatolalia', *Boletín de Filología* (Universidad de Chile), 8, pp. 355–78. (For a general survey of gestures.)

Rabelais, F. 1653. *The Works of Mr Francis Rabelais*. (First English edition, reprinted 1933 by the Navarre Society, London. See: Book 2, Ch. 19 for a 'battle of gestures', involving hand-pursing, nose-thumbing, and fig-signs. Also Book 4, Ch. 45 for fig insult.)

Read, A. W. 1963. 'The first stage in the history of "O.K."', *American Speech*, 38 (1), pp. 5–27

Reinach, S. 1924. 'L'Histoire des gestes', *Revue Archéologique* (Paris), 20, pp. 64–79.

Requena, V. 1797. *Scoperta della Chironomia osia dell'arte di gestire con le mani*. Parmi.

Robertson, W. 1693. *Phraseologia Generalis*. Cambridge. (See entry for 'finger', which gives early names for each digit.)

Rohrich, L. 1967. *Gebärde-Metapher-Parodie*. Düsseldorf.

Rolland, E. 1886–7. 'Les gestes, I', *Melusine*, 3, cols 116–19. (For gestures from Turkey and France.)

Rosa, L. A. 1929. *Espressione e Mimica*. Milan. (Includes 300 sketches of gesticulating Italians.)

Rose, H. A. 1919. 'The language of gesture', *Folk-Lore*, 30, pp. 312–15.

Roth, H. L. 1890. 'On salutations', *J. Anthropol. Inst.*, 19, p. 164.

Roth, W. E. 1897. *Ethnological Studies among the N.W. Central Queensland Aborigines*. Brisbane. (See Chapter 4 for Aboriginal gestures, 213 of which are illustrated in plates 2–10.)

Rous, F. and Z. Bogan. 1685. *Attick Antiquities*. London. (For reference to 'hay in his horns', regarding a cuckold, see p. 188.)

Rudkin, E. H. 1934. 'Witches and devils', *Folk-Lore*, 45, pp. 249–67. (For gesture used to protect oneself against witches.)

Ruesch, J. and W. Kees. 1969. *Nonverbal Communication*. University of California Press, Berkeley and Los Angeles.

Sainsbury, P. and W. R. Costain. 1971. 'The measurement of psychomotor activity: some clinical applications', *J. Psychosomatic Research*, 15, pp. 487–94.

Sainsbury, P. and E. Wood. 1977. 'Measuring gesture: its cultural and clinical correlates', *Psychol. Med.*, 7, pp. 63–72.

Saitz, R. L. and E. C. Cervenka. 1972. *Handbook of Gestures: Colombia and the United States*. Mouton, The Hague.

Sanford, E. M. 1928. 'De loquela digitorum', *The Classical Journal*, 23, pp. 588–93.

Scheflen, A. E. 1972. *Body Language and the Social Order*. Prentice-Hall, New Jersey.

Scheflen, A. E. 1973. *How Behavior Means*. Gordon and Breach, New York.

Schuler, E. A. 1944. 'V for Victory: a study in symbolic social control', *J. Soc. Psychol.*, 19, pp. 283–99.

Scott, G. R. 1966. *Phallic Worship*. Luxor Press, London. (See p. 86 for the fig-sign.)

Scott, H. L. 1893. 'The sign language of the Plains Indians', *Int. Folk-lore Assoc. Arch.*, 1, pp. 1–206.

Sebeok, T. A., A. S. Hayes and M. C. Bateson (editors). 1972. *Approaches to Semiotics*. Mouton, The Hague.

Seligmann, C. G. and A. Wilkin. 1907. 'The gesture language of the Western Islanders', *Camb. Anthrop. Exped. to Torres Straits Reports*, 3, pp. 255–60.

Seligmann, S. 1910. *Der böse Blick und Verwandtes*. Berlin.

Seligmann, S. 1922. *Die Zauberkraft des Auges und das Berufen*. Hamburg. (For gestures against the Evil Eye.)

Seligmann, S. 1927. *Die magischen Heil- und Schutzmittel aus der unbelebten Natur, mit besonderer Berücksichtigung der Mittel gegen den Bösen Blick; eine Geschichte des Amulettwesens.* Stuttgart. (For reference to the cornuta and the fig-sign.)

Seton, E. T. 1918. *Sign Talk; a Universal Signal Code without Apparatus.* Garden City, New York.

Shaftesbury, E. 1885. *Lessons in Acting.* (For codified bodily attitudes.)

Sharman, J. 1884. *A Cursory History of Swearing.* London.

Shawn, T. 1954. *Every Little Movement.* Pittsfield, Massachusetts.

Sherzer, J. 1972. 'Verbal and non-verbal deixis: the pointed lip gesture among the San Blas Cuna', in *Language in Society*, 2, pp. 117–31.

Siddons, H. 1807. *Practical Illustrations of Rhetorical Gesture and Action.* London.

Siegel, J. 1969. 'The Enlightenment and the evolution of a language of signs in France and England', *J. Hist. Ideas*, 30, pp. 96–115.

Sittl, K. 1890. *Die Gebärden der Griechen und Römer.* Leipzig. (For phallic and other gestures.)

Smith, H. 1972. *V is for Victory.* Kimber, London.

Smith, W. J., J. Chase and A. K. Lieblich. 1974. 'Tongue-showing: a facial display of humans and other primates', *Semiotica*, 11 (3), pp. 201–46.

Sorell, W. 1968. *The Story of the Human Hand.* Weidenfeld and Nicolson, London.

Spalding, A. C. B. 1826. *Portal to Rhetorical Delivery, with Questions, Exercises & Observations on the New System of Corporal Expression.* Dublin.

Spencer, B. and F. J. Gillen. 1927. *The Arunta.* Macmillan, London. (See Vol. 2, pp. 600–8 for Aboriginal gestures, 64 of which are illustrated.)

Stead, R. M. 1941. 'The secret V', *Current Hist. and Forum*, 53, p. 28.

Stebbins, G. 1901. *Delsarte System of Expression.* New York.

Stokoe, W. C. 1972. *Semiotics and Human Sign Languages.* Mouton, The Hague.

Story, W. W. 1877. *Castle S. Angelo and the Evil Eye.* London.

Strobridge, T. R. and B. C. Nalty. 1963. 'Hand Salute', *Leatherneck*, XLVI (No. 7), pp. 76–7.

Sullivan, F. A. 1968. 'Tendere manus; gestures in the *Aeneid*', *Classical Journal*, 63, pp. 358–62.

Taladoire, B. A. 1951. *Commentaires sur la mimique et l'expression corporelle du comédien romain.* Montpellier. (For Greek and Roman gestures.)

Taylor, A. 1956. 'The Shanghai gesture', *F. F. Communications*, No. 166. pp. 1–76.

Thomas, A. V. 1941. 'L'anthropologie du geste et les proverbes de la terre', *Revue Anthropol.*, Oct.–Dec. 1941, pp. 164–94. (For discussions of gestural origin of language.)

Tiger, L. 1969. *Men in Groups.* Nelson, London.

Tiger, L. and R. Fox. 1972. *The Imperial Animal.* Secker and Warburg, London.

Tinbergen, N. 1951. *The Study of Instinct.* O.U.P., Oxford.

Tomkins, S. S. 1962. *Affect Imagery Consciousness.* Springer, New York.

Tomkins, S. and C. E. Izard (editors). 1966. *Affect, Cognition and Personality*. Tavistock Publications, London.

Tomkins, W. 1969. *Indian Sign Language*. Dover, New York.

Trager, G. L. 1958. 'Paralanguage: a first approximation', *Studies in Linguistics*, 13, pp. 1–12.

Tylor, E. B. 1878. *Researches into the Early History of Mankind*. John Murray, London. (Chapters 2, 3 and 4 deal with gestures.)

Vanggaard, T. 1972. *Phallos*. Cape, London. (See p. 166 for fig-sign.)

Vasey, G. 1875. *The Philosophy of Laughter and Smiling*. Burns, London.

Vendrys, J. 1950. 'Langage oral et langage par gestes', *J. Psychol. Norm. et Path.*, 43, pp. 7–33.

Vine, I. 1973. 'The role of facial-visual signalling in early social development', in *Social Communication and Movement*. Academic Press, London. pp. 195–298.

Voegelin, C. F. 1958. 'Sign language analysis, on one level or two?', *Int. J. Amer. Ling.*, 24, pp. 71–7.

Walker, J. R. 1953. 'Sign language of the Plains Indians', *Chron. Oklahoma*, 31, pp. 168–77.

Ward, J. S. M. 1928. *The Sign Language of the Mysteries*. London. (See Vol. 2 for chronological listing of signs.)

Warman, E. B. 1892. *Gestures and Attitudes; an exposition of the Delsarte philosophy of expression*. Boston.

Weiss, P. 1943. 'The social character of gestures', *Phil. Rev.*, 52, pp. 182–6.

Wells, K. F. 1966. *Kinesiology*. Saunders, Philadelphia.

Whiteside, R. L. 1974. *Face Language*. Frederick Fell, New York.

Whitney, G. 1586. *A Choice of Emblems and other Devices*. Leiden. (Reprinted in Amsterdam by Da Capo, 1969.)

Whittick, A. 1960. *Symbols, Signs and their Meaning*. London. (See Chapter 16: 'The dance, gesture and ceremonies of everyday life'.)

Wickler, W. 1969. *The Sexual Code*. Weidenfeld and Nicolson, London.

Wildeblood, J. 1973. *The Polite World. A guide to English manners and deportment*. Davis-Poynter, London.

Williamson, G. C. 1923. *Curious Survivals*. Jenkins, London. (See p. 197 on the 'fig'.)

Wolff, C. 1945. *A Psychology of Gesture*. Methuen, London.

Wright, T. 1866. *The Worship of the Generative Powers During the Middle Ages of Western Europe*. London. (Reprinted by Julian Press, New York, 1957, in *Sexual Symbolism: A History of Phallic Worship*. See pp. 52 and 65–72 for a discussion of the fig-sign.)

Wundt, W. 1900. *Völkerpsychologie*. Volume One: *Die Sprache*. Stuttgart. (Chapter 2 'The Language of Gesture', was reprinted in English as a separate book by Mouton, The Hague, 1973.)

Zung, C. S. L. 1937. *Secrets of the Chinese Drama*. Shanghai. (For explanations of the symbolic gestures used.)

Index